P9-BJT-253

MUSICALS!

MUSICALS!

A Directory of Musical Properties Available for Production

by

Richard Chigley Lynch

JOHN TAGGART HINCKLEY LIBRARY
NORTHWEST COMMUNITY COLLEGE
POWELL WYOMING 82435

American Library Association
Chicago *1984*

Library of Congress Cataloging in Publication Data

Lynch, Richard Chigley, 1932–
   Musicals! : a directory of musical properties available for production.

   Includes index.
   1. Musical revue, comedy, etc.—Directories.
I. Title.
ML19.L9   1984   782.81'029'473   84-468
ISBN 0-8389-0404-1

Text designed by Marcia Rasmussen
Cover designed by Natalie Wargin
Composed by Modern Typographers in
   Linotron ITC Garamond
Printed on 55-pound Glatfelter, a pH-neutral
   stock, and bound in Kivar 6 cover stock
   by Edwards Brothers, Inc.

Copyright © 1984 by the American Library Association. All rights reserved except those which may be granted by Sections 107 and 108 of the Copyright Revision Act of 1976. Printed in the United States of America.

*For all my friends and colleagues at
The New York Public Library*

Contents

Introduction

Common opinion has it that musicals are not as popular today as they once were, that their quantity and quality have declined in recent years. Not true.

A survey of last season's theater scene in New York City showed, for example, that of the nearly 50 plays running on and off Broadway at one time, almost one-third were musicals, ranging from *The Fantasticks* (1960) to *Zorbá* (1968) to *La Cage aux Folles* (1983).

In addition, there has been summer stock. In one recent season in the Northeast, nearly 45 musicals were being produced. They included *Joseph and the Amazing Technicolor Dreamcoat* (1982), *I Do! I Do!* (1966), *The Sound of Music* (1959), *South Pacific* (1949), and *Show Boat* (1927).

The strongest evidence of the musical's continued appeal, however, is found in the thousands of amateur theater companies that stage musicals throughout the country each year. By involving local citizens in all phases of a musical's production—including acting, directing, conducting, costuming, publicity, financing, and many others—the amateur theater company thus informs, entertains, and ultimately enriches the lives of its members and of its community.

There are many books available on staging a musical, but none have adequately addressed the question that the amateur company asks itself when a musical finishes its run: "What musical shall we do next?" In the past, theater amateurs have had to rely on their memories for the answer.

Now *Musicals!* extends their reach by offering a detailed compilation of almost 400 musical properties available for production.

Listed in each entry are title, date of production, playwright, composer, lyricist, and a plot summary as well as other vital information. The book allows amateurs to sample shows by directing them to available sound recordings and librettos that might be used when the group gathers to discuss preferences.

What musical to do next? Take your pick.

On Using This Book

Musicals! consists of an alphabetical listing, by title, of nearly 400 currently available musical properties. The reader will also find these properties entered by composer, lyricist, and librettist in the index at the end of the book.

The date or dates found in each entry indicates New York City production(s). In those few cases where there was no New York City production, the originating city is given.

Credits for writers, composers, lyricists, and source materials have been borrowed from programs, posters, and record jackets. The descriptive paragraph about each show has been drawn from published reviews, catalogs, record liner notes, and personal recollection. It is intended to give an idea of the musical's plot, locale, time period, audience suitability, and anything else that might be of interest to the theater amateur.

For purposes of this directory, *piano-vocal score* refers to the complete score; *vocal selections* refers to the major songs. Occasionally, *music publisher* is indicated and refers to songbook or individual songs. A great deal of the published material, including recordings, is out of print but can be located through a library or collector. In addition, a licensing agency normally will provide you with scripts and scores on request. Each entry provides the name of the licensing agent, and the list of agents in the appendixes provides addresses of the 11 agencies that own the rights to these musicals.

The reader should note that licensing agents and script availability change from time to time. A successful revival on Broadway, for example, may result in sudden restrictions on amateur production. In any and all cases, amateur theater companies must obtain agency permission before beginning production on *any* musical.

Titles not included in the directory were not available for production at the time the book was being compiled. If you wish to stage a musical that is not listed here, first ask all the agencies if they control it, or if they know who does. If no one can help you, then you might seek out the copyright owners, or their estates, and make your own financial arrangements. If you have a script or score, contact first the publishers of the material. Other sources for help include:

Authors League of America, Inc. (for older or deceased writers)
    234 West 44th Street, New York, N.Y. 10036 (212) 391-9198
Dramatists Guild, Inc. (for current writers)
    234 West 44th Street, New York, N.Y. 10036 (212) 398-9366
American Society of Composers, Authors and Publishers (ASCAP)
    One Lincoln Plaza, New York, N.Y. 10023 (212) 595-3050
Broadcast Music, Inc. (BMI)
    320 West 57th Street, New York, N.Y. 10019 (212) 586-2000

In compiling *Musicals!*, the most recent catalogs of the 10 major licensing agents were examined. With a few exceptions, they control all of the properties currently available.

To obtain a listing of published material, the following sources were used: the *Play Index*, published by H. W. Wilson; *Books in Print*, published by R. R. Bowker; and the *Dictionary Catalog of the Research Libraries of the New York Public Library* (including the music and theater collections), published by G. K. Hall.

Musicals Available for Production

THE ADVENTURES OF MARCO POLO
(1956 TV musical adapted for the stage)

Book by William Friedberg and Neil Simon   *Music* by Clay Warnick and Mel Pahl; based on themes of Rimsky-Korsakov   *Lyrics* by Edward Eager   *Published libretto*: Samuel French, 1959   *Condensation*: None   *Anthology*: None   *Vocal selections*: None   *Licensing agent*: Samuel French   *Recording*: Columbia ML 5111 (original TV cast)   *Cast*: 7 M; 4 F; extras, chorus

Alfred Drake and Doretta Morrow starred in the original TV production. The plot deals with Marco Polo's visit to Kublai Khan's court in the thirteenth century. It was called a musical fantasy—a historical romance with deathless music and colorful locales. The musical numbers are based on such familiar compositions as "Scheherazade" and the "Antar Symphony."

AIN'T MISBEHAVIN'
(1978)

Music primarily by Thomas "Fats" Waller; based on an idea by Murry Horwitz and Richard Maltby, Jr.   *Published libretto*: None   *Condensation*: None   *Anthology*: None   *Vocal selections*: Big Three,

1

1978   *Licensing agent*: Music Theatre International   *Recording*: RCA CBL 2-2965 (original cast)   *Cast*: 2 M; 3 F

The small cast (variable) is backed by a piano and small band and presents 30 songs composed or performed by Fats Waller. This is a musical revue with solos, group numbers, and some instrumentals presented in a simple cabaret setting with no dialogue. There was a later TV production. Some of the songs, performed in 1930s and 1940s Harlem style, include "Honeysuckle Rose," "Mean to Me," and "The Joint Is Jumpin'." Strong musical talents and personalities are required. *Tony Award Winner (Best Musical)*

ALL AMERICAN
(1962)

Book by Mel Brooks; based on *Professor Fodorski* by Robert Lewis Taylor *Music* by Charles Strouse   *Lyrics* by Lee Adams   *Published libretto*: Dramatic, 1972   *Condensation*: None   *Anthology*: None   *Vocal selections*: Big Three (Morris, 1962)   *Licensing agent*: Dramatic *Recording*: Columbia CSP AKOS 2160 (original cast)   *Cast*: 6 M; 6 F; flexible chorus

This college musical was described as an audience show and good clean fun. The plot revolves around a shy immigrant professor from Austria who goes to an American southern college to teach engineering and ends up as the football coach. The professor was originally played by Ray Bolger, so strong dancing skills are needed.

ALL IN LOVE
(1962)

Book and lyrics by Bruce Geller; based on *The Rivals* by William Sheridan *Music* by Jacques Urbont   *Published libretto*: None   *Condensation*: None   *Anthology*: None   *Vocal selections*: None   *Licensing agent*: Music Theatre International   *Recording*: Mercury OCS 6204 (original cast) *Cast*: 9 M; 7 F

The famous Restoration comedy of eighteenth-century England has been transformed into a minuscule musical with rapid and involved period numbers and reminiscent tunes for operetta voices. The plot concerns an heiress infatuated with the "ideal lover" of romantic novels. There are incredible and mandatory complications before a finale of multiple marriages. Comedian Dom De Luise was in the original off-Broadway production.

ALLEGRO
(1947/1978/1984)

Book and lyrics by Oscar Hammerstein, II   *Music* by Richard Rodgers
Published libretto: Knopf, 1948   *Condensation*: *The Burns Mantle Best
Plays of 1947–1948*. John Chapman, ed. Dodd, Mead, 1948   *Anthology*:
Six Plays by Rodgers and Hammerstein. Random House, 1955 ☆ Modern
Library, 1959   *Piano-vocal score*: Williamson, 1948   *Licensing agent*:
Rodgers and Hammerstein Theatre Library   *Recording*: RCA LSO 1099(e)
(original cast)   *Cast*: 25 M; 15 F

This show followed such Rodgers and Hammerstein hits as *Oklahoma!*
and *Carousel* and was an attempt by the famous duo to do something
different and original. It was called a drama with music, rather than a
musical, and it was a stylized production with a minimum of scenery. The
story followed a small-town boy up to the age of 35. One famous song
from the score is "The Gentleman Is a Dope." *Allegro* has not been
filmed and is not as well known as most other Rodgers and Hammerstein
shows.

THE AMOROUS FLEA
(1964)

Book by Jerry Devine; based on Moliere's *School for Wives*   *Music and
lyrics* by Bruce Montgomery   *Published libretto*: Dramatists Play Service,
1964   *Condensation*: None   *Anthology*: None   *Vocal selections*:
None   *Licensing agent*: Dramatists Play Service   *Recording*: None
Cast: 6 M; 2 F

This is a modest musical with a small cast, simple sets, and an unpretentious air. It is classic nonsense in a most stylish vein, concerning a
Frenchman who has arranged for his future bride to be raised in complete seclusion until the wedding. The play was performed off-Broadway.

ANGEL
(1978)

Book by Ketti Frings and Peter Udell; based on the play *Look Homeward,
Angel* by Ketti Frings, which was based on Thomas Wolfe's novel   *Music*
by Gary Geld   *Lyrics* by Peter Udell   *Published libretto*: Samuel
French, 1979   *Condensation*: None   *Anthology*: None   *Vocal
selections*: None   *Licensing agent*: Samuel French   *Recording*: None
Cast: 10 M; 9 F

The original play won a Pulitzer Prize, but this musical adaptation by the
same author did not fare so well. The autobiographical Thomas Wolfe

novel concerns a youth's formative years, his mother's pursuit of property and security, and his drunken stonecutter father. A lot of color and "calico" touches are evident in this family show set in North Carolina in 1916. A unit set with cyclorama is used.

ANIMAL CRACKERS
(1928)

Book by George S. Kaufman and Morrie Ryskind   *Music and lyrics* by Bert Kalmar and Harry Ruby   *Published libretto*: Samuel French *Condensation*: None   *Anthology*: None   *Music publisher*: The Kalmar-Ruby Song Book. Random House, 1936   *Licensing agent*: Samuel French   *Recording*: None   *Cast*: Large mixed cast

"Hooray for Captain Spalding," the theme of Groucho Marx, comes from this stage hit that was revived in 1982 by Washington's Arena Stage. "There are lots of atrocious puns and non-sequiturs and sight gags which raise many, many laughs," reported a recent critic of that production. It was staged as a circus, with the band up high. The choreography reminded some of Busby Berkeley. The finale is a costume ball with the Groucho character as Louis XVII. "Show Me a Rose" and "Three Little Words" are from the score, and "Oh, By Jingo!" was interpolated. There was a Marx Brothers film version in 1930, but without most of the songs.

ANNE OF GREEN GABLES
(1971)

Adaptation by Donald Harron; based on the novel by Lucy Maud Montgomery   *Music* by Norman Campbell   *Lyrics* by Donald Harron and Norman Campbell   *Published libretto*: Samuel French, 1972 *Condensation*: None   *Anthology*: None   *Vocal selections*: None *Licensing agent*: Samuel French   *Recording*: CBS 70053 (British—1969 London original cast)   *Cast*: 12 M; 17 F

This cheerfully old-fashioned Canadian musical was created for the Charlottetown Festival on Prince Edward Island. It was done at New York's City Center in 1971 for the Christmas season. This is a real family show with folksy charms, based on a Canadian children's classic story of an orphan at the end of the nineteenth century. It works well simply produced in a small, intimate theater. *Variety* reported, "It's good for a smile, a twinge of nostalgia and perhaps even an occasional sniffle."

ANNIE
(1977)

Book by Thomas Meehan; based on *Little Orphan Annie* by Harold Gray
Music by Charles Strouse   *Lyrics* by Martin Charnin   *Published libretto*:
None   *Condensation*: *The Best Plays of 1976–1977*. Otis L. Guernsey, Jr.,
ed. Dodd, Mead, 1977   *Anthology*: None   *Piano-vocal score*: Big Three
(Morris, 1977)   *Vocal selections*: Big Three (Morris, 1977)   *Licensing
agent*: Music Theatre International   *Recording*: Columbia PS 34712
(original cast)   *Cast*: 8 M; 4 F; 6 orphans; chorus; and 1 dog

Everyone knows the comic strip of *Little Orphan Annie* as well as the
successful Broadway musical and film based on it. This is a show for the
whole family, and particularly for children. Costumes for both rich and
poor are required; the setting is New York City in 1933. The production
can be elaborate or moderate. The cast includes a dog for the role of
"Sandy."
Tony Award Winner (Best Musical)

ANNIE GET YOUR GUN
(1946/1966/1978)

Book by Herbert and Dorothy Fields   *Music and lyrics* by Irving Berlin
Published libretto: Dramatic, 1946, 1952 (without music)   *Condensation*:
American Musicals: Berlin. Time-Life, 1981   *Anthology*: None
Piano-vocal score: Irving Berlin Music, 1947, 1967   *Vocal selections*:
Irving Berlin Music, 1946   *Licensing agent*: Rodgers and Hammerstein
Theatre Library   *Recordings*: MCA 2031 E (original cast) ✩ RCA LSO 1124,
Time-Life STL-AMO7 (1966 revival cast)   *Cast*: 20 M; 10 F; seven children,
singers and dancers

Surely everyone has seen this show, either on the stage, in the MGM
movie version, or as a TV special. It is based on the exciting career of
Annie Oakley, an expert sharpshooter who performed in the Buffalo Bill
Wild West Show. It is full of simple, singable songs ("There's No Business
like Show Business!") that the audience will know and love, and nice
homely humor.

ANYONE CAN WHISTLE
(1964/1980)

Book by Arthur Laurents   *Music and lyrics* by Stephen Sondheim
Published libretto: Random House, 1965 ✩ Leon Amiel, 1976

Condensation: None   *Anthology*: None   *Piano-vocal score*: Chappell, 1968   *Vocal selections*: Chappell, 1964   *Licensing agent*: Music Theatre International   *Recording*: Columbia CSP AS 32608 (original cast)   *Cast*: 5 M; 3 F; variable chorus; dancers

Initially this show was a failure, but over the years and with the subsequent career of Sondheim it has become more and more respected. It takes place in an imaginary township under the control of a corrupt Mayor and her evil aides. A phony miracle is concocted to attract tourists to the area. There is also a plot dealing with madness. The local insane asylum is called "The Cookie Jar," and some of the staff there become involved in the town's activities. This is an interesting and challenging property.

ANYTHING GOES
(1934/1962)

Book by Guy Bolton and P. G. Wodehouse; revised by Howard Lindsay and Russel Crouse   *Music and lyrics* by Cole Porter   *Published libretto*: None   *Condensation*: None   *Anthology: American Musicals: Porter*. Time-Life, 1981   *Piano-vocal score*: Harms, 1936   *Licensing agent*: Tams-Witmark   *Recordings*: Smithsonian 2007 (original cast) ☆ Epic FLS 15100, Time-Life STL-AM02 (1962 revival cast)   *Cast*: 12M; 11 F

This is a great Cole Porter show that has been done many times on stage, screen, and television. It's all about a group of gangsters, nightclub performers and English nobility at sea and bound for England in the mid-1930s. The songs are the attraction . . . such evergreens as "I Get a Kick Out of You" and "Blow, Gabriel, Blow." This is sophisticated entertainment.

APPLAUSE
(1970)

Book by Betty Comden and Adolph Green; based on the film *All About Eve* and the original story by Mary Orr   *Music* by Charles Strouse   *Lyrics* by Lee Adams   *Published libretto*: Random House, 1971   *Condensation*: *The Best Plays of 1969–1970*. Otis L. Guernsey, Jr., ed. Dodd, Mead, 1970   *Anthology*: *Great Musicals of the American Theatre*, vol. 2. Stanley Richards, ed. Chilton, 1976   *Piano-vocal score*: Morris, 1970   *Vocal selections*: Big Three (Morris, 1970)   *Licensing agent*: Tams-Witmark   *Recording*: MCA 37100 (original cast)   *Cast*: 15 M; 6 F; singers, dancers

A musical about the theater—from the gypsies that make up the chorus to the superstars winning their awards. Due to the famous film, this show has much popular appeal. It has been updated to include disco rhythms. The plot centers on a female star (Margo Channing) who befriends and is betrayed by a young hopeful. A great deal of glamor is required for the part of Margo.

Tony Award Winner (Best Musical)

THE APPLE TREE
(1966)

Book by Jerry Bock and Sheldon Harnick; based on "The Diary of Adam and Eve" by Mark Twain, "The Lady or the Tiger?" by Frank R. Stockton, and "Passionella" by Jules Feiffer; additional material by Jerome Coopersmith. *Music* by Jerry Bock   *Lyrics* by Sheldon Harnick   *Published libretto*: Random House, 1967   *Condensation: The Best Plays of 1966–1967*. Otis L. Guernsey, Jr., ed. Dodd, Mead, 1967   *Anthology: The Best Short Comedies from Broadway and London*. Stanley Richards, ed. Random House, 1970   *Piano-vocal score*: Valando, 1968   *Licensing agent*: Music Theatre International   *Recording*: Columbia KOS 3020 (original cast)   *Cast*: 5M; 3F; chorus

A trio of short stories has been transformed into a three-act musical. Usually each act is performed by the same cast, but this is not necessary. In fact, the three one-act musicals can be performed singularly or as a trio. The first, naturally enough, is set in the Garden of Eden. The second is set in ancient Babylon, and the last from the chimney tops to glamorous Hollywood. Even though there is not a lot of dancing, this is a challenging show to stage. Strong comic talents are required.

archie and mehitabel
(1957)

Book by Joe Darion and Mel Brooks; based on stories and vignettes by Don Marquis   *Music* by George Kleinsinger   *Lyrics* by Joe Darion *Published libretto*: None   *Condensation*: None   *Anthology: The Best Short Plays of 1957–1958*. Margaret Mayorga, ed. Beacon, 1958   *Vocal selections*: Chappell, 1957   *Licensing agent*: Music Theatre International *Recordings*: Columbia CSP AOL 4963 (1955 studio recording) ✩ *Sound of Broadway* 300/1 (TV sound track and original cast)   *Cast*: 12 M; 8 F

This property started out as stories and then was made into a "back-alley opera" and recorded by Carol Channing and Eddie Bracken. From this record came a Broadway musical retitled *Shinbone Alley*. It is the wistful one-sided romance of a cockroach for an alley cat. These creatures symbolize human emotions and frailties. It was called novel and imaginative, with a happy and jazzy score. The Broadway cast featured Bracken with Eartha Kitt, and Jacques D'Amboise and Allegra Kent from the New York City Ballet.

AROUND THE WORLD IN 80 DAYS (1963)

Book by Sig Herzig; based on the motion picture and Jules Verne story
Lyrics by Harold Adamson   *Music* by Sammy Fain and Victor Young
Published libretto: None   *Condensation*: None   *Anthology*: None
Music publisher: Chappell, 1957 (film score, no vocals)   *Licensing agent*: Tams-Witmark   *Recording*: Everest LPBR 4001 (studio cast)   *Cast*: 20 M; 5 F; chorus

Michael Todd's gigantic 1956 film won five Academy Awards, including one to Victor Young for the musical score. After Todd's death, his son had the property transformed into a stage production. He presented it successfully in 1963 at Jones Beach on Long Island, outside New York City. All Jones Beach productions are spectacular, but this can be produced on a reasonably modest scale.

BABES IN ARMS (1937/1951)

Book by Rodgers and Hart   *Music* by Richard Rodgers   *Lyrics* by Lorenz Hart   *Published libretto*: None   *Condensation*: *American Musicals: Rodgers and Hart*. Time-Life, 1981   *Anthology*: None   *Vocal selections*: Chappell (Hansen), 1937   *Piano-vocal score*: Chappell (1959 version), 1960   *Licensing agent*: Rodgers and Hammerstein Theatre Library   *Recordings*: Columbia CSP AOS 2570E ☆ Time-Life STL-AM06 (studio cast)   *Cast*: 11 M; 8 F; chorus

At its opening in 1937, the critic for the *New York Telegram* called it "a musical of taste, smartness and delightful abandon." The children of touring vaudevillians are about to be sent to a summer work camp on Long Island. To escape, the kids put on a show! There's a lot of singing and dancing (including a dream ballet) by a young cast to some of of the most famous Rodgers and Hart songs. The score includes "My Funny Valentine" and "I Wish I Were in Love Again."

BABES IN TOYLAND
(1903/1929/1975)

Book and lyrics by Glen MacDonough   *Music* by Victor Herbert
Published libretto: None   *Condensation*: None   *Anthology*: None
Piano-vocal score: M. Witmark, 1903 (Warner Brothers Music)   *Licensing agent*: Tams-Witmark   *Recordings*: Reader's Digest RD 40-N3 (studio cast—*Treasury of Great Operettas*, Record 3)   *Cast*: Large mixed cast, including children

Sometimes described as a Christmas pantomime, this famous show is remembered for its large cast (with many children), vast ensembles, and elaborate and frequently changed settings. The plot concerns mean old Uncle Barnaby who is scheming to obtain the fortune of the Widow Piper's niece and nephew. As a result of Barnaby's attempts the niece and nephew are shipwrecked and finally wander into Toyland. Children will especially enjoy this family show.

BAJOUR
(1964)

Book by Ernest Kinoy; based on *The New Yorker* stories by Joseph Mitchell
Music and lyrics by Walter Marks   *Published libretto*: Dramatic, 1976
Condensation: None   *Anthology*: None   *Vocal selections*: Morris, 1965
Licensing agent: Dramatic   *Recording*: Columbia KOS 2700 (original cast)
Cast: 7 M; 5 F; chorus

A "bajour" is a major caper that enriches a whole tribe of modern gypsies. While the gypsies are plotting and fighting among themselves, a female anthropologist arrives to live with them and study them. She was played on Broadway by Nancy Dussault and stopped the show with her song, "Where Is the Tribe for Me?" This show has a contemporary setting in and around New York City, and strong dancing.

BAKER STREET
(1965)

Book by Jerome Coopersmith; adapted from the stories by Arthur Conan Doyle   *Music and lyrics* by Marion Grudeff and Raymond Jessel
Published libretto: Doubleday, 1966   *Condensation*: None   *Anthology*: None   *Vocal selections*: Marks, 1964   *Licensing agent*: Tams-Witmark
Recording: MGM SE 7000 OC (original cast)   *Cast*: 16 M; 3 F; singers, dancers

A musical adventure with those old friends, Sherlock Holmes and Doctor Watson. The plot deals with Irene Adler and Professor Moriarty—she is an American musical comedy star who is happy to be back in London, and he is out to steal the British crown jewels. Turn-of-the-century London lends itself to beautiful costumes and opulent sets. There is a tongue-in-cheek approach to all of this.

BALALAIKA
(1936)

Book and lyrics by Eric Maschwitz   *Music* by George Posford and Bernard Grum   *Published libretto*: None   *Condensation*: None   *Anthology*: None   *Vocal selections*: None   *Licensing agent*: Tams-Witmark   *Recording*: World Records (British) WRC T 794 (studio cast)   *Cast*: Large mixed cast

A spectacular British musical (some productions claim a cast of 100!) that has been done in many locations throughout the United States and the world, but not on Broadway. It has cossacks and gypsies and all the romance of Czarist Russia. The story deals with an Imperial Prince and an anarchist's daughter. They meet in Paris where he sings in a nightclub operated by exiled White Russians. This was made into a film with Nelson Eddy and Ilona Massey in 1939. "Dark Eyes" and "Two Guitars" are among the familiar songs in the production.

BALLAD OF BABY DOE
(1956/1958)

Music by Douglas Moore   *Book* by John Latouche   *Published libretto*: Program Pub. Co., 1958   *Condensation*: Milton Cross, *More Stories of the Great Operas*. Doubleday, 1971   *Anthology*: None   *Piano-vocal score*: Chappell, 1958   *Licensing agent*: Tams-Witmark   *Recording*: DGG 2709 061 (original cast)   *Cast*: 2 M; 5 F; chorus

This is the story of Colorado silver king Horace Tabor and the two women in his life—his first wife from New England and Elizabeth "Baby" Doe, the noted Oshkosh beauty who became his second wife. After a lavish premiere in Central City, Colorado, this American opera has since been performed many times by the New York City Opera. It was described as a solid contribution to the contemporary musical stage.

BALLROOM
(1979)

Book by Jerome Kass; adaptation of "The Queen of the Stardust Ballroom," TV musical special   *Music* by Billy Goldenberg   *Lyrics* by Alan and Marilyn Bergman   *Published libretto*: None   *Condensation*: None *Anthology*: None   *Vocal selections*: Schirmer, 1979   *Licensing agent*: Samuel French   *Recording*: Columbia 35762 (original cast)   *Cast*: 14 M; 17 F

A widow and a married man meet at a public dance hall in this bittersweet romance originally done on television. The Broadway production expanded the plot and score. A 1940s "big band" orchestra and many ballroom dancers are featured.

BARNUM
(1980)

Book by Mark Bramble   *Music* by Cy Coleman   *Lyrics* by Michael Stewart   *Published libretto*: Fireside Theatre Book Club, 1982 *Condensation*: None   *Anthology*: None   *Vocal selections*: Notable Music, 1980   *Licensing agent*: Tams-Witmark   *Recording*: CBS JS 36576 (original cast); includes lyrics   *Cast*: 11 M; 8 F

For this story of P. T. Barnum the theater in New York City was turned into a circus, with the stage as the main ring. Not only clowns and jugglers performed all over the auditorium, but street entertainers performed outside before the show. The band was frequently on stage and marched in the aisles. The ringmaster would announce high spots of Barnum's career, and then P. T. would proceed to enact them. Although the action covers 1835 to 1880, Barnum never ages. The plot concerns Barnum and his level-headed wife, and includes the possibility of Barnum's affair with Jenny Lind and his eventual merger with Bailey to form the "greatest show on earth." The highly praised score is made up of ballads, marches and ragtime struts. A great deal of energy is required, from all concerned, in staging this show.

BELLS ARE RINGING
(1956)

Book and lyrics by Betty Comden and Adolph Green   *Music* by Jule Styne *Published libretto*: Random House, 1957 ✰ *Theatre Arts* (magazine), April 1959   *Condensation*: *American Musicals: Styne*. Time-Life, 1981.

Anthology: *Comden and Green on Broadway*. Drama Book Specialists, 1981
Piano-vocal score: Chappell, 1967   *Licensing agent*: Tams-Witmark
Recordings: Columbia CSP AOS 2006, Time-Life STL-AM05 (original cast)
Cast: 22 M; 6 W; chorus

Judy Holliday was the original telephone answering service operator taking a more than routine interest in her customers. This show was later made into a film, and some of the songs ("Just in Time") have become standards. This musical has fun and romance in a New York setting.

BEN FRANKLIN IN PARIS
(1964)

Book and lyrics by Sidney Michaels   *Music* by Mark Sandrich, Jr.
Published libretto: Random House, 1965   *Condensation*: None
Anthology: None   *Vocal selections*: None   *Licensing agent*: Samuel
French   *Recording*: Capitol SVAS 2191 (original cast)   *Cast*: 18 M; 4 F;
singers; dancers

The setting is Paris and the court of Louis XVI. Some of the delights include a love song sung in the gondola of a balloon and monks singing "Hic Haec Hoc" as they go about their tasks in the vineyard. Ben goes to France to get aid for the American Revolution. He is helped by a Countess who loves him and has strong influence with the French king. The subplot is a romance between Ben's grandson and a poor Parisienne.

BERLIN TO BROADWAY WITH KURT WEILL
(1972/1983)

Music by Kurt Weill   *Text and format* by Gene Lerner   *Lyrics* by
Maxwell Anderson, Bertolt Brecht, Ira Gershwin, Michael Feingold, Paul
Green, Alan Jay Lerner, George Tabori, Marc Blitzstein, Jacques Deval,
Langston Hughes, Ogden Nash and Arnold Weinstein   *Published libretto*:
None   *Condensation*: None   *Anthology*: None   *Music publisher*:
Chappell, 1975   *Licensing agent*: Music Theatre International
Recording: Paramount PAS 4000 (original cast)   *Cast*: 2 M; 2 F; 1 narrator

This show is done as a selected biography of the composer with a narrator to bridge songs. Slide projections were used in the original off-Broadway production. Featured are some of the truly great songs of the musical theater, from *The Threepenny Opera* and *Lady in the Dark* to *Lost in the Stars*. The cast will have to be up to this material!

BEST FOOT FORWARD
(1941/1963)

Book by John Cecil Holm   *Music and lyrics* by Hugh Martin and Ralph
Blane   *Published libretto*: Dramatic, 1943   *Condensation*: None
Anthology: None   *Music publisher*: Chappell, 1941   *Licensing agent*:
Tams-Witmark   *Recording*: Stet DS 15003 (1963 cast)   *Cast*: 12 M; 9 F

A fading film star agrees to appear at the annual prom at Winsocki and as a
result causes confusion and pandemonium. This bright and appealing
musical has a number of good songs: "Just a Little Joint with a Juke Box,"
"The Three B's," and "Buckle Down Winsocki." This was filmed by MGM
with June Allyson. It was performed off-Broadway with Liza Minnelli.

THE BEST LITTLE WHOREHOUSE IN TEXAS
(1978)

Book by Larry L. King and Peter Masterson; based on an article by Larry L.
King   *Music and lyrics* by Carol Hall   *Published libretto*: None
Condensation: *The Best Plays of 1977–1978*. Otis L. Guernsey, Jr., ed. Dodd,
Mead, 1978   *Anthology*: None   *Vocal selections*: MCA Music, 1979
Licensing agent: Samuel French   *Recording*: MCA 3049 (original cast)
Cast: 13 M; 14 F; extras

This popular show and film takes place in a brothel called "The Chicken
Ranch" in a small Texas town. The plot revolves around a crusading TV
moralist who is out to close down the ranch. It is very funny on a low,
profane level. The original production was particularly praised for the
direction and choreography of Tommy Tune.

BILLION DOLLAR BABY
(1945/1951)

Book and lyrics by Betty Comden and Adolph Green   *Music* by Morton
Gould   *Published libretto*: None   *Condensation*: None   *Anthology*:
None   *Vocal selections*: None   *Licensing agent*: Tams-Witmark
Recording: None   *Cast*: 19 M; 12 F

A satire on the "terrific twenties," this show takes place during the time of
gangsters and gangster funerals—of Texas Guinan and her silly suck-
ers—of beauty contests and dance marathons—what John Chapman of
the *New York Daily News* called "the markhellinger era." There is a bit of
satire in the sets and costumes, and even in the production numbers,
when the chorines nasally sing, "A Lovely Girl Is like a Bird."

BITTER SWEET
(1929/1934)

Book, music and lyrics by Noel Coward　　*Published libretto*: Doubleday, 1929　　*Condensation*: None　　*Anthology*: *Play Parade*, vol. 1. Heinemann (London), 1934　　*Piano-vocal score*: Harms, 1929 *Licensing agent*: Tams-Witmark　　*Recordings*: Monmouth Evergreen 7062/3 E (London original cast) ✰ Angel S 35814 (studio cast)　　*Cast*: 22 M; 12 F

The time is the 1870s and the setting is Vienna. Sari has fallen in love with her music teacher and they have run away together; he leads the orchestra in a cafe and she works as a dance girl. This romantic operetta is called buoyant, light-hearted and graciously amusing. Coward songs such as "I'll See You Again" and "Zigeuner" are featured.

BLOOMER GIRL
(1944)

Book by Sig Herzig and Fred Saidy; based on the play by Lilith and Dan James　　*Music* by Harold Arlen　　*Lyrics* by E. Y. Harburg　　*Published libretto*: None　　*Condensation*: *American Musicals: Arlen*. Time-Life, 1982 *Anthology*: None　　*Vocal selections*: Chappell, 1944　　*Licensing agent*: Tams-Witmark　　*Recordings*: MCA 2072 E, Time-Life STL-AM11 (original cast)　　*Cast*: 18 M; 13 F; chorus

The original production was the biggest thing since *Oklahoma!*. Dolly Bloomer, in rebellion against the suppression of women's rights, starts an anti-hoopskirt fashion. Hence the term, bloomers. The time is 1861, so the Civil War figures in the plot. Ballets by Agnes de Mille were featured in the original production. There was a revival at Goodspeed in East Haddam, Connecticut in 1981.

BLOSSOM TIME
(1921/1943)

Book and lyrics by Dorothy Donnelly; from the play *Dreimaderlhaus* by A. M. Willner and Heinz Reichert; based on the novel *Schwammerl* by Rudolph Hans Bartsch　　*Music* from Franz Schubert and Heinrich Berte; adapted by Sigmund Romberg　　*Published libretto*: None *Condensation*: None　　*Anthology*: None　　*Vocal selections*: None *Licensing agent*: Shubert Organization　　*Recordings*: RCA K 5 (studio cast) ✰ Reader's Digest RD 40-N5 (studio cast—*Treasury of Great Operettas*, Record 5)　　*Cast*: 12 M; 11 F

The imaginary plot is set in Vienna around 1826. Schubert is in love with Mitzi Kranz, the daughter of the court jeweler. When Baron Schober offers to help Schubert, Mitzi falls in love with the Baron. This famous show has toured the country many times, and despite some shortcomings in production, the critics always find that the wonderful Schubert melodies are still there. This was done in England under the title *Lilac Time*.

THE BODY BEAUTIFUL
(1958)

Book by Joseph Stein and Will Glickman   *Music* by Jerry Bock   *Lyrics* by Sheldon Harnick   *Published libretto*: Samuel French, 1957 *Condensation*: None   *Anthology*: None   *Vocal selections*: Valando, 1962   *Licensing agent*: Samuel French   *Recording*: None   *Cast*: 20 M; 6 F; chorus

This spoof of the boxing industry features a wealthy young collegian boxer from Dartmouth who goes into professional fighting and has various mishaps. This was a late fifties show, so there is a rock and roll number by street kids in the Elvis Presley style.

THE BOY FRIEND
(1954/1970)

Book, music and lyrics by Sandy Wilson   *Published libretto*: Dutton, 1955 *Condensation*: *The Best Plays of 1954–1955*. Louis Kronenberger, ed. Dodd, Mead, 1955   *Anthology*: None   *Piano-vocal score*: Chappell, 1960 *Vocal selections*: Chappell, 1954   *Licensing agent*: Music Theatre International   *Recording*: RCA LOC 1018 (original cast)   *Cast*: 12 M; 13 F

This musical comedy of the 1920s has been consistently popular for over 25 years and has been performed many times throughout the world. It has been called perfectly conceived and a classic. The plot is all about a romance between a rich girl and boy, each believing the other to be poor. But never mind the plot, concentrate on the 1926 sets of the Riviera and all the flappers doing "Won't You Charleston with Me?" and all the clichés of twenties musicals! Julie Andrews was the first "Polly" on Broadway and Twiggy played the part in the film in 1971.

THE BOYS FROM SYRACUSE
(1938/1963)

Book by George Abbott; based on *The Comedy of Errors* by William
Shakespeare   Music by Richard Rodgers   Lyrics by Lorenz Hart
Published libretto: None   Condensation: American Musicals: Rodgers and
Hart. Time-Life, 1981   Anthology: None   Piano-vocal score: Chappell,
1965   Vocal selections: Chappell, 1938   Licensing agent: Rodgers and
Hammerstein Theatre Library   Recordings: Columbia CSP COS 2580,
Time-Life STL-AMO6 (studio cast) ☆ Capitol STAO 1933 (1963 revival cast) ☆
STET DS 15016 (1963 London cast)   Cast: 13 M; 7 F

Ephesus in ancient Greece is the scene for this tale of two sets of identical
twins reunited through a wild series of improbable complications. Most
critics agree that Rodgers and Hart were at their peak when they composed this famous score that includes "This Can't Be Love" and "Falling
in Love with Love." There was a film version in 1940 with Martha Raye and
Allan Jones.

BRIGADOON
(1947/1964/1980)

Book and lyrics by Alan Jay Lerner   Music by Frederick Loewe
Published libretto: Coward, McCann, 1947 ☆ *Theatre Arts* (magazine), August
1952   Condensation: Burns Mantle Best Plays of 1946–1947. Burns
Mantle, ed. Dodd, Mead, 1947 ☆ American Musicals: Lerner and Loewe.
Time-Life, 1981   Anthology: Ten Great Musicals of the American Stage.
Stanley Richards, ed. Chilton, 1973   Piano-vocal score: Big Three (S. Fox,
1948)   Vocal selections: Big Three (S. Fox, 1947)   Licensing agent:
Tams-Witmark   Recordings: RCA LSO 1001 E (original cast) ☆ Columbia
CL 1132, Time-Life STL-AMO4 (studio cast)   Cast: 12 M; 5 F; extras

Brigadoon is a town in Scotland that comes awake for only one day in a
century. Two Yanks stumble into the village and fall in love with two of
the local girls. Some critics feel that this is the best Lerner and Loewe
musical, and the score does contain "Almost Like Being in Love" and
"The Heather on the Hill." Gene Kelly starred in the film. Recent revivals
have emphasized the classical training of the dancers.

BRING BACK BIRDIE
(1981)

Book by Michael Stewart   Music by Charles Strouse   Lyrics by Lee
Adams   Published libretto: None   Condensation: None   Anthology:

None   *Piano-vocal score*: None   *Licensing agent*: Tams-Witmark
Recording: Original Cast OC 8132 (original cast)   *Cast*: 11 M; 8 F; chorus

This is a sequel to *Bye Bye Birdie*. It is 20 years later, and Albert and Rose set out to find Conrad Birdie so that he can appear on a special TV show saluting all-time great recording stars. Since Albert and Rose have teenage children there is also an opportunity to satirize current music and mores.

BY HEX
(1956)

Book by John Rengier; based on an idea suggested by Richard Gehman
Music and lyrics by Howard Blankman; additional lyrics by Richard Gehman and John Rengier   *Published libretto*: Dramatists Play Service, 1956
Condensation: None   *Anthology*: None   *Piano-vocal score*: None
Licensing agent: Dramatists Play Service   *Recording*: None   *Cast*: 9 M; 5 F; extras

A rebellious young Amish man named Jonas wants to go modern with tractors, television and red suspenders and ends up getting himself "shunned." Jonas learns his lesson and all ends well for him and his sweetheart. This small-scale musical with only one backdrop was first done in Lancaster (Pennsylvania) and later off-Broadway. A charming and easily presented score makes this an uncomplicated show for family audiences.

BY JUPITER
(1942/1967)

Book by Richard Rodgers and Lorenz Hart; based on the play *The Warrior's Husband* by Julian F. Thompson; additional material for the 1967 production by Fred Ebb   *Music* by Richard Rodgers   *Lyrics* by Lorenz Hart
Published libretto: None   *Condensation*: None   *Anthology*: None
Music publisher: Chappell, 1942   *Licensing agent*: Rodgers and Hammerstein Theatre Library   *Recording*: RCA LSO 1137 (1967 cast recording)   *Cast*: 9 M; 8 F

Set in ancient Greece, this is the tale of mighty Hercules, in a woman's world, who sets out to wrestle the girdle of domination from Hippolyta, Queen of the Amazons. The original production was called naughty and ribald; the songs include "Ev'rything I've Got" and "Nobody's Heart." This is a dancing show; Ray Bolger was the original star.

BY STROUSE
(1978)

Music by Charles Strouse   *Lyrics* by Lee Adams, Martin Charnin, Fred
Tobias, David Rogers, and Charles Strouse   *Published libretto*: None
Condensation: None   *Anthology*: None   *Vocal selections*: None (see
individual titles by Strouse)   *Licensing agent*: Samuel French
Recording: None (see individual titles by Strouse)   *Cast*: 1 M; 3 F

This show includes 46 numbers—"I-feel-great-songs, I-feel-blue-songs,
times-they-are-a-changing-songs,"said Rex Reed of the *New York Daily
News*—from a dozen different shows without dialogue or sets, and with
only a few props. There are two versions available: one cabaret-type that
is one hour long, and a full theatrical version that is almost twice as long
with one intermission. Songs are from such Strouse shows as *Annie*, *Bye
Bye Birdie*, *Applause*, and include the title song from the TV show *All in
the Family*.

BY THE BEAUTIFUL SEA
(1954)

Book by Herbert and Dorothy Fields   *Music* by Arthur Schwartz
Lyrics by Dorothy Fields   *Published libretto*: None   *Condensation*:
None   *Anthology*: None   *Vocal selections*: None   *Licensing agent*:
Music Theatre International   *Recording*: Capitol T 11652 (original cast)
Cast: 12 M; 7 F; chorus

The scene is Coney Island in the early 1900s. A boarding house proprietor falls in love with a Shakespearean actor who is down on his luck and
currently doing a vaudeville act. The sets include the Midway, the Old
Mill, the Dreamland Casino and the Brighton Beach Vaudeville Theater.
This show was particularly praised for its star, Shirley Booth.

BYE BYE BIRDIE
(1960)

Book by Michael Stewart   *Music* by Charles Strouse   *Lyrics* by Lee
Adams   *Published libretto*: Drama Book Shop, 1962   *Condensation*:
Broadway's Best, 1960. John Chapman, ed. Doubleday, 1960   *Anthology*:
None   *Piano-vocal score*: Big Three (Morris, 1962)   *Vocal selections*:
Big Three (Morris, 1963)   *Licensing agent*: Tams-Witmark   *Recording*:
Columbia CSP COS 2025 (original cast)   *Cast*: 22 M; 26 F

Conrad Birdie, a rock and roll singer, has been drafted! This satire on the
Elvis Presley incident was one of the earliest Broadway musicals to use

rock and roll rhythms. It first creeps into the "Telephone Hour" number with all the teenagers in different boxes. It was an amusing hit back then and has the added appeal now of nostalgia. There is also an adult story with traditional show tunes. This was a popular film with Ann-Margaret in 1963.
Tony Award Winner (Best Musical)

CABARET
(1966)

Book by Joe Masteroff; based on the play *I Am a Camera* by John van Druten and stories by Christopher Isherwood   *Music* by John Kander   *Lyrics* by Fred Ebb   *Published libretto*: Random House, 1967 (as "Harold Prince's Cabaret")   *Condensation*: *The Best Plays of 1966–1967*. Otis L. Guernsey, Jr., ed. Dodd, Mead, 1967   *Anthology*: *Great Musicals of the American Theatre*, vol. 2. Stanley Richards, ed. Chilton, 1976   *Piano-vocal score*: Sunbeam Music (Valando), 1968   *Vocal selections*: New York Times Music, 1972   *Licensing agent*: Tams-Witmark   *Recording*: Columbia KOS 3040 (original cast)   *Cast*: 13 M; 15 F

The time is 1930 and the city is Berlin. There are several intertwined plots: Sally, the young English girl who performs at the Kit Kat Club; the American writer, Cliff, who lives at the same boarding house as Sally; and Fraulein Schneider, the landlady, and her romance with Herr Schultz. All these stories come together with the rise of Nazism. The role of the Master of Ceremonies is one of the most theatrical in modern musical comedy and made a star of Joel Grey. This is an extremely popular adult musical that was even more popular as a film with Liza Minnelli in 1972.
Tony Award Winner (Best Musical)

CALAMITY JANE
(1953 film adapted for the stage)

Book adapted for the stage by Ronald Hammer and Phil Park; from the stage play by Charles K. Freeman after the James O'Hanlon screenplay   *Music* by Sammy Fain   *Lyrics* by Paul Francis Webster   *Published libretto*: None   *Condensation*: None   *Anthology*: None   *Vocal selections*: Harms-Witmark (London), 1962   *Licensing agent*: Tams-Witmark   *Recording*: Columbia CL 6273 (film sound track)   *Cast*: 12 M; 4 F; chorus

This western musical's plot is about Calamity's offer to present the ravishing Adelaide Adams to Deadwood City, and her subsequent problems while doing so. Calamity was described as "a western shrew magnificently worth the taming." The musical score includes the 1953

Academy-Award-winning "Secret Love" and several new songs for a total of 13 musical numbers. Doris Day was in the original film and Carol Burnett was Calamity on both regional stages and television.

CALL ME MADAM
(1950)

Book by Howard Lindsay and Russel Crouse   Music and lyrics by Irving Berlin   Published libretto: None   Condensation: American Musicals: Berlin. Time-Life, 1981   Anthology: None   Piano-vocal score: Irving Berlin Music (London), 1952   Licensing agent: Music Theatre International   Recordings: RCA CBM 1-2032 (Dinah Shore and original cast) ☆ MCA 2055E, Time-Life STL-AMO7 (Ethel Merman and studio cast) Cast: 15 M; 5 F; chorus

This fictional version of Mrs. Perle Mesta, a famous Washington hostess and once Minister to Luxembourg, was devised specifically with Ethel Merman in mind for the lead role. She goes to "Lichtenburg" and falls in love with a diplomat. There is a secondary romance between a princess and a young man from the State Department. The well-known score includes "You're Just in Love." This musical was filmed with Ethel Merman and George Sanders in 1953.

CAMELOT
(1960/1980)

Book and lyrics by Alan Jay Lerner; based on The Once and Future King by T. H. White   Music by Frederick Loewe   Published libretto: Random House, 1961   Condensation: American Musicals: Lerner and Loewe. Time-Life, 1981   Anthology: Great Musicals of the American Theatre, vol. 2. Stanley Richards, ed. Chilton, 1976   Piano-vocal score: Chappell, 1962 Licensing agent: Tams-Witmark   Recordings: Columbia JS 32602, Time-Life STL-AMO4 (original cast)   Cast: 14 M; 4 F; 1 dog; chorus

It is "a long time ago" at Camelot and the court of King Arthur and his Knights of the Round Table. His struggle to reconcile his difficult private life with his concepts of right and justice provides a moving and melancholy story. Beauty and pageantry are two terms frequently used to describe this show. The beauty may refer, at least in part, to the famous score, but it also refers to a show that lends itself to lavish sets and costumes. Richard Burton was the original King Arthur and Richard Harris starred in the film. Twenty years later Harris replaced Burton in the highly successful revival.

CAN-CAN
(1953/1959/1981)

Book by Abe Burrows   *Music and lyrics* by Cole Porter   *Published libretto*: None   *Condensation*: *American Musicals: Porter.* Time-Life, 1981   *Anthology*: None   *Piano-vocal score*: Chappell, 1954   *Licensing agent*: Tams-Witmark   *Recordings*: Capitol DW 452E, Time-Life STL-AMO2 (original cast) ✭ Monmouth Evergreen 7073E (London cast)   *Cast*: 15 M; 7 F; chorus

Pistache is the proprietor of a Montmartre bistro in Paris during the Toulouse Lautrec era in 1893. A young judge wants to close down the "Bal du Paradis" as they perform the forbidden Can-Can. The recent Broadway revival (1981) was quite lavish. It featured ballets by Roland Petit, but it was always a dancing show. Cole Porter's "I Love Paris" and "C'est Magnifique" are some of the jewels of the score. Frank Sinatra and Maurice Chevalier were in the 1960 film.

CANDIDE
(1973/1982)

Book by Hugh Wheeler; based on Voltaire's satire   *Music* by Leonard Bernstein   *Lyrics* by Richard Wilbur; with additional lyrics by Stephen Sondheim and John Latouche   *Published libretto*: Schirmer Books, 1976   *Condensations*: *American Musicals: Bernstein.* Time-Life, 1983   *Vocal selections*: Schirmer, 1974   *Licensing agent*: Music Theatre International   *Recording*: Columbia S2X 32923 (1973 production)   *Cast*: 11 M; 12 F

The original 1956 operetta by Lillian Hellman was considerably revised with a new book, but retaining the Bernstein score, and was a smash hit in 1973. It is this 1973 version that is currently available. The classic plot concerns optimistic Dr. Pangloss sending Candide and his friends out into a cynical and predatory world. The Broadway revival production featured a complex set of platforms, drawbridges, trap doors and ramps. The New York City Opera recently staged *Candide* in a production similar to the 1956 operetta and it was a sensational success.

CANTERBURY TALES
(1969/1979)

Book by Martin Starkie and Nevill Coghill; based on a translation from Chaucer by Nevill Coghill   *Music* by Richard Hill and John Hawkins   *Lyrics* by Nevill Coghill   *Published libretto*: None   *Condensation*: None

Anthology: None   *Vocal selections*: Blackwood Music, 1969   *Licensing agent*: Music Theatre International   *Recording*: Capitol SW 229 (original cast)   *Cast*: 12 M; 7 F; chorus

Four of Chaucer's famous tales have been musicalized. They are: The Miller's, The Steward's, The Merchant's and The Wife of Bath's. Some critics found these classic fourteenth century tales bawdy and in doubtful taste in their reviews of the stories told by pilgrims to while away their time along the way to the shrine of Thomas à Becket. The music is a blend of modern and medieval rhythms. This can be staged very economically.

CARMEN JONES
(1943)

Book and lyrics by Oscar Hammerstein, II; based on Bizet's opera *Carmen*
Music by Georges Bizet   *Published libretto*: Knopf, 1945
Condensation: None   *Anthology*: None   *Vocal selections*: Chappell,
1944   *Licensing agent*: Rodgers and Hammerstein Theatre Library
Recording: MCA 2054E (original cast)   *Cast*: 7 M; 6 F; chorus

Bizet's *Carmen*, its score intact, has been transported to the United States during World War II. Carmen still works in a factory and Joe is a soldier; the toreador has become a boxing champion. The show was traditionally performed by an all black cast, and the film starred Harry Belafonte. His voice was not used, however, as operatic voices are required.

CARNIVAL
(1961/1977)

Book by Michael Stewart; based on material by Helen Deutsch, the film *Lili*, and a short story by Paul Gallico   *Music and lyrics* by Bob Merrill
Published libretto: Drama Book Shop, 1968   *Condensation*: None
Anthology: None   *Vocal selections*: Big Three (Robbins Music, 1961)
Licensing agent: Tams-Witmark   *Recording*: MGM 3946 (original cast)
Cast: 13 M; 9 F

The orphan Lili comes to the circus seeking a friend of her father's and with the hope of finding a job. But the friend has gone and as she is about to give up hope she gets a job working with the puppet show. At first she thinks she loves the magician but eventually realizes that the lame puppeteer is the one for her. Some added attractions can include jugglers and other performers likely to be found in a small European circus.

CAROUSEL
(1945/1965)

Book and lyrics by Oscar Hammerstein, II; based on Ferenc Molnar's *Liliom*
Music by Richard Rodgers   *Published libretto*: Knopf, 1946
Condensation: *American Musicals: Rodgers and Hammerstein*. Time-Life,
1980   *Anthology*: *Six Plays by Rodgers and Hammerstein*. Random House,
1955 ☆ Modern Library, 1959   *Piano-vocal score*: Harms, 1945
Licensing agent: Rodgers and Hammerstein Theatre Library   *Recordings*:
MCA 2033E, Time-Life STL-AMO1 (original cast) ☆ RCA LSO 1114 (1965
Lincoln Center cast)   *Cast*: 12 M; 7 F; chorus

The setting is a coastal New England town in 1873. Julie, a shy small-town
girl, is attracted to Billy Bigalow, a barker at an amusement park. They
marry and he loses his job. In his famous "Soliloquy" Billy thinks about
the child they soon will have. In this show the characters do not all live
happily ever after. Agnes de Mille did the choreography for such famous
numbers as "June Is Bustin' Out All Over" and everyone knows the
beautiful "If I Loved You." There was a film in 1956.

THE CAT AND THE FIDDLE
(1931)

Book and lyrics by Otto Harbach   *Music* by Jerome Kern   *Published
libretto*: None   *Condensation*: None   *Anthology*: None
Piano-vocal score: Harms, 1932   *Vocal selections*: Harms, 1931
Licensing agent: Tams-Witmark   *Recording*: *Jerome Kern in London*
(London original cast) ☆ Monmouth-Evergreen 7064E (four selections)
Cast: 9 M; 7 F; chorus

Victor is a serious-minded young gentleman who goes in for classical
music. Shirley is not as serious, and doesn't mind at all jazzing up a score
Victor has written. Some famous Kern tunes are "The Night Was Made for
Love" and "She Didn't Say Yes." Eddie Foy, Jr., who was in the original,
stopped the show with "Ha Cha Cha!" There was a film with Jeanette
MacDonald in 1934.

CAVALCADE
(1931)

Book, music and lyrics by Noel Coward   *Published libretto*: Grosset and
Dunlop, 1933 ☆ Doubleday, 1933   *Condensation*: None   *Anthology*:
Sixteen Famous British Plays. Bennett Cerf, ed. Modern Library, 1942 ☆ *Play*

Parade, vol. 1. Heinemann (London), 1934   *Vocal selections*: None
Licensing agent: Samuel French   *Recording*: *Noel Coward the Master*,
World Records (British) SHB 50   *Cast*: Large mixed cast

This pageant of English history includes 22 scenes from the Boer War to the early 1930s. It portrays the shifting fortunes of the Marryot family and the Bridges family (respectively employers and servants, somewhat like "Upstairs, Downstairs"). The original production was a lavish spectacle that employed over 400 people at London's Drury Lane. A recent London revival featured a professional cast of 12 and scores of tightly-drilled amateurs. The music of the play is chiefly made up of popular songs of the times. Coward did compose "Twentieth Century Blues" and "Mirabelle." There was a 1933 film version using at least one Coward song.

CELEBRATION
(1969/1975)

Book and lyrics by Tom Jones   *Music* by Harvey Schmidt   *Published libretto*: None   *Anthology*: *Fantasticks and Celebration*. Drama Book Specialists, 1973   *Condensation*: *The Best Plays of 1968–1969*. Otis L. Guernsey, Jr., ed. Dodd, Mead, 1969   *Piano-vocal score*: Portfolio Music, 1970 (Chappell)   *Vocal selections*: Portfolio Music, 1969 (Chappell) *Licensing agent*: Music Theatre International   *Recording*: Capitol SW 198 (original cast)   *Cast*: 3 M; 1 F; singers; dancers

The celebration is New Year's Eve, and out of the masked crowds we meet a wistful but hopeful orphan. He becomes involved in a spiritual tug-of-war with a rich old man. These are symbolic characters who perform a parable of youth and age. The other two characters are the narrator and an angel (really a night club singer). The original production was noted for its costumes, particularly the masks, and the staging. The scenery consisted of an arrangement of trestle-like platforms. Highly original, this ritualistic morality play is a celebration of life.

CHARLIE AND ALGERNON
(1980)

Book and lyrics by David Rogers; based on the novel *Flowers for Algernon* by Daniel Keyes   *Music* by Charles Strouse   *Published libretto*: Dramatic, 1981   *Condensation*: None   *Anthology*: None   *Vocal selections*: None   *Licensing agent*: Dramatic   *Recording*: Original Cast OC 8021 (London original cast under title, *Flowers for Algernon*)   *Cast*: 5 M; 4 F; 1 child; 1 mouse (live or toy)

Charlie is a grown man with the mind of a child who is turned into a genius through a brain operation. Algernon is a mouse who also had the operation. Unfortunately the effects of the operations are not permanent. This was a popular film with Cliff Robertson. The lead roles are a challenge, as are the scenes with the mouse.

CHARLOTTE SWEET
(1982)

Libretto by Michael Colby   *Music* by Gerald Jay Markoe   *Published libretto*: Samuel French, 1983   *Condensation*: None   *Anthology*: None
Vocal selections: None   *Licensing agent*: Samuel French
Recording: John Hammond W2X 38680   *Cast*: 4 M; 4 F

Charlotte's father won't let her marry her beloved, so she joins a troupe of touring musicians and becomes "the incomparable" on the Victorian music-hall stage. When she begins to lose her high notes, the leader of the troupe puts her on helium, and she is soon addicted. There is no spoken dialogue in this music hall pastiche. There are 26 songs, ranging from ballad to tango to march rhythm to patter song. The off-Broadway production was praised by the critic of the *New York Post* for its scenery with "flat surfaces and illusory depths of a pop-up valentine." The costumes were described as "slightly demented" versions of the authentic style. There is also a touch of Victorian melodrama, with the audience constantly hissing the villain.

CHICAGO
(1975)

Book by Fred Ebb and Bob Fosse; based on the play *Chicago* by Maurine Dallas Watkins   *Music* by John Kander   *Lyrics* by Fred Ebb
Published libretto: Samuel French, 1976   *Condensation*: *The Best Plays of 1975–1976*. Otis L. Guernsey, Jr., ed. Dodd, Mead, 1976   *Anthology*: None   *Vocal selections*: Chappell, 1975   *Licensing agent*: Samuel French   *Recording*: Arista 9005 (original cast)   *Cast*: 9 M; 10 F; chorus; dancers

"Razzle Dazzle 'Em" goes the song, and that's just what this show does. The tale of Roxie Hart (a chorus girl who shoots a lover, but due to her slick lawyer, beats the rap) is told in the form of a 1920s vaudeville show. This is a cynical, but stylish and sophisticated show. Gwen Verdon and Liza Minnelli both played "Roxie" on Broadway with great success. The Bob Fosse choreography adds a great deal to the show's lurid and sensational mood.

CINDERELLA
(1957 TV musical adapted for the stage)

Book and lyrics by Oscar Hammerstein, II; adapted for the stage by Don Driver   *Music* by Richard Rodgers   *Published libretto*: None *Condensation*: None   *Anthology*: None   *Piano-vocal score*: Williamson Music, 1962   *Vocal selections*: Williamson Music, 1957   *Licensing agent*: Rodgers and Hammerstein Theatre Library   *Recording*: Columbia OS 2005 (original TV cast)   *Cast*: 10 M; 6 F; singing and dancing chorus

The classic tale of the prince and the glass slipper is followed in this production, with lavish costumes for the ball and a fairy tale atmosphere. There are no classic songs in the score, but any songs by Rodgers and Hammerstein are likely to please. This has been done successfully at the St. Louis Municipal Opera, in London, and off-Broadway (in 1977).

CINDY
(1964)

Book by Joe Sauter and Mike Sawyer   *Lyrics and music* by Johnny Brandon   *Published libretto*: None   *Condensation*: None *Anthology*: None   *Vocal selections*: None   *Licensing agent*: Tams-Witmark   *Recording*: ABC S-OC-2 (original cast)   *Cast*: 6 M; 6 F

The leading lady's name is "Cindy Kreller"—say that aloud! A lively twentieth-century version of the classic Cinderella, this contemporary teen musical is set in a Jewish delicatessen. There is a lot of Lower East Side (New York) Jewish humor. In the original off-Broadway production, the good fairy also played an insolent housemaid.

THE CLUB
(1976)

Devised by Eve Merriam; musical direction and arrangements by Alexandra Ivanoff   *Pubished libretto*: Samuel French, 1977   *Condensation*: None *Anthology*: None   *Vocal selections*: None   *Licensing agent*: Samuel French   *Recording*: None   *Cast*: 7 F

In the off-Broadway production of this show, two platforms connected by a long, narrow ramp made up the acting area. It was here that the audience was introduced to the members of an all-male club, circa 1905. They talked and sang about their wives, alimony, card games, and the stock market. But they were all played by women disguised as men. They sang old songs (from the period 1894 to 1905) and exchanged anti-feminist and sometimes smutty jokes. Merriam is deeply involved in the women's liberation movement and used this show as a vehicle of feminist protest.

Off-Broadway (OBIE) Award Winner

COLE
(1974)

Devised by Benny Green and Alan Strachan   *Lyrics and music* by Cole Porter   *Published libretto*: None   *Condensation*: None   *Anthology*: None   *Music publisher*: Music and Lyrics by Cole Porter. 2 vols. Chappell, 1972–1975   *Licensing agent*: Samuel French   *Recording*: RCA CRL 2-5054 (London original cast)   *Cast*: 5 M; 5 F

Today Cole Porter stands for great show tunes, sophistication, wit, and nostalgia. This revue was originally presented at the Mermaid Theatre in London. It takes us from 1916 to the mid-1950s, with about 50 songs. Although there are some biographical details in the first part, it is basically a song and dance show. It is performed in an art deco set that serves as an ocean liner, or a Broadway stage, or a bar, or, in other words, the world of Cole Porter. Some slide projections were used in the original production.

COMIN' UPTOWN
(1979)

Book by Philip Rose and Peter Udell; based on *A Christmas Carol* by Charles Dickens   *Music* by Garry Sherman   *Lyrics* by Peter Udell   *Published libretto*: None   *Condensation*: None   *Anthology*: None   *Vocal selections*: None   *Licensing agent*: Samuel French   *Recording*: None   *Cast*: 11 M; 8 F; chorus

Dickens' tale of London has been modernized and set in Harlem, in New York City. Scrooge is now a black slum landlord. The music has a modern beat with African ethnic and gospel touches. Gregory Hines was the Broadway star and received much praise for his singing and dancing, as did the elaborate, maneuverable settings.

COMPANY
(1970/1980)

Book by George Furth   Music and lyrics by Stephen Sondheim
Published libretto: Random House, 1970   Condensation: The Best Plays of
1969–1970. Otis L. Guernsey, Jr., ed. Dodd, Mead, 1970 ☆ American
Musicals: Sondheim. Time-Life, 1982   Anthology: Ten Great Musicals of
the American Stage. Stanley Richards, ed. Chilton, 1973   Piano-vocal
score: Valando, 1971   Vocal selections: Valando, 1970   Licensing agent:
Music Theatre International   Recordings: Columbia OS 3550, Time-Life
STL-AM12 (original cast)   Cast: 6 M; 8 F; small chorus

This musical takes a stinging look at the state of matrimony, particularly
in a big city—New York City. Various married couples try to convince a
35-year-old bachelor that he should marry, but they do not present very
good role models for marriage. This musical has been hailed as a
landmark in American theater. The original set resembled a modern
building skeleton with many different levels, stairs, and two elevators.
Tony Award Winner (Best Musical)

A CONNECTICUT YANKEE
(1927/1943)

Book by Herbert Fields; musical adaptation of A Connecticut Yankee in King
Arthur's Court by Mark Twain   Music by Richard Rodgers   Lyrics by
Lorenz Hart   Published libretto: None   Condensation: None
Anthology: None   Vocal selections: None   Licensing agent:
Tams-Witmark   Recording: AEI 1138 (1943 cast recording)   Cast: 7 M;
5 F; chorus

Martin Barratt is knocked unconscious at his bachelor's dinner party in
Connecticut, and awakes to find himself in King Arthur's court in Camelot
in 543 A.D. The 1943 production was considerably revised from the
original, and several new songs were added to the score, including the
famous "To Keep My Love Alive." The two biggest numbers, however,
come from the original, and are "My Heart Stood Still" and "Thou Swell."
This musical was described as clever, smart, amiable and engaging.

THE CONTRAST
(1972)

Book adapted by Anthony Stimac; based on the play The Contrast (the first
American comedy, written in 1787) by Royall Tyler   Music by Donald

Pippin   *Lyrics* by Steve Brown   *Published libretto*: Samuel French, 1972
Condensation: None   *Anthology*: None   *Vocal selections*: None
Licensing agent: Samuel French   *Recording*: None   *Cast*: 5 M; 5 F

This off-Broadway musical version of the first American comedy (written
in 1787) was described as being filled with satire and innuendo. For
example, the cast also moves the props and scenery about, taking more
and more elaborate bows after each shift. A sense of comic timing is
required, as the cast scurries about with split-second synchronization.
The plot (and title) involves exaggerated European manners and the
straightforwardness of Americans in the late eighteenth century. The
score was described as a blend of everything from square dance to
George M. Cohan, with a bit of rock thrown in.

COTTON PATCH GOSPEL
(1981)

Book by Tom Key and Russell Treyz; based on *The Cotton Patch Version of
Matthew and John* by Clarence Jordan   *Music and lyrics* by Harry Chapin
Published libretto: Dramatic, 1982   *Condensation*: None   *Anthology*:
None   *Vocal selections*: None   *Licensing agent*: Dramatic
Recording: Chapin Productions CP 101 (original cast)   *Cast*: 1 M (plus
back-up group—may be done by large cast)

Described as a down-home retelling of the Christ story, this show asks
the question, "What if Jesus was born 40 years ago in Georgia?" The one
actor/singer portrays Matthew and 33 other characters. The country band
comments on the narrative through the songs. Politicians, the moral
majority, TV evangelists, the Klu Klux Klan and racial prejudice are just
some of the topics brought into the story. Jesus is born behind the Dixie
Delight Motor Lodge. Three scholars from the East give him a gold
American Express card, peach-scented candles and a bottle of Jade East!
The 16 songs are described as rousing country and western songs and
gospel tunes. Simple to stage, the whole show hinges on the music and
the satire.

COWARDY CUSTARD
(1972)

Devised by Gerald Frow, Alan Strachan and Wendy Toye   *Words and
music* by Noel Coward   *Published libretto*: Samuel French, 1977
Condensation: None   *Anthology*: None   *Vocal selections*: Noel Coward

Songbook. Simon and Schuster, 1953   *Licensing agent*: Samuel French
Recording: RCA LSO 6010 (London original cast)   *Cast*: 6 M; 6 F

In this revue, the songs and sketches of Noel Coward are bound together by autobiographical material. This all takes us back to a smart era, with crisp, impertinent dialogue, and familiar and witty songs. There is a London sequence ("London Pride"), a travel sequence ("Mad Dogs and Englishmen"), and a party sequence ("I've Been to a Marvelous Party"), and there are excerpts from "Tonight at 8:30" and "Present Laughter." This material of Noel Coward, Gertrude Lawrence, and Bea Lillie calls for an extraordinary cast.

THE CRADLE WILL ROCK
(1937/1964/1983)

A play in music by Marc Blitzstein   *Published libretto*: Random House, 1938   *Condensation*: None   *Anthology*: *The Best Short Plays of the Social Theatre*. William Kozlenko, ed. Random House, 1939   *Vocal selections*: Chappell, 1938   *Licensing agent*: Tams-Witmark
Recordings: American Legacy 1001 (original cast) ☆ Composers Recordings 2-CRI SD 266 (1964 cast)   *Cast*: 10 M; 7 F

Subtitled "a worker's opera," this pro-labor union, anti-big business work features the "Good Guys" against the "Bad Guys" and moves in and out of court. Everyone is a caricature instead of a person. But never mind the dated social message. What's important now is the jazzy, mock-popular and craggy musical score somewhat in the style of Kurt Weill. The songs are strung together by bits of dialogue. This is traditionally performed without scenery or costumes and usually with only a piano.

CURLEY MCDIMPLE
(1967)

Book by Mary Boylan and Robert Dahdah   *Music and lyrics* by Robert Dahdah   *Published libretto*: Samuel French, 1967   *Condensation*: None
Anthology: None   *Vocal selections*: Chappell, 1968   *Licensing agent*: Samuel French   *Recording*: Capitol 45-2116 (original cast—two songs)
Cast: 3 M; 3 F; 1 young girl

Two young song-and-dance vaudevillians are trying for success on Broadway. There's an Irish landlady and every other 1930s movie musical cliché you can imagine—plus an eight-year-old girl with Shirley Temple curls who must carry the bulk of the show all by herself. Curley has been left on the doorstep in a large laundry basket. Be prepared for lots of tap-dancing. This show has simple sets and costumes, and the off-Broadway production used a combo of three musicians.

DAMES AT SEA
(1968)

Book and lyrics by George Haimsohn and Robin Miller   *Music* by Jim Wise   *Published libretto*: Samuel French, 1969   *Condensation*: None *Anthology*: None   *Vocal selections*: Big Three, 1969   *Licensing agent*: Samuel French   *Recording*: Columbia OS 3330 (original cast)   *Cast*: 4 M; 3 F

This spoof of elaborate movie musicals of the thirties started out in a coffee house in Greenwich Village. The production was staged "in the round" on a postage stamp-sized stage with only a piano. It went on to off-Broadway, London, and television with Ann Miller. It has the standard backstage plot of the young chorus girl going on at the last minute to save the show. The finale takes place on the deck of a battleship. All of the songs are meant to recall the famous movie musical songs, and the young lovers are appropriately named Dick and Ruby.

DAMN YANKEES
(1955/1981)

Book by George Abbott and Douglass Wallop; based on the novel *The Year the Yankees Lost the Pennant* by Douglass Wallop   *Music and lyrics* by Richard Adler and Jerry Ross   *Published libretto*: Random House, 1956 ☆ *Theatre Arts* (magazine), November 1956   *Condensation*: None *Anthology*: None   *Piano-vocal score*: Frank Music, 1957   *Vocal selections*: Frank Music, 1958   *Licensing agent*: Music Theatre International   *Recording*: RCA LSO 1021E (original cast)   *Cast*: 14 M; 7 F; chorus; children

In a slight twist of the Faust legend, Joe Hardy makes a deal with the Devil to regain his youth and lead the Washington Senators baseball team to victory. When Joe shows signs of exercising his "escape clause," the Devil sends in his helper, Lola, to convince Joe. This is one of the very few successful baseball musicals. "You Gotta Have Heart" and "Whatever Lola Wants" were some popular songs from the score. It was filmed in 1958 featuring the Broadway cast and Bob Fosse choreography, plus Tab Hunter. It was performed later at Jones Beach with Joe Namath. *Tony Award Winner (Best Musical)*

THE DANCING YEARS
(1939)

Devised, written and composed by Ivor Novello   *Lyrics* by Christopher
Hassall   *Published libretto*: None   *Condensation*: None   *Anthology*:
None   *Music publisher*: *Ivor Novello Song Album*. Chappell, 197-
Licensing agent: Samuel French   *Recordings*: *Ivor Novello: The Great
Shows* EMI SHB 23 (British) (original London cast) ☆ Philips 6308 225,
Columbia TWO 188 (British—studio cast)   *Cast*: Large mixed cast

The settings are Vienna and the Tyrol during the period from 1911 to
1938. Described as a Viennese confection, the plot concerns Rudi Kleber,
a composer, and his bittersweet love for Maria Ziegler, a celebrated
prima donna. The scenes include performances at the Theater an der
Wien, Tyrolean dancers at the Chalet, and a masked ball. This British
spectacle had its American premiere in St. Louis in 1947. There was a
color film version in 1950 with Dennis Price.

A DAY IN HOLLYWOOD—A NIGHT IN THE UKRAINE
(1980)

Book and lyrics by Dick Vosburgh; additional lyrics by Jerry Herman
Music by Frank Lazarus; additional music by Jerry Herman   *Published
libretto*: Samuel French   *Condensation*: None   *Anthology*: None
Vocal selections: Big Three, 1980   *Licensing agent*: Samuel French
Recording: DRG SBL 12580 (original cast)   *Cast*: 4 M; 4 F

Despite its title, this musical double feature started out in Hampstead and
moved on to London before becoming a big hit on Broadway. The first
half is a spoof of Hollywood in the 1930s, with reenactments of legendary
anecdotes and many popular songs of the era, including a Richard
Whiting medley. Particularly praised was the "dancing feet" routine. The
audience sees the dancers only from the knees down, but quickly iden-
tifies Astaire and Rogers, Mickey Mouse, and a host of others. Part two is a
burlesque of Chekhov's *The Bear* done in the style of the Marx Brothers.
An extremely versatile cast is needed to handle both the musical numbers and the Marx Brothers parody.

DEAR WORLD
(1969)

Book by Jerome Lawrence and Robert E. Lee; based on *The Madwoman of
Chaillot* by Jean Giraudoux, as adapted by Maurice Valency   *Music and
lyrics* by Jerry Herman   *Published libretto*: None   *Condensation*: None
Anthology: None   *Vocal selections*: Morris, 1969   *Licensing agent*:

Tams-Witmark   *Recording*: Columbia CSP ABOS 3260 (original cast)
Cast: 14 M; 4 F; singers; dancers

This musical very closely follows the play upon which it is based. So we have the "Madwoman" in her clothes of yesteryear, various picturesque sets of Paris, and even a trip to the sewers. The "Madwoman" and her friends are out to save Paris from the money-hungry capitalists who want to destroy the city by digging for oil. This is a real tour de force for the leading lady, with outlandish makeup, eccentric costumes, and big numbers with lots of singing. Angela Lansbury was the star of the lavish Broadway production.

DEAREST ENEMY
(1925)

Book by Herbert Fields   *Music* by Richard Rodgers   *Lyrics* by Lorenz Hart   *Published libretto*: None   *Condensation*: None   *Anthology*: None   *Vocal selections*: None   *Licensing agent*: Rodgers and Hammerstein Theatre Library   *Recording*: Beginners Productions BRP-1 (British studio cast)   *Cast*: 12 M; 7 F

This musical is set in the revolutionary war period in New York City. Betsy Burke has fallen in love with Captain (Sir John) Copeland, although her loyalty to the Continentals causes her to betray him. A true historical incident is reenacted as Mrs. Murray serves cake to the British to distract them while the patriots regroup their forces under George Washington in Harlem. "Here in My Arms" is the best-remembered song from the score. This was done on television in 1955 with Anne Jeffreys and at the Goodspeed Opera in East Haddam, Connecticut, in 1976.

THE DESERT SONG
(1926/1946/1973)

Book and lyrics by Otto Harbach, Oscar Hammerstein, II, and Frank Mandel   *Music* by Sigmund Romberg   *Published libretto*: Samuel French, 1932   *Condensation*: None   *Anthology*: None   *Piano-vocal score*: Harms, 1927 (Warner Brothers)   *Licensing agent*: Samuel French   *Recordings*: Columbia CSP ACL 831, Angel S 37319 (studio cast)   *Cast*: 12 M; 6 F; singers; dancers

Pierre Birabeau, the lackluster son of a general, is in fact the "Red Shadow," a mysterious leader of the Riffs in French Morocco back in the 1920s. In this show there is ample opportunity for fun and excitement with the French Foreign Legion, Arabian and Spanish dancing girls, and the romantic music that everybody knows. This is an old-fashioned, vintage operetta and should be staged accordingly; it certainly should not be modernized or mocked. There were several filmed versions—Dennis Morgan in the 1940s production, and Gordon MacRae in the 1950s.

DESTRY RIDES AGAIN
(1959)

Book by Leonard Gershe; based on the story by Max Brand   *Music and lyrics* by Harold Rome   *Published libretto*: None   *Condensation*: None   *Anthology*: None   *Piano-vocal score*: Chappell, 1959   *Licensing agent*: Tams-Witmark   *Recording*: Decca DL 79075 (original cast)   *Cast*: 14 M; 6 F; chorus

This lavish Broadway musical is a western melodrama with song and dance. The plot revolves around the town of Bottleneck, which is under the control of a tough gambler named Kent. Destry is brought in to maintain law and order. Frenchy is the star entertainer at the Last Chance Saloon. The choreography by Michael Kidd (particularly the "Whip Dance") was highly praised by the critics. The costumes were called flashy and fun, particularly those of the dance-hall girls. The score is in the traditional mood of cowboy music with some ragtime flourishes for the saloon festivities. A London production was done "in the round" and the bar used in the set was also used as a refreshment stand during the intermission.

DIAMOND STUDS
(1975)

Book by Jim Wann   *Original music and lyrics* by Bland Simpson and Jim Wann   *Published libretto*: Samuel French, 1976   *Condensation*: None   *Anthology*: None   *Vocal selections*: None   *Licensing agent*: Samuel French   *Recording*: Pasquotank 003 (original cast)   *Cast*: 12 M; 2 F

The off-Broadway production was an example of "environmental theater." The theater was transformed into a frontier saloon with dance-hall girls serving beer, and peanut shells were scattered on the floor. This show is primarily a concert of country music (both traditional and original) rather than a play. The story line concerns Jesse James and is told through narration and sketchy scenes. The performers are musicians first, and actors second.

DIVORCE ME, DARLING!
(1965)

Book, music, and lyrics by Sandy Wilson   *Published libretto*: None
Condensation: None   *Anthology*: None   *Vocal selections*: None
Licensing agent: Music Theatre International   *Recording*: DRG DS 15009
(London original cast)   *Cast*: 18 M; 15 F

This is Wilson's sequel to his very popular *The Boy Friend*. Many of the same characters are used and are now ten years older. It's the 1930s and they are in Nice on a holiday. They all are contemplating the possibility of being single again. Dance numbers are "à la Fred Astaire" and the music sometimes parodies Cole Porter. A Noel Coward terrace scene presents a golden opportunity for displaying high-fashion costumes of the period. This is very British and has never been done on Broadway.

DO BLACK PATENT LEATHER SHOES REALLY REFLECT UP?
(1982)

Book by John R. Powers; based on his novel   *Music and lyrics* by James
Quinn and Alaric Jans   *Published libretto*: None   *Condensation*: None
Anthology: None   *Vocal selections*: None   *Licensing agent*: Mavin
Productions   *Recording*: None   *Cast*: 5 M; 9 F

This musical written and produced in Chicago enjoyed a healthy run there and in other cities before moving to New York. It takes a rather irreverent look at Roman Catholic education. The plot line involves a group of children (played by adults) progressing through grade school and high school. Nuns and priests guide them in religious indoctrination, sex education, and other subjects that Catholic audiences are sure to enjoy. The score was described as "hummable" with a "snappy, bouncy beat." One dance number has the entire company lie on their backs and wave their oversized shoes in the air. The sets were designed to look like cartoons.

DO I HEAR A WALTZ?
(1965/1975)

Book by Arthur Laurents; based on his play *The Time of the Cuckoo*
Music by Richard Rodgers   *Lyrics* by Stephen Sondheim   *Published
libretto*: Random House, 1966   *Condensation*: None   *Anthology*: None
Piano-vocal score: Williamson Music, 1965   *Vocal selections*: Williamson
Music, 1965   *Licensing agent*: Rodgers and Hammerstein Theatre Library

Recording: Columbia CSP AKOS 2770 (original cast)   *Cast*: 6 M; 6 F; chorus

A vacationing spinster visits Venice, meets a handsome Italian, and falls in love. Before being turned into a musical, the original play was filmed as *Summertime* with Katharine Hepburn. The cast includes a young married couple, a worldly Italian landlady, and a young boy. This is a bittersweet love story that can be staged quite simply. Despite the title, there is little dancing. The critics of this show found Richard Rodgers a bit old-fashioned; but Stephen Sondheim was on his way up.

DO RE MI
(1961)

Book by Garson Kanin   *Music* by Jule Styne   *Lyrics* by Betty Comden and Adolph Green   *Published libretto:* None   *Condensation*: None *Anthology*: None   *Piano-vocal score*: Chappell, 1961   *Licensing agent*: Tams-Witmark   *Recording*: RCA LSOD 2002 (original cast)   *Cast*: 8 M; 2 F; chorus; dancers

The original Broadway production had the benefit of two top comedians as stars: Phil Silvers and Nancy Walker. The plot concerns the world of juke box rackets and deals with underworld characters in New York. There is a secondary pair of young lovers and they get to sing the score's bit hit, "Make Someone Happy." The critics mentioned the extravagant production and the numerous scene changes. There are takeoffs on "The Late Late Show," Zen Buddhism and other aspects of life in 1960.

A DOLL'S LIFE
(1982)

Book and lyrics by Betty Comden and Adolph Green   *Music* by Larry Grossman   *Published libretto*: Samuel French   *Condensation*: None *Anthology*: None   *Vocal selections*: Fiddleback (Valando), 1982 *Licensing agent*: Samuel French   *Recording*: Original Cast Records OC 8241 (original cast)   *Cast*: Large mixed cast

The curtain goes up on a present-day rehearsal of Ibsen's *A Doll's House*. After Nora's final exit we are suddenly whisked back to Norway in 1879 to find out what happened to Nora after she left her husband and children. This is a serious work concerning women's rights and equality and was given a lavish Broadway production. The show's design in dark colors was based on the works of Edvard Munch. The score for this musical was described as quasi-operatic, or operetta-like, indicating a need for strong trained voices.

DONNYBROOK!
(1961)

Book by Robert E. McEnroe; based on *The Quiet Man* by Maurice Walsh
Music and lyrics by Johnny Burke   *Published libretto*: None
Condensation: None   *Anthology*: None   *Vocal selections*: None
Licensing agent: Samuel French   *Recording*: Kapp KD 8500 S (original
cast)   *Cast*: 9 M; 5 F; chorus

John Enright, a prizefighter who has killed an opponent in the ring, returns to Ireland seeking peace. Once there he falls in love with a vixenish colleen. Her bullyboy brother tries to get him to fight, and eventually we have an old-fashioned knockdown for the second act finale. This show was described as loud and lusty. The male dancers sometimes wear kilts.

DON'T BOTHER ME, I CAN'T COPE
(1972)

Music by Micki Grant; conceived and directed by Vinnette Carroll
Published libretto: Samuel French, 1972   *Condensation*: None
Anthology: None   *Vocal selections*: Fiddleback Music (Valando), 1973
Licensing agent: Samuel French   *Recording*: Polydor PD 6013 (original
cast)   *Cast*: 7 M; 5 F; 4 musicians

A black revue that consists primarily of songs about being black and human and sensitive. There are also dancers and a gospel choir. There is no plot; this is a musical "happening," and can be done in a simple setting.

DOWNRIVER
(1975)

Book by Jeff Tambornino; based on *The Adventures of Huckleberry Finn* by Mark Twain   *Music and lyrics* by John Braden   *Published libretto*: None   *Condensation*: None   *Anthology*: None   *Vocal selections*: None   *Licensing agent*: Music Theatre International   *Recording*: Take Home Tunes THT 7811 (original cast)   *Cast*: 14 M; 7 F

The off-Broadway production was noted for its abstract settings, which utilized overhead projectors that gave an impressionistic atmosphere. The story is the familiar one about the misadventures of Huck and Jim, the freed slave. This bit of Americana can be simply staged for the whole family.

DRAT! THE CAT!
(1965/1974)

Book and lyrics by Ira Levin   *Music* by Milton Schafer   *Published libretto*: None   *Condensation*: None   *Anthology*: None   *Vocal selections*: Morris (distributed by C. Hansen), 1966   *Licensing agent*: Samuel French   *Recording*: None   *Cast*: 9 M; 6 F; chorus

Around the turn of the century, a "cat burglar" has all of New York in a state of panic! "The Cat" turns out to be the daughter of a millionaire who falls in love with a rookie cop (the son of a former detective chief). This high-spirited comedy is played somewhat in a "Keystone Cop" style. One popular song from the score is "He Touched Me." This was an elaborate Broadway musical with a Japanese kabuki scene, a uniformed 1890s band on stage at one point, and a basement pipe that leaked real water.

THE DRUNKARD
(1970)

Adaptation by Bro Herrod; based on the melodrama by W. H. S. Smith   *Music and lyrics* by Barry Manilow   *Published libretto*: None   *Condensation*: None   *Anthology*: None   *Vocal selections*: None   *Licensing agent*: Music Theatre International   *Recording*: None   *Cast*: 4 M; 4 F

A good old-fashioned "hiss and cheer" melodrama (with olio curtain). A young husband is ruined by drink, then rescued by last minute faith. This show has been popular since 1844! "Do You Want to Be Saved?" was a Salvation Army number most of the critics liked. The score is in traditional style. The off-Broadway production offered free beer (or root beer) and group singing between the acts. Simple to stage and it's good fun.

DU BARRY WAS A LADY
(1939/1972)

Book by B. G. De Sylva and Herbert Fields   *Music and lyrics* by Cole Porter   *Published libretto*: None   *Condensation*: None   *Anthology*: None   *Music publisher*: *Music and Lyrics by Cole Porter*. 2 vols. Chappell, 1972–1975   *Licensing agent*: Tams-Witmark   *Recording*: None   *Cast*: 12 M; 10 F; singers; dancers

The story begins at the Club Petite nightclub in New York City, circa 1939. The main characters are a former bathroom attendant who has just come into a lot of money, and the female star of the floor show. He dreams they are at the palace of Versailles, and that he is Louis XV and she is Madame Du Barry. There is ample opportunity for elaborate costumes and powdered wigs. This show was described as rowdy and boisterous, almost a burlesque show. Some famous tunes from the score include "Friendship" and "Do I Love You." This was filmed by MGM in 1943 with Lucille Ball.

EAST WIND
(1931)

Musical play by Oscar Hammerstein, II, and Frank Mandel   *Music* by Sigmund Romberg   *Published libretto*: None   *Condensation*: None *Anthology*: None   *Vocal selections*: None   *Licensing agent*: Tams-Witmark   *Recording*: None   *Cast*: 12 M; 10 F; chorus

A large and animated musical, the original Broadway production was staged with lavishness. Set in Paris and Saigon, the melodramatic plot includes mysterious Indo-Chinese secret societies, sinister half-caste dancers, and other exotic elements. Some of the sets include a gilded Chinese boat along the riverfront and an equatorial cabaret, as well as the Gare de Lyon, Paris. The eminent critic John Mason Brown declared, "a book which makes O'Neill's trilogy seem simple!" This show has been very popular at the St. Louis Municipal Opera.

THE EDUCATION OF H*Y*M*A*N K*A*P*L*A*N
(1968)

Book by Benjamin Bernard Zavin; based on stories by Leo Rosten   *Music and lyrics* by Paul Nassau and Oscar Brand   *Published libretto*: Dramatic, 1968   *Condensation*: None   *Anthology*: None   *Vocal selections*: None   *Licensing agent*: Dramatic   *Recording*: None   *Cast*: 9 M; 7 F

Mr. Kaplan is a Jewish immigrant who wants to become a United States citizen. The time is 1920 and the setting is New York City's Lower East Side. Mr. Kaplan attends night school and is threatened with deportation, but the story has a predictably happy ending. The critic at *Women's Wear Daily* summed it up as "singing . . . dancing . . . and other paraphernalia of the Lower East Side—Broadway style."

ERNEST IN LOVE
(1964)

Book and lyrics by Anne Croswell; based on Oscar Wilde's *The Importance of Being Earnest*   *Music* by Lee Pockriss   *Published libretto*: None   *Condensation*: None   *Anthology*: None   *Vocal selections*: None   *Licensing agent*: Music Theatre International   *Recording*: Columbia OS 2027 (original cast)   *Cast*: 10 M; 6 F

This is an off-Broadway musical version of Wilde's classic comedy. While this production obviously did not improve on the original, most critics felt that it did not betray it, either. There was a small musical ensemble of five that was praised, and the overture was compared to chamber music. The small, jewel-like production was a very stylish show.

FADE OUT—FADE IN
(1964)

Book and lyrics by Betty Comden and Adolph Green   *Music* by Jule Styne   *Published libretto*: Random House, 1965   *Condensation*: None   *Anthology*: None   *Vocal selections*: Stratford Music, 1964   *Licensing agent*: Tams-Witmark   *Recording*: ABC OC 3 (original cast)   *Cast*: 26 M; 9 F

"Oh Those Thirties" goes the opening number, and we go back to Hollywood in its golden era. Hope Springfield, by mistake, has been signed by a major studio to become a film star. Carol Burnett was "Hope" on Broadway, and this was a big musical. The sets can be elaborate, and there is ample opportunity for dancing, spectacle, and comedy. The original production even included a live seal!

A FAMILY AFFAIR
(1962)

By James Goldman, John Kander and William Goldman   *Published libretto*: None   *Condensation*: None   *Anthology*: None   *Vocal selections*: Valando, 1960   *Licensing agent*: Music Theatre International   *Recording*: United Artists UAS 5099 (original cast)   *Cast*: 5 M; 9 F; chorus

Set in Chicago, the story begins with a proposal of marriage and ends with the wedding ceremony. In between are all the wedding preparations, and all the members of the families of the bride and groom trying to run the show. The families are Jewish, so there are a lot of Yiddish words and some ethnic humor. One critic called it a burlesque of a large Jewish wedding. The Broadway production included no elaborate sets or big production numbers.

FANNY
(1954)

Book by S. N. Behrman and Joshua Logan; based on Marcel Pagnol's trilogy, *Marius, Fanny*, and *Cesar*   *Music and lyrics* by Harold Rome   *Published libretto*: Random House, 1954   *Condensation: Theatre '55*. John Chapman, ed. Random House, 1955   *Anthology*: None   *Piano-vocal score*: Chappell, 1956   *Vocal selections*: Chappell, 1954   *Licensing agent*: Tams-Witmark   *Recording*: RCA LSO 1015 E (original cast)   *Cast*: 10 M; 6 F; large chorus; dancers

Cesar is the proprietor of a waterfront bistro in Marseilles "not so long ago" and Panisse is his lifelong friend. Panisse marries Cesar's daughter, Fanny, who really loves Marius. The original Broadway production was described as big, opulent, costly; the belly dance number was called spectacular. The score was unusually rich (helped by voices like Ezio Pinza's) and the show was a big hit. It was subsequently filmed, with the background music from Mr. Rome's score, but no songs!

THE FANTASTICKS
(1960)

Book and lyrics by Tom Jones; based on the play *Les Romanesques* by Edmond Rostand   *Music* by Harvey Schmidt   *Published libretto*: Drama Book Shop, 1964   *Condensation*: None   *Anthology: Fantasticks and Celebration*. Drama Book Specialists, 1973 ☆ *The Best American Plays*, 6th Series, 1963–1967. John Gassner and Clive Barnes, eds. Crown, 1971   *Piano-vocal score*: Chappell, 1963   *Vocal selections*: Chappell, 1963   *Licensing agent*: Music Theatre International   *Recording*: MGM 3872 OC (original cast)   *Cast*: 8 M; 1 F; piano and harp

This is the ageless tale that love conquers all. It is a harlequinade, a variation of the Pierrot and Columbine theme. The girl and boy have purposefully been kept apart by their parents to foster a romance. The first act takes place at night, and the parents have dreamed up a kidnapping of the girl, so the boy can rescue her. The sun shines in the second act, and all ends well. This simple off-Broadway musical ran for more than 20 years and broke all records for longevity. "Try to Remember" is the most popular song from the score.

FASHION
(1974)

Book adapted by Anthony Stimac; based on the 1845 drama by Anna Cora Mowatt   *Music* by Don Pippin   *Lyrics* by Steve Brown   *Published*

libretto: Samuel French, 1974   *Condensation*: None   *Anthology*: None
Vocal selections: None   *Licensing agent*: Samuel French   *Recording*:
None   *Cast*: 1 M; 8 F

Using the play-within-a-play device, the authors present a production that
was popular back in 1845 which reflected American society and manners.
But now it is a musical, done very simply as a chamber-ensemble. The
score was described as having a rollicking charm and the production was
stylishly mounted. The plot is a spoof about women who turn their
husbands' bank accounts into clothes. Some of the women double as
men in the play they are rehearsing. This off-Broadway production was
also done on Public Television.

FESTIVAL
(1979)

Book and lyrics by Stephen Downs and Randal Martin; additional material by
Bruce Vilanch; based on the chantefable "Aucassin and Nicolette"   *Music*
by Stephen Downs   *Published libretto*: None   *Condensation*: None
Anthology: None   *Vocal selections*: None   *Licensing agent*: Samuel
French   *Recording*: Original Cast OC 7916 (original cast)   *Cast*: 6 M;
4 F

This zany musical begins with the pianist walking across the stage in tails,
and unexpectedly doing a cartwheel! Members of the cast play multiple
roles in modern dress in this fantasy with a carnival setting. The story
concerns young lovers, their family quarrels and their world-hopping
adventures before their final fulfillment. This show has a soft rock
musical score; it played successfully around America before an off-
Broadway presentation.

FIDDLER ON THE ROOF
(1964/1976/1981)

Book by Joseph Stein; based on Sholem Aleichem's stories   *Music* by
Jerry Bock   *Lyrics* by Sheldon Harnick   *Published libretto*: Crown, 1964
☆ Pocket Books (paperback), 1965   *Condensation*: *The Best Plays of
1964–1965*. Otis L. Guernsey, Jr., ed. Dodd, Mead, 1965 ☆ *American
Musicals: Bock and Harnick*. Time-Life, 1982   *Anthology*: *Ten Great
Musicals of the American Stage*. Stanley Richards, ed. Chilton, 1973 ☆ *The
Best American Plays*, 6th series, 1963–67. John Gassner and Clive Barnes,
eds. Crown, 1971 ☆ *Fifty Best Plays of the American Theatre*, vol. 4. Clive
Barnes, ed. Crown, 1969   *Piano-vocal score*: Valando, 1965   *Vocal
selections*: Times Square, 1964   *Licensing agent*: Music Theatre

International   *Recordings*: RCA LSO 1093, Time-Life STL-AM14 (original cast) ✩ Columbia SX 30742 (London cast)   *Cast*: 12 M; 10 F; chorus; and dancers

The time is 1905 and the place is Anatevka, a hamlet in Russia. The plot concerns Tevye and his daughters, and how their lives are changed by Czarist repression of the Jews. This show is one of the most popular and long-running in the history of musical theater. "If I Were a Rich Man" and "Matchmaker" are just two of the many famous songs. There was a film version in 1971.

Tony Award Winner (Best Musical)

FINIAN'S RAINBOW
(1947/1960/1977)

Book by E. Y. Harburg and Fred Saidy   *Music* by Burton Lane   *Lyrics* by E. Y. Harburg   *Published libretto*: Random House, 1947 ✩ *Theatre Arts* (magazine), January 1949   *Condensation*: None   *Anthology*: None   *Piano-vocal score*: Chappell, 1968   *Vocal selections*: Chappell (De Sylva, 1946)   *Licensing agent*: Tams-Witmark   *Recordings*: Columbia CS 2080E (original cast) ✩ RCA LSO 1057 (1960 cast)   *Cast*: 23 M; 12 F; chorus

Finian has stolen the Glocca Morra pot of gold, and is pursued by its guardian leprechaun to rural America. The book of this show contains a satiric plot line that deals with bigotry and politics that may seem a bit dated now; but the lovely score is not dated. "Old Devil Moon" and "How Are Things in Glocca Morra" are just two of the big hits from this show. It was recently revived at the open-air Jones Beach Theater outside New York City. There was a film version in 1968 with Fred Astaire.

FIORELLO!
(1959/1976)

Book by Jerome Weidman and George Abbott   *Music* by Jerry Bock   *Lyrics* by Sheldon Harnick   *Published libretto*: Random House, 1960 ✩ *Theatre Arts* (magazine), November 1961   *Condensation*: *Broadway's Best, 1960*. John Chapman, ed. Doubleday, 1960 ✩ *The Best Plays of 1959–1960*. Louis Kronenberger, ed. Dodd, Mead, 1960 ✩ *American Musicals: Bock and Harnick*. Time-Life, 1982   *Anthology*: *Great Musicals of the American Theatre*, vol. 2. Stanley Richards, ed. Chilton, 1976   *Vocal selections*: New York Times Music, 1960   *Licensing agent*: Tams-Witmark   *Recordings*: Capitol SWAO 1321, Time-Life STL-AM14 (original cast)   *Cast*: Large mixed cast

A musicalized biography of the little Italian who became the mayor of New York City. It covers the time from World War I to World War II. "Little Tin Box" is one of the examples of political satire, and "Gentleman Jimmy" is a jazzy salute to Mayor Jimmy Walker. This is one of the few musical comedies to win the Pulitzer Prize.
Tony Award Winner (Best Musical)
Pulitzer Prize

THE FIREFLY
(1912/1931/1983)

Book and lyrics by Otto Harbach   *Music* by Rudolf Friml   *Published libretto*: None   *Condensation*: None   *Anthology*: None *Piano-vocal score*: Schirmer, 1912   *Vocal selections: Album of Song Hits.* Schirmer, 1955   *Licensing agent*: Tams-Witmark   *Recording*: RCA LM 121 (studio cast)   *Cast*: Large mixed cast

This popular operetta has been revived many times—usually with the critics complaining that the book or score had been altered. One of the most famous songs, "The Donkey Serenade" comes from the 1937 film version with Jeanette MacDonald and Allan Jones. "Giannina Mia" and "Sympathy" are well-loved Friml songs from the original score. Nina, the heroine, disguises herself as a boy and stows away on a Bermuda-bound vessel to be near the one she loves. Set in the period from 1910 to 1913, the production features various resort fashions of the era. This has been done at Jones Beach (New York) and other summer "spectacle" theaters.

THE FIRST
(1981)

Book by Joel Siegel with Martin Charnin   *Music* by Bob Brush   *Lyrics* by Martin Charnin   *Published libretto*: None   *Condensation*: None *Anthology*: None   *Vocal selections*: None   *Licensing agent*: Samuel French   *Recording*: None   *Cast*: Large mixed cast

Set during the postwar period (1945–47), this is the story of how Jackie Robinson became the first black major league baseball player. Although there is very little dancing, there is considerable choreography required in staging the baseball game scenes. For the Broadway production the sets were particularly praised for their Brooklyn ambiance and some abstract effects for Ebbets Field. Jackie's fans provide some needed humor. This is not an easy show to stage, but sports fans will enjoy it.

FIRST IMPRESSIONS
(1959)

Book by Abe Burrows; based on Jane Austen's *Pride and Prejudice* and the play by Helen Jerome   *Music and lyrics* by Robert Goldman, Glenn Paxton and George Weiss   *Published libretto*: Samuel French, 1962 *Condensation*: None   *Anthology*: None   *Vocal selections*: None *Licensing agent*: Samuel French   *Recording*: Columbia CSP AOS 2014 (original cast)   *Cast*: 12 M; 12 F; chorus

Set in England in the early 1800s, the story concerns a mother's desperate antics to marry off her five daughters. One daughter's first impression of her beau is that he is conceited and proud; he thinks she is prejudiced and distant. Many critics mentioned the massive sets and lavish gowns and called the production dazzling. The dancing includes gavottes, schottisches and polkas. This is a charming and proper family show.

THE FIVE O'CLOCK GIRL
(1927/1981)

Book by Guy Bolton and Fred Thompson   *Music and lyrics* by Bert Kalmar and Harry Ruby   *Published libretto*: None   *Condensation*: None   *Anthology*: None   *Vocal selections*: None   *Licensing agent*: Tams-Witmark   *Recording*: None   *Cast*: 4 M; 4 F; singers; dancers

The hero of the story is a wealthy Beekman Place playboy who loves a poor but honest laundry girl. She has been anonymously telephoning him each afternoon at five. In order to carry on the affair, she poses as a society girl. The revival on Broadway of this show was a Goodspeed Opera production, which means that there was careful attention to period costumes and decor. There was some outstanding choreography. "Thinking of You" is a popular song from the score.

FLORODORA
(1899/1920/1981)

Book by Owen Hall   *Music* by Leslie Stuart   *Lyrics* by E. Boyd Jones and Paul Rubens   *Published libretto*: None   *Condensation*: None *Anthology*: None   *Piano-vocal score*: Harms, 1899   *Licensing agent*: Tams-Witmark   *Recording*: None   *Cast*: 10 M; 9 F

The setting for Act I is a mythical island in the Philippines. A wealthy American has a factory there where he manufactures perfume. There is some confusion about the actual ownership of the island, but our young heroine, Dolores, claims her right and is happily married in Wales in Act II. This show is remembered for its famous sextet of beauties, "The Florodora Girls" who flirted with the audience. A recent New York revival proved that this show still has an audience and that it can be simply staged.

FLOWER DRUM SONG
(1958)

Book by Oscar Hammerstein, II, and Joseph Fields; based on the novel by C. Y. Lee   *Music* by Richard Rodgers   *Lyrics* by Oscar Hammerstein, II *Published libretto*: Farrar, Straus, 1959   *Condensation*: *Broadway's Best, 1959*. John Chapman, ed. Doubleday, 1959   *Anthology*: None *Piano-vocal score*: Williamson Music, 1959   *Licensing agent*: Rodgers and Hammerstein Theatre Library   *Recording*: Columbia OS 2009 (original cast)   *Cast*: 11 M; 7 F; chorus

The new and old collide in this story of Chinese-Americans in San Francisco. Wang Ta is torn between two girls. Linda Low is a thoroughly Americanized nightclub entertainer, while Mei Li has just arrived from China. Although various others performed in the original Broadway production, the leading roles are supposed to be Chinese. The choreography by Carol Haney was particularly praised by critics and utilized paper lanterns and umbrellas. There was a film version in 1961.

FLY WITH ME
(1920/1980)

Book by Milton Kroopf and Phillip Leavitt; 1980 adaptation by Michael Numark   *Music* by Richard Rodgers   *Lyrics* by Lorenz Hart; additional lyrics by Oscar Hammerstein, II, and Richard Rodgers   *Published libretto*: None   *Condensation*: None   *Anthology*: None   *Vocal selections*: None   *Licensing agent*: Dramatic   *Recording*: Original Cast OC 8023 (1980 revival cast)   *Cast*: 7 M; 4 F; chorus

The original 1920 Columbia University Varsity show was done with an all-male cast. The 1980 revival, however, included females. It was a college show, and projected the cast 50 years forward to 1970. The theme of futurism included an island off the coast of America run by the Bolsheviks! One song from the score, "College on Broadway" has remained popular at Columbia through the years.

FOLLIES
(1971/1976)

Book by James Goldman   *Music and lyrics* by Stephen Sondheim
Published libretto: Random House, 1971   *Condensation*: *The Best Plays of 1970–1971*. Otis L. Guernsey, Jr., ed. Dodd, Mead, 1971   *Anthology*: None   *Piano-vocal score*: Columbia Pictures (Hansen, 1974)   *Vocal selections*: Valando, 1971   *Licensing agent*: Music Theatre International
Recording: Capitol SO-761 (original cast)   *Cast*: 4 M; 8 F; large mixed cast

Various cast members of the old Weismann shows gather at a reunion just before the theater is to be torn down and replaced with a parking lot. As they recall their youth, we see them as young performers doing their numbers. We also find out about their lives, as the title of the show has a double meaning. For most of the action, the set is a stage of a decrepit theater, but suddenly it is transformed into a Ziegfeld Follies-type setting for the finale. One appeal of the original Broadway production was seeing old stars return to the spotlight. Sondheim's score has been described as "an incredible display of musical virtuosity." One of the popular songs from the score is "Losing My Mind."

FOLLOW THRU
(1929)

Book by Laurence Schwab and B. G. De Sylva   *Songs* by B. G. De Sylva, Lew Brown, and Ray Henderson   *Published libretto*: None
Condensation: None   *Anthology*: None   *Vocal selections*: De Sylva, Brown, and Henderson, 1929   *Licensing agent*: Tams-Witmark
Recording: None   *Cast*: 8 M; 10 F; boys; girls; caddies

Subtitled, "a musical slice of Country Club life," this show begins in 1908, and then jumps up to 1928 for the bulk of the plot. Although most critics were confused about the plot, they all agreed it concerned two female golfers in competition, not only for a championship, but for a man as well. All agreed that the "romping, stomping" cast had a good time and the songs were "crisp, crazy, lusty, ankle-loosing and hip-seizing." One very popular song is "Button Up Your Overcoat."

THE FORTUNE TELLER
(1898/1929/1980)

Book and lyrics by Harry B. Smith   *Music* by Victor Herbert
Published libretto: None   *Condensation*: None   *Anthology*: None

Piano-vocal score: Warner Brothers Music (Dennison, 1955) *Vocal selections:* M. Witmark, 1898 *Licensing agent:* Tams-Witmark *Recording:* Smithsonian R 017 (several selections recorded by the original cast) *Cast:* 10 M; 6 F; chorus

Irma, a ballet student in Budapest at the turn of the century, is in love with Captain Ladislas. Count Berezowski, however, wants to marry her for her money. When she runs away with the Captain, the Count finds a gypsy fortune teller who resembles Irma and attempts to pass her off as the heiress. A recent off-Broadway revival (by the Light Opera of Manhattan) was praised for its authentic style and charm. Featured are dashing Czardas dances and the famous "Gypsy Love Song," one of Herbert's most beloved melodies.

FRANK MERRIWELL (or Honor Challenged)
(1971)

Book by Skip Redwine, Larry Frank and Heywood Gould; based on *Frank Merriwell's School Days* by Burt L. Standish *Music and lyrics* by Skip Redwine and Larry Frank *Published libretto:* Samuel French, 1971 *Condensation:* None *Anthology:* None *Vocal selections:* None *Licensing agent:* Samuel French *Recording:* None *Cast:* 7 M; 6 F; 1 boy

Frank Merriwell was a dime novel hero around the turn of the twentieth century. He stood for courage, fair play, and honesty. The plot of this gentle spoof concerns Frank's adventures at college; he becomes involved with a spy ring; and saves the fair Inez from a death "worse than fate." Although it was done on Broadway, this show is ideally suited for a small production, simply mounted. It is a wholesome, family show.

THE FROGS
(1984)

Book freely adapted for today by Burt Shevelove; based on Aristophanes' comedy *Music and lyrics* by Stephen Sondheim *Published libretto:* Dramatic, 1975 *Condensation:* None *Anthology:* None *Vocal selections:* None *Licensing agent:* Dramatic *Recording:* RCA CBL 2-4745 *Sondheim Evening* (2 selections) *Cast:* 10 M; 2 F; large chorus; dancers; swimmers

The plot concerns the god Dionysus, dissatisfied with the current crop of playwrights, going down into Hades to bring back Bernard Shaw and restore him to life. This 90-minute farce was originally staged at Yale around a swimming pool and was later produced in New York City. Reviews indicate that there were various water ballets à la Busby Berkeley. There was also dancing at poolside, and the actors were sometimes out in the pool in a rowboat. The Yale production was quite spectacular, with about 125 people involved in the show.

FUNNY GIRL
(1964)

Book by Isobel Lennart; from her original story based on the early life of Fanny Brice   *Music* by Jule Styne   *Lyrics* by Bob Merrill   *Published libretto*: Random House, 1964   *Condensation: American Musicals: Styne.* Time-Life, 1981.   *Anthology*: None   *Piano-vocal score*: Chappell, 1964 *Vocal selections*: Chappell, 1968   *Licensing agent*: Tams-Witmark *Recordings*: Capitol STAO 2059, Time-Life STL-AM05 (original cast)   *Cast*: Large mixed cast

This musical comedy biography of Fanny Brice made a superstar of Barbra Streisand. She later starred in the film version. The story begins with Fanny as a homely, gawky girl on the Lower East Side. We follow her career as a Ziegfeld star, and her romance with gambler Nick Arnstein. The plot ends there (and was later continued in the film sequel, *Funny Lady*). There are numerous musical numbers in the style of the period from 1914 to 1918. There are wonderful character parts, and a juicy one for the lead. "People" was the hit song from the score. The Broadway production was described as sumptuous.

A FUNNY THING HAPPENED ON THE WAY TO THE FORUM
(1962/1972)

Book by Burt Shevelove and Larry Gelbart; based on the plays of Plautus *Music and lyrics* by Stephen Sondheim   *Published libretto*: Dodd, Mead, 1963   *Condensation: American Musicals: Sondheim.* Time-Life, 1982 *Anthology*: None   *Piano-vocal score*: Chappell, 1964   *Licensing agent*: Music Theatre International   *Recording*: Capitol SW 1717, Time-Life STL-AM12 (original cast)   *Cast*: Large mixed cast

Hero, in love with a slave girl he cannot afford to buy, turns his problems over to a fast-talking slave, Pseudolus, who is the real star of the show. After a good deal of low comedy and confusion, all is straightened out—lovers are united and Pseudolus is set free. Zero Mostel starred on Broadway and in the film version and Phil Silvers later starred in a revival.

Set in ancient Rome, this show is very funny and popular. It is physical, energetic, unpretentious, and for adults only! Audiences love it. *Tony Award Winner (Best Musical)*

GAY'S THE WORD
(1951)

Book and music by Ivor Novello; from an idea by Jack Hulbert   *Lyrics by* Alan Melville   *Published libretto*: None   *Condensation*: None *Anthology*: None   *Vocal selections*: *English Musical Comedies*. Chappell, 1947–1952   *Licensing agent*: Samuel French   *Recording*: World Records SH 216 (London original cast)   *Cast*: 16 M; 24 F

The show opens with the final performance of a musical play somewhere in the British provinces. Gay Daventry, now out of work, sets up an acting school at Folkstone. There are some run-ins with a gang of foreign smugglers before the final school performances that are a tribute to the headmistress. This show was written for the style and personality of Cicely Courtneidge, and along the way Novello makes gentle fun of his own past successes. There is plenty of opportunity for energetic dancing. "Vitality" is the big first act finale.

GEORGE M!
(1968)

Book by Michael Stewart and John and Fran Pascal   *Music and lyrics* by George M. Cohan; lyric and musical revisions by Mary Cohan   *Published libretto*: None   *Condensation*: None   *Anthology*: None   *Vocal selections*: Cohan Music, 1968   *Licensing agent*: Tams-Witmark *Recording*: Columbia KOS 3200 (original cast)   *Cast*: Large mixed cast

The life, career, loves and songs of George M. Cohan in this show provide a strong part for a song-and-dance man; this was Joel Grey's first starring role. The story line is the usual backstage melodrama, with nostalgia and sentiment. The period is primarily around World War I and the staging and dancing should reflect this spirit. Certainly the famous Cohan songs will—"Yankee Doodle Boy," "Over There," and many more. This a flag-waving family show!

THE GIFT OF THE MAGI
(1958 TV musical adapted for the stage)

Book by Ronald Alexander; a musical version of the short story by O. Henry
Music and lyrics by Richard Adler   *Published libretto*: None
Condensation: None   *Anthology*: None   *Vocal selections*: None
Licensing agent: Tams-Witmark   *Recording*: United Artists UAL 4013
(original TV cast with Allen Case replacing Gordon MacRae)   *Cast*: Small
mixed cast

This famous short story has been done several times as a musical, both on
the stage and on television. This particular version was first done with
Gordon MacRae and Sally Ann Howes on television in 1958. It is a
Christmas show set in New York City in 1905. The plot concerns a young
married couple without money for Christmas gifts and their sacrifices of
personal treasures to buy presents for each other.

GIGI
(1973)

Book and lyrics by Alan Jay Lerner; based on the novel by Colette   *Music*
by Frederick Loewe   *Published libretto*: None   *Condensation*: None
Anthology: None   *Piano-vocal score*: Chappell, 1975   *Vocal selections*:
Chappell, 1974   *Licensing agent*: Tams-Witmark   *Recording*: RCA ABL
1-0404 (original cast)   *Cast*: 14 M; 4 F; singers; dancers

Lerner and Loewe again struck paydirt with the film *Gigi*, with Leslie
Caron and Maurice Chevalier. When the film was made into a stage
musical a number of new songs were added to the score. Set in Paris at
the turn of the century, this is a sentimental tale of a child in a family of
courtesans who grows up rapidly and converts a playboy into a honest
and adoring husband. The Broadway production was described as lavish
with handsome costumes. "Thank Heaven for Little Girls" and "I Remember It Well" are a couple of the famous songs in the score.

GIRL CRAZY
(1930)

Book by Guy Bolton and John McGowan   *Music* by George Gershwin
Lyrics by Ira Gershwin   *Published libretto*: None   *Condensation*:
American Musicals: Gershwin. Time-Life, 1982   *Anthology*: None
Piano-vocal score: New World Music, 1954   *Licensing agent*:

Tams-Witmark   *Recording*: Columbia CL 822, Time-Life STL-AM09 (studio cast)   *Cast*: 7 M; 6 F; male quartet; singers; dancers

This famous Gershwin show set in the Wild West introduced Ethel Merman to Broadway with her sensational rendition of "I Got Rhythm." Ginger Rogers was the star and introduced "Embraceable You." Wealthy Danny arrives from the East for a two-year rest cure, opens a dude ranch, and imports Broadway talent. (A 1960 modernized version dealt with a TV western star!) There was a 1943 film version with Mickey Rooney and Judy Garland.

GODSPELL
(1971)

Music and new lyrics by Stephen Schwartz; based upon the gospel according to St. Matthew   *Published libretto*: None   *Condensation*: None   *Anthology*: None   *Piano-vocal score*: Hansen, 1973   *Vocal selections*: Valando, 1971 ✫ Columbia Pictures, 1980   *Licensing agent*: Theatre Maximus   *Recording*: Arista 4001 (original cast)   *Cast*: 5 M; 5 F

Described as a musical circus, *Godspell* is a combination of vaudeville, clown and minstrel show, with sweet rock sounds. Ten young performers dressed as clowns bring the Bible to life. The performance includes mime, magic, song and dance, charade, clowning, and children's games. This was one of the most popular shows of the 1970s and has been performed many times all over the world. There was also a film version.

GOING UP
(1917/1976)

Book and lyrics by Otto Harbach; based on *The Aviator* by James Montgomery   *Music* by Louis A. Hirsch   *Published libretto*: None   *Condensation*: None   *Anthology*: None   *Piano-vocal score*: M. Witmark, 1918   *Licensing agent*: Tams-Witmark   *Recording*: None   *Cast*: 11 M; 6 F

A young novelist writes a best-seller about flying and then gets involved in a contest to win the girl he loves although he has never actually been in an airplane. This was recently revived on Broadway by the Goodspeed Opera from Connecticut and was noted for its high-spirited choreography. A period piece, subtitled *An Uplifting Musical Comedy*.

THE GOLDEN APPLE
(1954/1962)

Book and lyrics by John Latouche; based on the Homeric legend of Ulysses
Music by Jerome Moross   *Published libretto*: Random House, 1954
Condensation: The Best Plays of 1953–1954. Louis Kronenberger, ed. Dodd,
Mead, 1954 ☆ *Theatre '54.* John Chapman, ed. Random House, 1954
Anthology: None   *Music publisher*: Chappell, 1954   *Licensing agent*:
Tams-Witmark   *Recordings*: RCA LOC 1014 (original cast), reissued as
Elektra EKL 5000   *Cast*: 16 M; 6 F

This critically acclaimed musical was taken from the Greek and done
entirely in song and dance. It has been transposed to America at the turn
of the century. The New York revival was done with twin pianos and
bright, simple sets. The principals and chorus should be musicians first
and foremost. "Lazy Afternoon" is the most famous song from the score.

GOLDEN BOY
(1964)

Book by Clifford Odets and William Gibson; based on the play by Clifford
Odets   *Music* by Charles Strouse   *Lyrics* by Lee Adams   *Published
libretto*: Atheneum, 1965 ☆ Samuel French, 1965   *Condensation*: None
Anthology: None   *Vocal selections*: Big Three (Morris, 1965)   *Licensing
agent*: Samuel French   *Recording*: Capitol SVAS 2124 (original cast)
Cast: 9 M; 2 F; chorus

The famous 1937 Odets play was musicalized in the 1960s and changed to
a black boxer's resentment of racial prejudice and his desire for accept-
ance in the white world. Along the way he has a romance with his
manager's white secretary-mistress. Sammy Davis starred on broadway
with a cast that included Billy Daniels and Lola Falana. The settings were
simple, but projections on a back screen were used to show Harlem and
other locations.

GOLDEN RAINBOW
(1968)

Book by Ernest Kinoy; based on the play *A Hole in the Head* by Arnold
Schulman   *Music and lyrics* by Walter Marks   *Published libretto*: None
Condensation: None   *Anthology*: None   *Vocal selections*: Damila
Music, 1967   *Licensing agent*: Samuel French   *Recording*: Calendar
KOS 1001 (original cast)   *Cast*: 8 M; 4 F; 1 boy; chorus; show girls

A third-rate hotel in Las Vegas is about to go under. Larry Davis, its owner and a widower, is busy trying to concoct money-making schemes and leaves the management of the place to his ten-year-old son. But Larry's sister-in-law enters the picture and all ends happily. This show was tailored for the well-known husband-and-wife team, Steve Lawrence and Eydie Gorme. Their nightclub expertise was well used. A popular song from the score is "I've Got to Be Me."

GOLDILOCKS
(1958/1971)

Book by Walter and Jean Kerr   *Music* by Leroy Anderson   *Lyrics* by Joan Ford, Walter and Jean Kerr   *Published libretto*: Doubleday, 1959 ☆ Samuel French, 1970   *Condensation*: None   *Anthology*: None *Vocal selections*: None   *Licensing agent*: Samuel French   *Recording*: Columbia CSP COS 2007 (original cast)   *Cast*: 8 M; 3 F; chorus

Featuring choreography by Agnes de Mille, this bouncy tale of early nickelodeon days around 1913 concerns a movie director and a Pearl White-like actress. She is about to leave a Broadway musical and marry a millionaire but eventually succumbs to both the movie director and the medium. Some of the musical numbers burlesque classics like "Intolerance," and the best numbers were "The Pussy Foot" and the "Town House Maxixe." Some critics felt that the original production was overproduced, and mentioned excessively elaborate scenery. The off-Broadway revival was a much simpler production.

GOOD NEWS
(1927/1974)

Book by Laurence Schwab, B. G. De Sylva and Frank Mandel   *Words and music* by B. G. De Sylva, Lew Brown and Ray Henderson   *Published libretto*: Samuel French, 1932   *Condensation*: None   *Anthology*: None *Vocal selections*: Chappell, 1974   *Licensing agent*: Samuel French *Recording*: None   *Cast*: 10 M; 5 F; chorus

The football coach at Tait College has a problem. His star player is temporarily ineligible to play in the big game because he's flunked his astronomy test. (In the 1947 film version with June Allyson, it was a French exam.) Energy and enthusiasm will be required from a youthful cast. "The Varsity Drag" is a big production number, and "The Best Things in Life Are Free" is the big song hit. The 1974 Broadway revival was described as being corny but fetching.

GOODTIME CHARLEY
(1975)

Book by Sidney Michaels   *Music* by Larry Grossman   *Lyrics* by Hal
Hackady   *Published libretto*: None   *Condensation*: None
Anthology: None   *Vocal selections*: None   *Licensing agent*: Samuel
French   *Recording*: RCA ARL 1-1011 (original cast)   *Cast*: 15 M;
7 F; chorus

This musical presents the Dauphin of France as a weakling, dominated by
those surrounding him. When he comes into contact with Joan of Arc she
leads him on to drive the English out of France. The role of the Dauphin,
played on Broadway by Joel Grey, is the starring one, rather than that of
Joan. The original production was praised for its lavish costumes and
medieval sets.

GOREY STORIES
(1978)

Adaptation by Stephen Currens; based on illustrated stories by Edward
Gorey   *Music* by David Aldrich   *Published libretto*: Samuel French
Condensation: None   *Anthology*: None   *Vocal selections*: None
Licensing agent: Samuel French   *Recording*: None   *Cast*: 5 M; 4 F

Gorey has written and illustrated over 40 little volumes of mock-Gothic
black-humor tales, sketches, rhymes and limericks. He also designed the
very successful revival of *Dracula*. For this revue, 18 sketches are spoken,
sung, and occasionally danced as deadpan spoofs. While this is all very
sophisticated, it nevertheless appeals to young children and the innocent
elderly. Martin Gottfried of *Saturday Review* described the music as
"new classical music . . . a quirky score for a chamber group." The staging
must be highly stylized. The two abstract sets represent a drawing room
and a summer house. Costumes must be appropriately bizarre.

THE GRAND TOUR
(1979)

Book by Michael Stewart and Mark Bramble; based on the original play
Jacobowsky and the Colonel by Franz Werfel and the American play based
on the same by S. N. Behrman   *Music and lyrics* by Jerry Herman
Published libretto: Samuel French, 1980   *Condensation*: None
Anthology: None   *Vocal selections*: Schirmer, 1979   *Licensing agent*:
Samuel French   *Recording*: Columbia JS 35761 (original cast)   *Cast*: 29
roles; extras; singers; dancers

The theme is survival and the scene is France as the Germans begin their occupation during World War II. The hero is a Jew on the run. He joins a Polish Colonel and they flee to the coast of France where they hope to get a boat to England. There are numerous scene changes—from crowded trains to a traveling circus. There is also a big Jewish wedding number. This was a big Broadway musical.

EL GRANDE DE COCA COLA
(1973)

Words and music by Ron House and other cast members; based on an idea by Ron House and Diz White   *Published libretto*: Samuel French, 1973
Condensation: None   *Anthology*: None   *Vocal selections*: None
Licensing agent: Samuel French   *Recording*: Bottle Cap 1001 (original cast)   *Cast*: 2 M; 3 F; piano and drum

Subtitled *A Refreshment*, this revue has an accent on comedy rather than music. Pepe Hernandez, a third-rate Honduran impresario, tries to pass off some of his relatives as an "International Parade of Stars" at a run-down nightclub in Trujillo. First of all, no English is spoken. The entire one hour floor show is done in fractured Spanish, with German and other languages occasionally creeping in. This was a big success all over America and Europe. It is a simple show to produce, but a great deal of comic skill is required.

THE GRASS HARP
(1971/1977/1979)

Book and lyrics by Kenward Elmslie; based on the novel by Truman Capote
Music by Claibe Richardson   *Published libretto*: Samuel French, 1971
Condensation: None   *Anthology*: None   *Vocal selections*: Thackaray
Falls Music, 1971   *Licensing agent*: Samuel French   *Recording*: Painted
Smiles PS 1354 (original cast)   *Cast*: 4 M; 5 F; small chorus

An important part of this musical is the set—a tree house. The original Broadway production filled the stage with a huge loop of swirling branches. The plot concerns a Southern family, one of whom knows the secret recipe for their famous "Dropsy Cure." The older sister wants the secret so they can become rich. The big number is "Yellow Drum." Called charming, modest, tasteful and unpretentious, this whimsical story is ideal for a family audience production.

GREASE
(1972)

Book, music and lyrics by Jim Jacobs and Warren Casey *Published libretto*: Winter House, 1972 ☆ Samuel French, 1972 ☆ Pocket Books, 1972 *Condensation*: None *Anthology*: *Great Rock Musicals*. Stanley Richards, ed. Stein and Day, 1979 *Vocal selections*: Morris, 1972 *Licensing agent*: Samuel French *Recording*: MGM 1SE-34 (original cast) *Cast*: 10 M; 7 F

The current success story in musical comedy is to have a start off-Broadway, move to Broadway and run for years, be made into a hit movie, and then be made into a movie sequel or a TV series. And that is what has happened with *Grease*. Described as a "loud, coarse, aggressively cheerful rock-and-roll parody" it is set in 1959 and clearly strikes a note of response in all of us. Stars from the 1950s like Elvis Presley, Sandra Dee, and James Dean are all immortalized in this very popular musical.

THE GREAT AMERICAN BACKSTAGE MUSICAL
(1976)

Book by Bill Solly and Donald Ward *Music and lyrics* by Bill Solly *Additional lyrics* by Dick Vosburgh *Published libretto*: Samuel French, 1979 *Condensation*: None *Anthology*: None *Vocal selections*: None *Licensing agent*: Samuel French *Recording*: AEI 1101 (original cast) *Cast*: 3 M; 3 F

This is a good-humored spoof of Hollywood musicals before and during World War II. The story begins with a group of youngsters putting on a show in a New York cabaret. When the war begins they go to England with the U.S.O. This West Coast musical is small and simple to stage. This is the era of the jitterbug, the torch song, and Broadway vaudeville.

GREAT SCOT!
(1965)

Book by Mark Conradt and Gregory Dawson *Music* by Don McAfee *Lyrics* by Nancy Leeds *Published libretto*: Dramatists Play Service, 1969 *Condensation*: None *Anthology*: None *Vocal selections*: None *Licensing agent*: Dramatists Play Service *Recording*: None *Cast*: 8 M; 9 F

Set in eighteenth-century Edinburgh, this musical portrays the early life of poet Robert Burns. The plot revolves around his true love, and how he finally returns to marry her after running off to sample the high life of the big city. There's plenty of dancing, including a balletic Highland Game and an Edinburgh ball. Costumes should include lots of colorful tartans and tam-o-shanters. The off-Broadway production had an orchestra of four.

THE GREAT WALTZ
(1934)

Book by Moss Hart   *Music* by Johann Strauss and his son, Johann Strauss, Jr.   *Lyrics* by Desmond Carter   *Published libretto*: None
Condensation: None   *Anthology*: None   *Vocal selections*: L. Feist, 1944 (from 1938 film version)   *Licensing agent*: Tams-Witmark   *Recordings*: Capitol SVAS 2426 (1965 Los Angeles production) ☆ Columbia SCX 6429 (1970 London production)   *Cast*: Large mixed cast

Called "the spectacle of the century," this play is the story of Johann Strauss and his jealousy of his son. Set in Vienna around 1850, the plot concerns a Russian countess and how she helps the son prove he has a talent of his own. The original New York production was lavish, and it has been revived many times. The recordings listed above are of revised versions by Jerome Chodorov, Robert Wright and George Forrest. For the "Blue Danube" waltz the stage should be filled with suitably costumed dancers. This was filmed several times, most recently in 1972 with Mary Costa.

GUYS AND DOLLS
(1950/1955/1966/1976)

Book by Jo Swerling and Abe Burrows; based on "The Idyll of Sarah Brown" and characters by Damon Runyon   *Music and lyrics* by Frank Loesser
Published libretto: None   *Condensation*: *The Best Plays of 1950–1951*. John Chapman, ed. Dodd, Mead, 1951 ☆ *American Musicals: Loesser*. Time-Life, 1981   *Anthology*: *The Modern Theatre*, vol. 4. Eric Bentley, ed. Doubleday, 1956   *Piano-vocal score*: Frank Music, 1953   *Vocal selections*: Frank Music, 1955   *Licensing agent*: Music Theatre International   *Recordings*: MCA 2034 (E), Time-Life STL-AM08 (original cast) ☆ Motown M6-876S1 (1976 revival cast)   *Cast*: 12 M; 5 F; chorus

There are two love stories involved in this musical set in New York City in the 1950s. One is between Nathan Detroit, who runs a floating crap game, and Adelaide, a hoofer and chanteuse. The other romance is between big time gambler Sky Masterson and Sarah Brown, a Salvation Army lass. It's all very "Damon Runyon-New Yorkese," with such hit tunes as "A Bushel and a Peck" and "If I Were a Bell." There is also a Spanish interlude in Cuba. This was a big hit in 1982 at Britain's National Theatre. The film version in 1955 starred Marlon Brando and Frank Sinatra. *Tony Award Winner (Best Musical)*

GYPSY
(1959/1974)

Book by Arthur Laurents; suggested by the memoirs of Gypsy Rose Lee *Music* by Jule Styne   *Lyrics* by Stephen Sondheim   *Published libretto*: Random House, 1960 ☆ *Theatre Arts* (magazine), June 1962 *Condensation*: *Broadway's Best, 1959*. John Chapman, ed. Doubleday, 1959 ☆ *American Musicals: Styne*. Time-Life, 1981   *Anthology: Ten Great Musicals of the American Stage*. Stanley Richards, ed. Chilton, 1973 *Piano-vocal score*: Chappell, 1960   *Vocal selections*: Chappell, 1959 *Licensing agent*: Tams-Witmark   *Recordings*: Columbia S 32607, Time-Life STL-AM05 (original cast) ☆ RCA LBL 1-5004 (London cast)   *Cast*: Large mixed cast

The plot of this musical has been called unpleasant because it deals with a demanding mother determined to make "show biz" stars of her children. It has also been said that it presents a romanticized version of the "grubby" world of burlesque. The original production was the climax of the brilliant career of Ethel Merman. Costumes are late 1920s and there's plenty of opportunity for children and adults to put over such great numbers as "Let Me Entertain You" and "Everything's Coming Up Roses." The 1962 film featured Rosalind Russell.

HAIR
(1967/1968)

Book and lyrics by Gerome Ragni and James Rado   *Music* by Galt MacDermot   *Published libretto*: Pocket Books, 1969   *Condensation*: None   *Anthology*: *Great Rock Musicals*. Stanley Richards, ed. Stein and Day, 1979   *Vocal selections*: United Artists Music, 1968   *Licensing agent*: Tams-Witmark   *Recordings*: RCA LSO 1143 (original off-Broadway cast) ☆ RCA LSO 1150 (original Broadway cast)   *Cast*: 12 M; 10 F

Called a "hippie rock-musical," this show sparked a long stream of theatrical productions reflecting new themes, new mores, and new music. But this is the one with "The Age of Aquarius" and "Frank Mills." There is a bit of a plot about a flower boy who is going to be drafted, but otherwise it's the songs and dances that make the show. Some brief nudity caused a sensation, but it was not included in the original production and is not necessary. It was filmed in 1979.

HALF A SIXPENCE
(1965)

Book by Beverley Cross; based on *Kipps* by H. G. Wells   *Music and lyrics* by David Heneker   *Published libretto*: Dramatic, 1967   *Condensation*: None   *Anthology*: None   *Piano-vocal score*: Chappell (London), 1967 *Vocal selections*: Chappell, 1965   *Licensing agent*: Dramatic *Recording*: RCA LSO 1110 (original cast)   *Cast*: 12 M; 11 F; chorus

This was a big English musical hit that starred Tommy Steele, and he later filmed it in 1968. Set around the turn of the century, a poor but honest shop clerk inherits a fortune and travels to the seaside resort of Folkstone for fun and romance. This musical is remembered for its spirited music, bright dances, lovely costumes, and simple but highly effective sets.

HALLELUJAH, BABY!
(1967)

Book by Arthur Laurents   *Music* by Jule Styne   *Lyrics* by Betty Comden and Adolph Green   *Published libretto*: None   *Condensation*: None *Anthology*: None   *Vocal selections*: Stratford Music, 1967   *Licensing agent*: Music Theatre International   *Recording*: Columbia KOS 3090 (original cast)   *Cast*: Large mixed cast

This is a musical about racial problems in the United States, starting in 1900 and continuing to the 1960s. The leading characters never age as we see blacks in transition from servants to leaders. This allows a variety of styles in music, dancing, singing and costume. The production featured the dancing of "Tip and Tap" and a very funny Aunt Jemima-type parody. This was a big and brassy musical.
Tony Award Winner (Best Musical)

HANS CHRISTIAN ANDERSEN
(1974)

New book by John Fearnley, Beverley Cross and Tommy Steele; based on the Samuel Goldwyn film (1952) and the life of Hans Christian Andersen

Music and lyrics by Frank Loesser; additional material by Marvin Laird
Published libretto: None   *Condensation*: None   *Anthology*: None
Vocal selections: Frank Music, 1952 (from the film)   *Licensing agent*:
Music Theatre International   *Recordings*: PYE NSPL 18451 (1974 London
cast) ✫ PYE NSPL (British) 18551 (1974; and 1977 revision featuring Sally Ann
Howes)   *Cast*: 11 M; 5 F; singers; dancers; children

Back in 1952 Frank Loesser wrote a film musical for Danny Kaye. Some
years later it was adapted for the stage and has been done several times in
London with Tommy Steele. Our hero sets off for "Wonderful
Copenhagen" where he meets Jenny Lind. She helps him with his writ-
ing, but rejects him as a suitor. This is a family show, with happy songs
such as "Thumbelina" and "The Ugly Duckling" which will please all
audiences. A recent production by the St. Louis Municipal Opera re-
verted to the original film plot dealing with a ballerina rather than Jenny
Lind.

THE HAPPIEST GIRL IN THE WORLD
(1961)

Book by Fred Saidy and Henry Myers; story by E. Y. Harburg; based on the
Greek play *Lysistrata* by Aristophanes   *Music* by Jacques Offenbach
Lyrics by E. Y. Harburg   *Published libretto*: None   *Condensation*: None
Anthology: None   *Vocal selections*: None   *Licensing agent*: Tams-
Witmark   *Recording*: Columbia KOS 2050 (original cast)   *Cast*: Large
mixed cast

This is the familiar story of Lysistrata and how she gets the ladies of
ancient Athens to go on a sex strike until the men stop making war. The
Broadway production was noted for its wonderful music, sly antics,
gorgeous settings and pretty girls. Offenbach's music (particularly the
"Barcarolle") was well liked in this adaptation. The male lead plays nine
roles, and the female lead should dance as well as sing. Back in 1960s this
show was considered racy!

HAPPY END
(1929/1970/1977/1984)

Book and lyrics by Michael Feingold; based on the original German play by
Elisabeth Hauptmann   *Music* by Kurt Weill   *Lyrics* by Bertolt Brecht
Published libretto: Methuen, 1982 ✫ Samuel French, 1983   *Condensation*:
None   *Anthology*: None   *Piano-vocal score* (in German): Universal
Edition (Wien), 1958   *Licensing agent*: Samuel French   *Recording*:
Columbia CSP COS 2032 (German studio cast)   *Cast*: 9 M; 6 F; small
chorus

In Chicago in 1919, a group of second-rate gangsters is led by a mysterious lady called "The Fly." The Salvation Army enters the story and a humorous situation develops over the struggle for souls. This work is vintage Brecht-Weill—an animated cartoon of the 1920s with a message that is similar to the one in their more famous work, *The Threepenny Opera*. The songs are the most important part of this musical, and will require a definite style and flair from the cast.

HAPPY HUNTING
(1956)

Book by Howard Lindsay and Russel Crouse   *Music* by Harold Karr *Lyrics* by Matt Dubey   *Published libretto*: Random House, 1957 *Condensation*: None   *Anthology*: None   *Vocal selections*: Chappell, 1957   *Licensing agent*: Music Theatre International   *Recording*: RCA LOC 1026 (original cast)   *Cast*: Large mixed cast

For many years after this show closed, its star Ethel Merman usually opened her concert appearances with "Gee, But It's Good to Be Here" from its score. This musical revolves around a big wedding in Monaco with Merman playing the part of a wealthy Philadelphia matron who was not invited to the wedding. She hopes to marry her daughter to the pretender to the Spanish throne, but ends up in love with him herself. Scenes not only include the Riviera, but the Atlantic crossing and Philadelphia as well. Another popular song from the score is "Mutual Admiration Society."

HAPPY NEW YEAR
(1980)

Book by Burt Shevelove; adapted from the play *Holiday* by Philip Barry *Music and lyrics* by Cole Porter; songs edited by Buster Davis   *Published libretto*: Samuel French, 1982   *Condensation*: None   *Anthology*: None *Music publisher*: *Music and Lyrics by Cole Porter*, 2 vols. Chappell, 1972–1975 *Licensing agent*: Samuel French   *Recording*: None   *Cast*: 14 M; 11 F

The plot of this musical is about a nonconformist young man who almost marries the conventional daughter of the country's richest banker. The time is the mid-1930s, and the ladies' fashions were highly praised in the Broadway production. This is a Philip Barry play originally done in 1928; it has been refashioned into a musical with familiar Cole Porter songs. It is done as a "memory play" with an older man narrating the story. This is a chic, glamorous, nostalgic and sophisticated show.

THE HAPPY TIME
(1968)

Book by N. Richard Nash; suggested by the characters in the stories by Robert L. Fontaine   *Music* by John Kander   *Lyrics* by Fred Ebb *Published libretto*: Dramatic, 1969   *Condensation*: None   *Anthology*: None   *Vocal selections*: Valando, 1967   *Licensing agent*: Dramatic *Recording*: RCA LSO 1144 (original cast)   *Cast*: Large mixed cast, including children

A well-traveled photographer returns to St. Pierre, his French-Canadian home town. He considers taking his young nephew, Bibi, with him on his travels. The wise old Grandpère convinces him otherwise. There is a love story between the photographer and the girl he left behind. The sets were not overly elaborate for this big Broadway musical, but slide projections were used.

HARK!
(1972)

Music by Dan Goggin and Marvin Solley   *Lyrics* by Robert Lorick *Published libretto*: None   *Condensation*: None   *Anthology*: None *Vocal selections*: None   *Licensing agent*: Samuel French   *Recording*: None   *Cast*: 4 M; 2 F

This is a lighthearted cabaret show that consists entirely of songs and a bit of dancing with no attempt at a story. Growing up in America is the theme. The cast start as children and begin the life cycle. Overpopulation, pacifism and funerals as big business are some of the universal subjects covered. The off-Broadway production used a circular, relatively bare playing area with changing lights and projections. The score was described as "melodious and literate in variety and scope."

HAZEL FLAGG
(1953)

Book by Ben Hecht; based on a story by James Street and the film *Nothing Sacred*   *Music* by Jule Styne   *Lyrics* by Bob Hilliard   *Published libretto*: None   *Condensation*: None   *Anthology*: None   *Vocal selections*: None   *Licensing agent*: Tams-Witmark   *Recording*: RCA CBM 1-2207 (original cast)   *Cast*: Large mixed cast

A small-town girl in Vermont is diagnosed as dying from radium poisoning. An expense-paid trip to New York meant to boost the circulation of a magazine sets the stage for her sudden fame. She doesn't have radium poisoning, but does manage to fall in love. This musical is set in the 1930s. The big number was the Mayor of New York doing a "soft-shoe" to "Every Street's a Boulevard in Old New York."

HEAD OVER HEELS
(1981)

Book by William S. Kilborne, Jr. and Albert T. Viola; based on the play *The Wonder Hat* by Kenneth Sawyer Goodman and Ben Hecht   *Music* by Albert T. Viola   *Lyrics* by William S. Kilborne, Jr.   *Published libretto*: Samuel French   *Condensation*: None   *Anthology*: None   *Vocal selections*: None   *Licensing agent*: Samuel French   *Recording*: None   *Cast*: 3 M; 2 F

Described by critics as a brief harlequinade about potions, spells and suddenly requited love, this off-Broadway musical was particularly recommended for children during the Christmas season. It is rooted in commedia dell'arte with a plot about three charms in Punchinello's carpetbag, one of which is a hat that makes the wearer invisible.

HEIDI
(1955 TV musical adapted for the stage)

Book adaptation by William Friedberg and Neil Simon; based on the novel by Johanna Spyri   *Musical* adaptation by Clay Warnick; based on themes by Robert Schumann   *Lyrics* by Carolyn Leigh   *Published libretto*: Samuel French, 1955, 1959   *Condensation*: None   *Anthology*: None   *Vocal selections*: None   *Licensing agent*: Samuel French   *Recording*: None   *Cast*: 6 M; 6 F; singing chorus

This tale of the little Swiss girl is well-known. Some very big Broadway names contributed to this show early in their careers. The television cast included Natalie Wood and Wally Cox. This stage adaptation calls for two interiors and three exteriors.

HELLO DOLLY!
(1964/1978)

Book by Michael Stewart; based on *The Matchmaker* by Thornton Wilder   *Music and lyrics* by Jerry Herman   *Published libretto*: Drama Book Shop, 1966   *Condensation*: *The Best Plays of 1963–1964*. Henry Hewes, ed.

Dodd, Mead, 1964 ☆ *American Musicals: Willson and Herman*. Time-Life, 1982   *Anthology*: None   *Piano-vocal score*: Morris, 1964   *Vocal selection*: Big Three (Morris, 1964)   *Licensing agent*: Tams-Witmark *Recordings*: RCA AYL 1-3814, Time-Life STL-AM13 (original cast) ☆ RCA ANL 1-2849 (Pearl Bailey and cast)   *Cast*: 8 M; 6 F; chorus

The widowed Dolly Gallagher Levi makes a precarious living as a matchmaker. Wealthy store owner Horace Vandergelder needs a wife and Dolly secretly sets out to marry him herself. Set in Yonkers and New York City around 1890, this show provides ample opportunity for lavish costumes, big production numbers, and a large cast. A staircase is needed for the big title number at the Harmonia Gardens Restaurant on 14th Street. This was filmed in 1969 with Barbra Streisand.
Tony Award Winner (Best Musical)

HENRY, SWEET HENRY
(1967)

Book by Nunnally Johnson; based on *The World of Henry Orient* by Nora Johnson   *Music and lyrics* by Bob Merrill   *Published libretto*: Samuel French, 1969   *Condensation*: None   *Anthology*: None   *Vocal selections*: None   *Licensing agent*: Samuel French   *Recording*: ABC S-OC-4 (original cast)   *Cast*: 8 M; 8 F; singers; dancers

Henry Orient is a small-time conductor. Valerie, a fourteen-year-old schoolgirl, has a crush on him. Valerie and her school chums shadow Henry, just to be near him. This show featured choreography by Michael Bennett with a lot of young girls and a colorful set that was constantly in motion. The locale is New York City and the time is the 1960s. One dance number is a hippie event in Washington Square Park.

HERE'S LOVE
(1963)

Book, music and lyrics by Meredith Willson; based on the film *The Miracle on 34th Street*; story by Valentine Davies; screenplay by George Seaton *Published libretto*: None   *Condensation*: None   *Anthology*: None *Vocal selections*: Frank Music, 1963   *Licensing agent*: Music Theatre International   *Recording*: Columbia KOS 2400 (original cast)   *Cast*: Large mixed cast

This contemporary New York show features the Macy's Thanksgiving Day Parade at the center of the plot. There is a love story between a professional woman who works for Macy's and an ex-Marine. There is also a charming old gentleman who is hired as Santa Claus, and then claims he really is Kris Kringle. Big production numbers (the parade, naturally), a good part for a young girl, and all the warmth of the Christmas season are features of this family show.

HIGH BUTTON SHOES
(1947)

Book by Stephen Longstreet; based on his short stories   *Music* by Jule Styne   *Lyrics* by Sammy Cahn   *Published libretto*: None *Condensation*: None   *Anthology*: None   *Vocal selections*: None *Licensing agent*: Tams-Witmark   *Recording*: RCA LSO 1107(e) (original cast)   *Cast*: 10 M; 4 F; singers; dancers

This popular Broadway show that originally starred Phil Silvers, has been successfully revived at the Goodspeed Opera in Connecticut. A big hit song from the score is "Papa, Won't You Dance with Me?" Set in 1913, the story involves a con man in New Brunswick (New Jersey), a Rutgers–Princeton football game, a "Keystone Comedy" sequence at the beach in Atlantic City, and various other old-fashioned musical activities. This is a clean family show.

HIGH SPIRITS
(1964)

Music, lyrics and book by Hugh Martin and Timothy Gray; based on *Blithe Spirit* by Noel Coward   *Published libretto*: None   *Condensation*: None *Anthology*: None   *Vocal selections*: Cromwell Music, 1964   *Licensing agent*: Tams-Witmark   *Recording*: ABC S-OC-1 (original cast)   *Cast*: 4 M; 6 F; singers; dancers

Noel Coward's very popular play was turned into a musical in 1964 and starred his old friend Beatrice Lillie as Madame Arcati. The plot concerns a happily married man who is haunted by the spirit of his first wife. The comedy begins when a medium arrives for a seance. This was a lavish Broadway and London musical, which featured the spirit "flying" about the stage. This is a suave, sophisticated, drawing room comedy.

HIJINKS!
(1980)

Book by Robert Kalfin, Steve Brown and John McKinney; adapted from *Captain Jinks of the Horse Marines* by Clyde Fitch   *Published libretto:* Samuel French, 198-   *Condensation:* None   *Anthology:* None
Vocal selections: None   *Licensing agent:* Samuel French   *Recording:* None   *Cast:* 9 M; 6 F

The setting is New York City—in the era of gaslit streets and the music of Stephen Foster. Our hero is Jinks, a man about town, who makes a wager with his pals about which of them can first have a "flirtation" with a beautiful opera singer. The recent off-Broadway production featured familiar songs of the period and the audience was encouraged to sing along in some of the numbers. The sets were described as flexible and resembling lithographs. This show is simple to stage and is for the entire family.

A HISTORY OF THE AMERICAN FILM
(1978)

Book and lyrics by Christopher Durang   *Music* by Mel Marvin
Published libretto: Samuel French, 198- ☆ Avon (paperback), 1978
Condensation: None   *Anthology:* None   *Vocal selections:* None
Licensing agent: Samuel French   *Recording:* None   *Cast:* 9 M; 6 F

Called a social history of America during the past 60 years, the premise of Durang's musical is that it is often difficult to separate life on the silver screen from real life. The show begins in a theater, with the cast as the audience watching a film. Then they step forward and become the characters they are watching. They are thrown into situations we instantly recognize, and then they progress into absurd variations. Characters include Loretta, Bette, Hank, Mickey and a host of others as the small cast play many different parts. The songs and dancing take second place to the comedy and the content of this show.

HIT THE DECK
(1927/1960)

Book by Herbert Fields; adapted from the play *Shore Leave* by Hubert Osborne   *Music* by Vincent Youmans   *Lyrics* by Leo Robin and Clifford Grey   *Published libretto:* None   *Condensation:* None   *Anthology:* None   *Piano-vocal score:* Harms, 1925   *Licensing agent:*

Tams-Witmark   *Recording*: EPIC LN 3569 (studio cast)   *Cast*: 14 M; 5 F; chorus

Lulu is a coffeehouse manager who falls in love with a sailor and follows him around the world until she gets him. This has been a popular show for many years. It was lavishly mounted at Jones Beach once, and also filmed in 1930 and 1955. Some of the big numbers are "Hallelujah" and "Sometimes I'm Happy." There's a lot of "hoofing" by the sailors, and a good time is had by all.

HOW NOW, DOW JONES
(1967)

Book by Max Shulman; based on an original idea by Carolyn Leigh
Music by Elmer Bernstein   *Lyrics* by Carolyn Leigh   *Published libretto*:
Samuel French, 1968   *Condensation*: None   *Anthology*: None
Vocal selections: United Artists Music (Carwin, 1968)   *Licensing agent*:
Samuel French   *Recording*: RCA LSO 1142 (original cast)   *Cast*: 14 M;
9 F; singers; dancers

This is a musical about the New York Stock Exchange. Kate reads the Dow Jones quotations over the radio each day. She is loved by two gentlemen, one of whom promises to marry her when the Dow Jones average hits 1,000. There is also a secondary romance between an absent-minded tycoon and a stock exchange guide. The snappy score is by the Hollywood composer Elmer Bernstein. The big number is "Will Everyone Here Kindly Step to the Rear." The sets are offices and Wall Street environs in this contemporary musical.

HOW TO SUCCEED IN BUSINESS WITHOUT REALLY TRYING
(1961/1966/1972)

Book by Abe Burrows, Jack Weinstock and Willie Gilbert; based on the novel by Shepherd Mead   *Music and lyrics* by Frank Loesser   *Published libretto*: None   *Condensation*: *The Best Plays of 1961–1962*. Henry Hewes, ed. Dodd, Mead, 1962 ☆ *American Musicals: Loesser*. Time-Life, 1981 *Anthology*: None   *Piano-vocal score*: Frank Music, 1962   *Vocal selections*: Frank Music, 1961   *Licensing agent*: Music Theatre International   *Recordings*: RCA LSO 1066, Time-Life STL-AM08 (original cast)   *Cast*: Large mixed cast

This is the story of how ruthless but charming J. Pierpont Finch works his way to the top of the World Wide Wicket Company. A 1972 off-Broadway revival was noted for its use of a few doors, sparse furniture, and some

sliding elevator panels to simulate offices and lobbies. This contemporary story set in New York's business world is a jovial lampoon of a business office in operation. Stars Robert Morse and Rudy Vallee also appeared in the 1967 film version.
Tony Award Winner (Best Musical)
Pulitzer Prize

I, ANASTASIA
(1965 as *Anya*)

Book by Guy Bolton; based on *Anastasia* by Marcelle Maurette and Guy Bolton   *Lyrics and musical adaptation* by Robert Wright and George Forrest; musical score based on themes from Sergei Rachmaninoff
Published libretto: None   *Condensation*: None   *Anthology*: None
Vocal selections: Frank Music, 1965   *Licensing agent*: Music Theatre International   *Recording*: United Artists UAS 5133 (original cast of *Anya*)
Cast: Large mixed cast

This is a musical version of the play that was originally done on Broadway in 1954 as *Anastasia*. It is Berlin in 1925 and a former Cossack general is looking for a way to get at the impounded fortune of the Russian Czars. He finds a young woman in a sanatorium and attempts to pass her off as a princess who survived the massacre. Is she really the Princess Anastasia? This is a big operetta-style musical that was given a lavish production at New York's Ziegfeld Theatre.

I CAN GET IT FOR YOU WHOLESALE
(1962)

Book by Jerome Weidman; based on his novel   *Music and lyrics* by Harold Rome   *Published libretto*: Random House, 1962   *Condensation*: None   *Anthology*: None   *Piano-vocal score*: Chappell, 1963
Licensing agent: Tams-Witmark   *Recording*: Columbia CSP AKOS 2180 (original cast)   *Cast*: 18 M; 13 F; singers; dancers

The time is 1937 in New York City. Harry quickly rises in the 7th Avenue garment business by brashness, ruthlessness and chicanery. His mother, up in the Bronx, helps him charm his friends. There are also a couple of girl friends and an office secretary (a part that started Barbra Streisand). The scenes include showrooms, a nightclub, homes, and offices. There is a bit of ethnic color, including a Bar Mitzvah at the beginning of Act II. One critic called this show "a semi-serious song-and-dancer."

I DO! I DO!
(1966)

Book and lyrics by Tom Jones; based on The Fourposter by Jan de Hartog
Music by Harvey Schmidt   Published libretto: None   Condensation:
None   Anthology: None   Piano-vocal score: Portfolio Music, 1968
(Chappell)   Vocal selections: Portfolio Music, 1966 (Chappell)
Licensing agent: Music Theatre International   Recording: RCA LSO 1128
(original cast)   Cast: 1 M; 1 F

The show, with a cast of two, begins with a wedding (and the bride
tossing her bouquet to the audience). We then follow the couple through
50 years of matrimony as they raise their family, despite an occasional
roving eye. The Broadway set consisted of a bed in center stage and a few
graceful screens for walls. A few props and simple costumes carry the
audience along through the years. There are 17 songs including some
vaudeville turns as well as some tender moments.

I LOVE MY WIFE
(1977)

Book and lyrics by Michael Stewart; from the play Viens Chez Moi! by Luis
Rego   Music by Cy Coleman   Published libretto: Samuel French, 1980
Condensation: None   Anthology: None   Vocal selections: Big Three
(Notable Music), 1977   Licensing agent: Samuel French   Recording:
Atlantic SD 19107 (original cast)   Cast: 6 M; 2 F

The plot of this very contemporary musical set in Trenton, New Jersey,
involves wife-swapping. But never fear, the group sex is mostly talk and
each person winds up with his or her proper mate. In addition to the two
couples, there are four musicians on stage. They change costumes and
occasionally play small parts, in addition to providing the music. This
mildly sexy musical was quite popular and was one of several Broadway
shows that switched to an all-black cast at one point in its run.

I MARRIED AN ANGEL
(1938)

Book by Richard Rodgers and Lorenz Hart; adapted from the play by John
Vaszary   Lyrics by Lorenz Hart   Music by Richard Rodgers
Published libretto: None   Condensation: None   Anthology: None
Vocal selections: None   Licensing agent: Rodgers and Hammerstein
Theatre Library   Recording: None   Cast: Large mixed cast

An angel comes down to console an idealistic Budapest banker, marries him, loses her wings, and almost ruins his banking business. The angel was originally played by ballerina Vera Zorina with choreography by George Balanchine. The show features some great Rodgers and Hart songs, including "At the Roxy Music Hall" and the title tune. This show was described as "an imaginative, opulent and tuneful frolic." There was a 1942 film version with Jeanette MacDonald.

I REMEMBER MAMA
(1979)

Book by Thomas Meehan; based on the play *I Remember Mama* by John Van Druten and stories by Kathryn Forbes   *Music* by Richard Rodgers *Lyrics* by Martin Charnin and Raymond Jessel   *Published libretto*: None *Condensation*: None   *Anthology*: None   *Vocal selections*: None *Licensing agent*: Rodgers and Hammerstein Theatre Library   *Recording*: None   *Cast*: Large mixed cast, including children

This well-remembered play, film, and TV series was Richard Rodgers' final Broadway musical. The period is just before World War I. The plot concerns a Norwegian immigrant in San Francisco who is married to a ship's carpenter and is having a hard time keeping her family fed and clothed. This was a big, expensive musical, featuring Liv Ullman as "Mama." This old-fashioned family show is upbeat and cheerful.

ILLYA DARLING
(1967)

Book by Jules Dassin; based on the film *Never on Sunday*   *Music* by Manos Hadjidakis   *Lyrics* by Joe Darion   *Published libretto*: None *Condensation*: None   *Anthology*: None   *Vocal selections*: None *Licensing agent*: Tams-Witmark   *Recording*: United Artists UAS 9901 (original cast)   *Cast*: Large mixed cast

This musical was a vehicle for Melina Mercouri, who had starred in the original film version. An American tourist in Greece learns all about life from a wild assortment of locals, and in particular a strumpet from the seaport of Piraeus. The show features energetic male folk dancers, and bouzouki music. The very popular "Never on Sunday" theme from the film is included. This is a big, Greek-flavored musical.

I'M GETTING MY ACT TOGETHER AND TAKING IT ON THE ROAD
(1978)

Book and lyrics by Gretchen Cryer   *Music* by Nancy Ford   *Published libretto*: Samuel French, 1980   *Condensation*: None   *Anthology*: None   *Piano-vocal score*: Fiddleback Music, 1978   *Licensing agent*: Samuel French   *Recording*: Columbia CSP X14885 (original cast)   *Cast*: 6 M; 4 F

This musical deals with complex feminist questions. The central plot concerns Heather, a 39-year-old performer and songwriter who is launching her comeback act. Her manager wants her to continue in her old image, but Heather has more progressive ideas. It all takes place in a club as she rehearses. This is a show of the 1970s and was a very popular off-Broadway hit. The score was variously described as one of pleasant tunes and sweet rock music.

INNER CITY
(1972)

Based on the book *The Inner City Mother Goose* by Eve Merriam   *Music* by Helen Miller   *Lyrics* by Eve Merriam   *Published libretto*: None   *Condensation*: None   *Anthology*: None   *Vocal selections*: None   *Licensing agent*: Samuel French   *Recording*: RCA LSO 1171 (original cast)   *Cast*: 4 M; 5 F

Members of the small cast play a wide variety of roles—all types that would be found deep in the inner city ghetto. This cynical revue has almost no dialogue and is billed as a "street cantata" with no overall plot. The show is about subjects such as muggers, corrupt cops, garbage disposal, overpopulation, and prostitution. Some critics were taken with the setting—a pyramid of gorgeous junk: bedsprings, car mufflers, garbage cans, stove pipes, etc. The rock musical score should be performed with great spirit and liveliness by an integrated company.

IRENE
(1919/1973)

Book by Hugh Wheeler and Joseph Stein; from an adaptation by Harry Rigby; based on the play by James Montgomery   *Music* by Harry Tierney   *Lyrics* by Joseph McCarthy; additional lyrics and music by Charles Gaynor and Otis Clements   *Published libretto*: None   *Condensation*: None

Anthology: None   *Vocal selections*: Big Three, 1973   *Licensing agent*:
Tams-Witmark   *Recordings*: Columbia KS 32266 (1973 revival cast) ☆
Monmouth Evergreen 7057E (London original cast—1919)   *Cast*: Large
mixed cast

The original musical was considerably revised for its 1973 Broadway
revival with Debbie Reynolds. Irene is a piano tuner. At a wealthy home
where she is working she is spotted by a clothes designer who asks her to
become a model. Naturally she falls in love with the heir to a Long Island
fortune. The designer ends up with Irene's Irish mother. This is a big
musical set in 1919, with lavish costumes and a large cast. Some of the
best numbers are "Alice Blue Gown" and "You Made Me Love You." The
dances include tango, tap, soft shoe and an Irish jig. This is a family show.

IRMA LA DOUCE
(1960)

Original book and lyrics by Alexandre Breffort; *English book and lyrics* by
Julian More, David Heneker and Monty Norman   *Music* by Marguerite
Monnot   *Published libretto*: None   *Condensation*: None   *Anthology*:
None   *Vocal selections*: None   *Licensing agent*: Tams-Witmark
Recording: Columbia CSP AOS 2029 (New York original cast)   *Cast*: 15 M;
1 F; singers; dancers

Irma is a streetwalker in modern-day Paris. A young law student falls in
love with her, and in order to keep other men away, he masquerades as
an elderly gentleman who pays her 10,000 francs a day. This show started
out in Paris (the music is by the composer who wrote many of Edith Piaf's
hits) and then became a long-run success in London before coming to
Broadway. *Irma La Douce* is a dancing show with accordion music part
of the atmosphere. There was a film version with the background music
from the score, but no songs! One critic claims that this tale of French
prostitution could offend no one but another warned it was not for the
prudish.

IS THERE LIFE AFTER HIGH SCHOOL?
(1982)

Book by Jeffrey Kindley; suggested by the book by Ralph Keyes   *Music*
and lyrics by Craig Carnelia   *Published libretto*: Samuel French
Condensation: None   *Anthology*: None   *Vocal selections*: None
Licensing agent: Samuel French   *Recording*: Original Cast OC 8240
(original cast)   *Cast*: 5 M; 4 F

Described as gentle and low-key, this musical concerns high school days as we remember them—how high school affected us and is still with us. It is not really a play, but a revue of song, anecdotes, monologue and vignettes. The cast not only portrays the characters as they were in high school, but as they are today as well. The set for the New York production was multilevel and functioned as the gym, the locker rooms, and other school areas. The costumes were primarily street clothes with a suggestion of band uniforms and other high school modes. For an added touch of nostalgia, ring a bell when intermission time is over.

IT'S A BIRD   IT'S A PLANE   IT'S SUPERMAN (1966)

Book by David Newman and Robert Benton; based on the comic strip
Superman   Music by Charles Strouse   Lyrics by Lee Adams
Published libretto: None   Condensation: The Best Plays of 1965–1966.
Otis L. Guernsey, Jr., ed. Dodd, Mead, 1966   Anthology: None   Vocal
selections: Big Three (Morris, 1966)   Licensing agent: Tams-Witmark
Recording: Columbia CSP AKOS 2970 (original cast)   Cast: Large mixed
cast

Superman is the familiar hero of this tale. Other characters include reporter Lois Lane and the mad atomic scientist Abner Sedgwick, who is out to put an end to Superman. There are also a miserable newspaper gossip columnist named Max Mencken and some villainous Chinese acrobats. This big musical was done in a "pop art" style that was fashionable in the 1960s. Superman flies about the stage à la Peter Pan. There are no messages, just comic strip adventure. The whole show is a parody, with energetic dances and some spectacular effects.

JACQUES BREL IS ALIVE AND WELL AND LIVING IN PARIS (1968/1972/1974/1983)

Music by Jacques Brel   Production, conception, English lyrics and
additional material by Eric Blau and Mort Shuman; based on Jacques Brel's
lyrics and commentary   Published libretto: Dutton, 1971
Condensation: None   Anthology: None   Vocal selections: Big Three,
1972   Licensing agent: Music Theatre International   Recording:
Columbia D2S 779 (original cast)   Cast: 3 M; 1 F

This very popular show is made up of 26 songs sung by four performers. The songs are by the late Belgian composer and performer and have been translated into English. There are no sets. This cabaret show has proved extremely popular over the years and was elaborately filmed in 1975. The songs describe and celebrate the struggles of Paris low-life and the bustle of the streets. They have a lot to do with death, but they are mainly about love. Dramatic interpretations are essential.

JAMAICA
(1957)

Book and lyrics by E. Y. Harburg   *Music* by Harold Arlen   *Published libretto*: None   *Condensation: American Musicals: Arlen*. Time-Life, 1982 *Anthology*: None   *Vocal selections*: Morris, 1963   *Licensing agent*: Tams-Witmark   *Recordings*: RCA LOC 1036, Time-Life STL-AM11 (original cast)   *Cast*: 11 M; 6 F; chorus

The plot revolves around Savannah, a Caribbean island girl who wants to go to New York. "Push the Button" is how she describes life there, and that song is still sung by this show's star, Lena Horne. But her fisherman fiance doesn't want her to go. This big, lush Broadway musical has lots of tropical song and dance costumed in the hot colors of the Caribbean. This show was described as buoyant, spirited and wholesome.

JERRY'S GIRLS
(1981)

Music and lyrics by Jerry Herman; based on a concept by Jerry Herman and Larry Alford   *Published libretto*: None   *Condensation*: None *Anthology*: None   *Piano-vocal score*: Hal Leonard, 1982   *Licensing agent*: Samuel French   *Recording*: None (see individual cast albums) *Cast*: 4 F

This is a revue made up of the songs of Jerry Herman. The cast of four females in the original New York cabaret production was accompanied by a female three piece combo. But this is not a feminist revue, just Broadway show tunes arranged as medleys (optimist, vaudeville, movies, etc.) and sung singularly. The songs come from *Mame, Hello, Dolly!, Milk and Honey, Mack and Mabel, The Grand Tour, Dear World, Hollywood/ Ukraine* and *Parade*. This can be simply staged with only suggestions of costume changes.

JESUS CHRIST SUPERSTAR
(1971/1977)

Lyrics by Tim Rice   *Music* by Andrew Lloyd Webber   *Published libretto*: (see vocal selections listed below)   *Condensation*: None
Anthology: *Great Rock Musicals*. Stanley Richards, ed. Stein and Day, 1979
Vocal selections: Leeds Music, 1973 (MCA Music); includes libretto
Licensing agent: Music Theatre International   *Recording*: MCA 7-1503
(original cast)   *Cast*: Large mixed cast

The last seven days in the life of Jesus are portrayed in this musical. Passion Plays have been around since the Middle Ages, and this is simply a contemporary, or "rock opera," version. This was originally a lavish Broadway musical that later returned in a scaled-down version after touring most major cities. The critics found that it was a serious work with sincere intentions told entirely in song, the most familiar one being "I Don't Know How to Love Him." The show was staged on a basically bare, raked stage with drapes and platform sets lowered from the flies. There was also a film version.

JO
(1964)

Book and lyrics by Don Parks and William Dyer; based on Louisa May Alcott's *Little Women*   *Music* by William Dyer   *Published libretto*: Dramatists Play Service, 1964   *Condensation*: None   *Anthology*: None
Vocal selections: None   *Licensing agent*: Dramatists Play Service
Recording: None   *Cast*: 10 M; 12 F (3 girls)

This is the famous story of four girls growing up in Harmony, Massachusetts during the Civil War. The off-Broadway production was noted for its picture book sets which were edged in red velvet and gilt frames. The costumes were described as valentines made of ribbons and lace. This was considered an ideal family show and extra matinee performances were given for children. Twin pianos provided the accompaniment.

JOHNNY JOHNSON
(1936/1956)

Book and lyrics by Paul Green   *Music* by Kurt Weill   *Published libretto (revised and rewritten)*: Samuel French, 1971   *Condensation*: None   *Anthology*: *Twenty Best Plays of the Modern American Theatre*.

John Gassner, ed. Crown, 1939   *Vocal selections*: None   *Licensing agent*: Samuel French   *Recordings*: Heliodor HS 25024, MGM E3447 (1956 studio cast)   *Cast*: 49 M; 6 F

Despite the doubling up by the male cast members, this was one of the most expensive undertakings of the Group Theatre in the 1930s. At the original production handbills proclaiming "this is a play with songs, not a musical show" were handed out, so afraid were they that it would be considered light and frivolous. The plot concerns a young Southern boy who enlists during World War I to end all wars. He is wounded in France, sent back home to a mental hospital, and eventually becomes a peddler of toys. Pacifist viewpoints are expressed in satire and song. The Kurt Weill score was described as haunting. The later off-Broadway production used slides as projected backgrounds.

JOSEPH AND THE AMAZING TECHNICOLOR DREAMCOAT (1982)

Lyrics by Tim Rice; from the biblical story of Joseph and his brethren *Music* by Andrew Lloyd Webber   *Published libretto*: Holt, Rinehart and Winston, 1982   *Condensation*: None   *Anthology*: None *Piano-vocal score*: Sevenoaks, Kent, Novello, 1975   *Vocal selections*: Theodore Presser (Novello, 1982)   *Licensing agent*: Music Theatre International   *Recording*: Chrysalis CHR 1387 (Broadway original cast); includes libretto   *Cast*: Large mixed cast

This musical version of the biblical story pre-dates the hit show *Jesus Christ Superstar*. *Joseph and the Amazing Technicolor Dreamcoat* is the first show Webber and Rice composed back in 1967. It is perhaps the most performed musical in schools and universities although it was not performed on Broadway until 1982, when it transferred from off-Broadway. The latest version runs 90 minutes—entirely sung. Some of the numbers are done in a country and western style, while Pharaoh's number is strictly Elvis style. This musical appeals to young people.

THE KING AND I (1951/1964/1977)

Book and lyrics by Oscar Hammerstein, II; based on Margaret Landon's *Anna and the King of Siam*   *Music* by Richard Rodgers   *Published libretto*: Random House, 1951   *Condensation*: None   *Anthology*: *Six Plays by Rodgers and Hammerstein*. Random House, 1955 ✩ Modern Library,

1959   *Piano-vocal score*: Williamson Music, 1951   *Vocal selections*:
Williamson Music, 1951   *Licensing agent*: Rodgers and Hammerstein
Theatre Library   *Recordings*: MCA 2028E (original cast) ☆ RCA ABL 1-2610
(1977 revival)   *Cast*: 9 M; 4 F; children; singers; dancers

One of the most popular Rodgers and Hammerstein shows, this has been
presented all over the Western world many times and was beautifully
filmed in 1956. The story is about an English teacher who goes to Siam in
the 1860s to instruct the royal children, and all her confrontations with
the customs and the king of the land. There is a good deal of oriental
color and decor required and some exotic dancing. But the famous score
is sure to please, with such numbers as "Getting to Know You" and "Shall
We Dance." This is most effective if given a lavish production.
Tony Award Winner (Best Musical)

KING OF SCHNORRERS
(1979)

Book, music and lyrics by Judd Woldin; based on Israel Zangwill's *The King
of Schnorrers*   *Published libretto*: Samuel French, 1981   *Condensation*:
None   *Anthology*: None   *Vocal selections*: None   *Licensing agent*:
Samuel French   *Recording*: None   *Cast*: 5 M; 2 F; chorus

This show is also known as *Petticoat Lane*. "Schnorrer" is a Jewish term
for a moocher or beggar who is able to get something free, while making
you feel he has done you a favor. This musical is set in the Jewish quarter
of London around 1790. There are rival sects of Jews, and the son of one
falls in love with the daughter of another. For the off-Broadway production, multipanel curtains strung on wires were used, along with occasional chairs and tables to suggest different locales. The costumes were
brightly hued. This production was directed by a dancer, and the cast was
described as nimble. This show is particularly appealing to those interested in Jewish culture and tradition.

KING'S RHAPSODY
(1949)

Book and music by Ivor Novello   *Lyrics* by Christopher Hassall
Published libretto: None   *Condensation*: None   *Anthology*: None
Vocal selections: Chappell, 1949 ☆ *Song Album*. Chappell, 197– (two
selections)   *Licensing agent*: Samuel French   *Recordings*: *Ivor Novello:
The Great Shows*, World (British) EMI SHB 23 (original cast) ☆ Studio 2
Stereo (British) EMI TWO 270 (studio cast)   *Cast*: 18 M; 10 F; singers;
dancers

This musical romance of the 1880s involves a southern European king who weds a princess from the North. Some years later he is forced to abdicate in favor of his young son. He attends his son's coronation unrecognized. The original London production was noted for its elaborate staging and grandeur. This was a big post-war production with several lavish ballet numbers. It has been featured at large open-air summer theaters in England. There was a 1955 British film with Errol Flynn and Anna Neagle.

KISMET
(1953/1965/1974)

Book by Charles Lederer and Luther Davis; based on the play by Edward Knoblock   *Music and lyrics* by Robert Wright and George Forrest; from themes of Alexander Borodin   *Published libretto*: Random House, 1954   *Condensation*: None   *Anthology*: None   *Piano-vocal score*: Frank Music, 1955   *Licensing agent*: Music Theatre International   *Recording*: Columbia S 32605 (original cast)   *Cast*: Large mixed cast

This is a popular story of a king of beggars who pretends to be a visiting nobleman to the court of the Caliph of ancient Bagdad. This Arabian Nights fantasy fills the stage with colorful sets, costumes and dancing girls. It has been produced as a straight play and film, and then in a musical version which was filmed in 1955 with Howard Keel. A lavish production will certainly be expected. This story seems to lend itself well to ethnic adaptations; it was performed by the Puerto Rican Traveling Theater and a recent black version was called *Timbuktu!*
Tony Award Winner (Best Musical)

KISS ME, KATE
(1948/1965)

Book by Bella and Samuel Spewack; Shakespeare's *The Taming of the Shrew* is the play-within-the-play   *Music and lyrics* by Cole Porter   *Published libretto*: Knopf, 1953 ☆ *Theatre Arts* (magazine), January 1955   *Condensation*: *American Musicals: Porter*. Time-Life, 1981   *Anthology*: *Ten Great Musicals of the American Stage*. Stanley Richards, ed. Chilton, 1973   *Piano-vocal score*: Harms, 1967 (Chappell)   *Licensing agent*: Tams-Witmark   *Recordings*: Columbia S 32609, Time-Life STL-AM02 (original cast)   *Cast*: 17 M; 5 F; chorus

A production of *The Taming of the Shrew* is overshadowed by the on and off stage battles of the stars, plus a secondary plot of a dancer in trouble

with some gangsters. Some of the musical numbers are done in Shakespearean costume and style, while others are offstage and backstage. The score is considered the best of Cole Porter, and includes "So in Love" and "Wunderbar." This sophisticated Broadway show was a big hit all over the world, and it was filmed in 1953.
Tony Award Winner (Best Musical)

KNICKERBOCKER HOLIDAY
(1938/1975/1977)

Book and lyrics by Maxwell Anderson; suggested by Washington Irving's *Father Knickerbocker's History of New York*   *Music* by Kurt Weill   *Published libretto*: Anderson House, 1938   *Condensation*: None   *Anthology*: None   *Piano-vocal score*: Crawford Music, 1951   *Licensing agent*: Rodgers and Hammerstein Theatre Library   *Recording*: Joey 7243 (radio version with Walter Huston)   *Cast*: 14 M; 6 F; soldiers; citizens; Indians

The setting is New Amsterdam (old New York) in 1647. Tyrannical Peter Stuyvesant with a peg-leg sings the show's famous "September Song." The story includes Washington Irving as a narrator, a pair of young lovers, and a chorus of Dutch beauties. There is a message about tyranny and democracy. This has been done on a lavish scale, or in a concert version without costumes or sets. There was a film version (minus much of the score) in 1944 with Nelson Eddy.

KNIGHTS OF SONG
(1938)

Book by Glendon Allvine and Adele Gutman Nathan   *Music* by Arthur Sullivan   *Lyrics* by W. S. Gilbert   *Published libretto*: None   *Condensation*: None   *Anthology*: None   *Vocal selections*: None   *Licensing agent*: Tams-Witmark   *Recording*: None   *Cast*: 11 M; 3 F; chorus

Subtitled *A Musical Romance about Gilbert and Sullivan*, the book presents some biographical incidents from the lives of the famous team of composers. It begins with a rehearsal of *Pinafore* and ends after the death of Sullivan. Some of the characters include D'Oyly Carte, Oscar Wilde, Bernard Shaw and Queen Victoria. But it is really the musical excerpts the audience will be waiting to hear. This is a show for all good Savoyards.

KURT VONNEGUT'S GOD BLESS YOU, MR. ROSEWATER
(1979)

Book and lyrics by Howard Ashman; additional lyrics by Dennis Green; based on the novel by Kurt Vonnegut   Music by Alan Menken   Published libretto: Samuel French, 1979   Condensation: None   Anthology: None   Vocal selections: None   Licensing agent: Samuel French   Recording: None   Cast: 10 M; 4 F

The plot deals with an American millionaire who gives his money away in an effort to help the poor. It is a satire, a social commentary, and a plea for brotherhood. For the off-Broadway production an all purpose tri-level set was used. It was unpretentiously staged with energy and humor. The score was described as cheerful and pleasant.

LADY BE GOOD!
(1924)

Book by Guy Bolton and Fred Thompson   Music by George Gershwin   Lyrics by Ira Gershwin   Published libretto: None   Condensation: None   Anthology: None   Vocal selections: Harms, 1924–1925   Licensing agent: Tams-Witmark   Recordings: Smithsonian Collection R008, Monmouth Evergreen 7036E (London original cast)   Cast: Large mixed cast

In the original production, Adele Astaire played a poor girl who impersonates a Spanish heiress to collect four million dollars. Her brother Fred played her brother who she tries to keep out of a bad marriage. Cliff (Ukelele Ike) Edwards also participated, and stopped the show. The Gershwin score (even then) was hailed as brilliant. The Astaires seem to have swept all the critics right into their pockets—particularly Adele, who charmed them all. A London revival (1968) changed the period to the glamorous thirties but retained such famous songs as "Fascinating Rhythm" and the title tune.

LADY IN THE DARK
(1941/1969)

Book by Moss Hart   Music by Kurt Weill   Lyrics by Ira Gershwin   Published libretto: Random House, 1941 ☆ Dramatists Play Service, 1941   Condensation: The Best Plays of 1940–1941. Burns Mantle, ed. Dodd, Mead, 1941 ☆ American Musicals: Weill. Time-Life, 1982   Anthology: Great Musicals of the American Theatre, vol. 2. Stanley Richards, ed. Chilton, 1976

Piano-vocal score: Chappell, 1941   *Licensing agent*: Tams-Witmark
Recordings: RCA LPV 503 (original cast) ☆ Columbia CSP COS 2390, Time-Life
STL-AM10 (studio cast)   *Cast*: 9 M, 11 F; chorus

This famous show is officially billed as a "musical play." The plot concerns psychoanalysis and an editor of a fashion magazine who cannot
make up her mind. This was a lavish production with revolving stages
and a large cast. The production numbers are fantasies, including the
circus one with the famous "Saga of Jenny" number. This was Gertrude
Lawrence's show, and her famous songs include "My Ship." Danny Kaye
also stopped the show with "Tschaikowsky." There was a film version in
1944 with Ginger Rogers, and Angela Lansbury appeared in a concert
version at Lincoln Center.

THE LAST SWEET DAYS OF ISAAC
(1970)

Book and lyrics by Gretchen Cryer   *Music* by Nancy Ford   *Published
libretto*: None   *Condensation*: None   *Anthology*: None   *Vocal
selections*: None   *Licensing agent*: Samuel French   *Recording*: RCA
LSO 1169 (original cast)   *Cast*: 1 M; 1 F; chorus

This 1970 show is, in fact, two one-act musicals (an Isaac character is in
both). The first involves a couple trapped in an elevator. The second
takes place in jail, with two who have been arrested. Isaac believes that a
person's whole life can be taped, recorded, and photographed and
preserved so that future generations can relive his experiences. This is a
spoof on "the age of technology has arrived." Some names that popped
up in most reviews were Marshall McLuhan and Woody Allen, although
neither were in any way involved in the production. This can be simply
staged with a cast of two and a small back-up group. The rock score was
described as loud but agreeable.
Off-Broadway (OBIE) Award Winner

LEAVE IT TO JANE
(1917/1959)

Book and lyrics by Guy Bolton and P. G. Wodehouse; based on George
Ade's play, *The College Widow*   *Music* by Jerome Kern   *Published
libretto*: None   *Condensation*: None   *Anthology*: None   *Vocal
selections*: Harms, 1961   *Licensing agent*: Tams-Witmark   *Recording*:
Stet DS 15002 (1959 cast recording)   *Cast*: 9 M; 3 F; chorus

This musical is considered a landmark in musical comedy history as it uses purely American characters, locale and spirit, rather than the traditions of European operetta. It is the story of how a college professor's daughter manages to lure a football player away from a rival institution. The off-Broadway revival retained the pre-World War I setting and the music was provided by a piano, saxaphone-clarinet, banjo and drums. The critics found the show a nostalgic antique but all enjoyed the Jerome Kern score. June Allyson sang several of the songs in the 1946 film, " 'Till the Clouds Roll By." This can be simply staged with a relatively small cast, and for maximum charm should not be spoofed.

LEND AN EAR
(1948/1959/1969)

Sketches, music and lyrics by Charles Gaynor   *Published libretto*: Samuel French, 1971   *Condensation*: None   *Anthology*: None   *Vocal selections*: None   *Licensing agent*: Samuel French   *Recording*: None   *Cast*: 10 M; 11 F

This is a revue, and revues generally do not stand the test of time for revivals. But in this case the author wisely avoided topical material, and this show has been brought back twice off-Broadway. There are skits about travel, psychiatry, school, operas, and other timeless subjects. The original star was Carol Channing and her "Gladiola Girl" routine is the most famous number.

LI'L ABNER
(1956)

Book by Norman Panama and Melvin Frank; based on comic strip characters created by Al Capp   *Music* by Gene de Paul   *Lyrics* by Johnny Mercer   *Published libretto*: None   *Condensation*: None   *Anthology*: None   *Vocal selections*: Commander, 1959 (Twentieth Century Music)   *Licensing agent*: Tams-Witmark   *Recording*: Columbia OL 5150 (original cast)   *Cast*: Large mixed cast

This big Broadway musical is based on the popular comic strip characters, and it was filmed with members of the original cast in 1959. There is a complicated plot and some political satire. The sets are usually done in cartoon style, and there are lots of regional/hoe-down dances. A collection of barnyard animals will add to the fun. "Jubilation T. Cornpone" is a big production number and "Namely You" is one of the nicer ballads.

There is a big "Sadie Hawkins Day" ballet. The family will enjoy this popular regional show for all.

LITTLE MARY SUNSHINE
(1959)

Book, music and lyrics by Rick Besoyan   *Published libretto*: Samuel French (London), 1960 ☆ *Theatre Arts* (magazine), December 1960
Condensation: None   *Anthology*: None   *Piano-vocal score*: Sunbeam (Valando), 1965   *Vocal selections*: New York Times Music, 1962
Licensing agent: Samuel French   *Recording*: Capitol SWAO 1240 (original cast)   *Cast*: 13 M; 10 F

This is a musical spoof of the operettas of the 1920s. Echoes of the most famous shows are either seen or heard in this very popular off-Broadway show. Set in Colorado "early in this century," little Mary (an orphan found by the last of the Kadota Indians) runs a mountain inn. Some of the guests include a group of finishing school girls and a visiting opera star. There is also a troop of handsome forest rangers nearby. (Yes, there is a "Colorado Love Call.") This can be done very simply with a small cast and twin pianos. Some of the critical comments referred to the show as side-splitting and wonderful fun.

LITTLE ME
(1962/1982)

Book by Neil Simon; based on a novel by Patrick Dennis   *Music* by Cy Coleman   *Lyrics* by Carolyn Leigh   *Published libretto*: None
Condensation: None   *Anthology*: None   *Vocal selections*: Morris (Hansen), 1962   *Licensing agent*: Tams-Witmark   *Recording*: RCA LSO 1078 (original cast)   *Cast*: Large mixed cast

In the original production Sid Caesar played a number of different roles, but in the revival the parts were divided among several different men. This is a wild farce told in flashbacks about the career of Belle Poitrine. She is a vaudeville entertainer, a gangster's moll, a film star, and a passenger on the Titanic. The time is around World War I and there are some scenes with the soldiers in France. "Real Live Girl" and "I've Got Your Number" are two of the more familiar songs from the score. This is a big musical requiring a number of sets and costumes and involved dance numbers. The leading roles present a challenge to the cast.

LITTLE NELLIE KELLY
(1922)

Book, music and lyrics by George M. Cohan   *Published libretto*: None
Condensation: None   *Anthology*: None   *Vocal selections*: None
Licensing agent: Tams-Witmark   *Recording*: None   *Cast*: Large mixed
cast

The original production was described as the snappiest, liveliest, danciest, cleanest, and most wholesome show that had been presented in some time. The last act was particularly praised for its gorgeous set and costumes. The plot concerns the loss of a pearl necklace and how Nellie saves the day and finds her true love. This was meant to be a satire of popular mystery plays of the day. "Till My Luck Comes Rolling Along" was a hit number in the show. There was a Judy Garland film version which barely used the original plot and only one song ("Nellie Kelly, I Love You") from the score.

A LITTLE NIGHT MUSIC
(1973/1981)

Book by Hugh Wheeler; suggested by a film by Ingmar Bergman   *Music and lyrics* by Stephen Sondheim   *Published libretto*: Dodd, Mead, 1974
Condensation: *The Best Plays of 1972–1973*. Otis L. Guernsey, Jr., ed. Dodd, Mead, 1973 ☆ *American Musicals: Sondheim*. Time-Life, 1982   *Anthology*: *The Great Musicals of the American Theatre*, vol. 2. Stanley Richards, ed. Chilton, 1976 ☆ *Best American Plays*, 8th ser. Clive Barnes, ed. Crown, 1983
Piano-vocal score: Revelation Music, 1974   *Vocal selections*: Revelation Music, 1973   *Licensing agent*: Music Theatre International   *Recordings*: Columbia JS 32265, Time-Life STL-AM12 (original cast) ☆ RCA LRL 5090 (London cast)   *Cast*: Large mixed cast

Called a musical with elegance, this show is set in Sweden at the turn of the century. The central character is a middle-aged actress, and the plot concerns her family and loves. Most of the music is in three-quarter time, and there is almost no dancing. This show was highly praised for its style and imagination and its combination of humor and sadness. The big song is "Send In the Clowns." There was a film version in 1977 with Elizabeth Taylor. An opulent production is recommended.
Tony Award Winner (Best Musical)

LOCK UP YOUR DAUGHTERS
(1959)

Adaptation by Bernard Miles; based on Henry Fielding's comedy *Rape upon Rape*   *Music* by Laurie Johnson   *Lyrics* by Lionel Bart   *Published libretto*: Samuel French, 1967   *Condensation*: None   *Anthology*: None   *Vocal selections*: None   *Licensing agent*: Samuel French   *Recording*: London 5766 (London original cast)   *Cast*: 15 M; 4 F

The plot of this musical is about a villainous British magistrate who extorts money from those whom he judges. In this farce some of his victims plan revenge. This musical was a hit in London at the Mermaid Theatre in 1959 but closed "out of town" when it tried for Broadway. It has been successfully staged at the Goodspeed Opera in Connecticut. The London setting in 1730 requires various streets, taverns and courtrooms, as well as wigs, breeches, and dresses of the period. The plot is somewhat bawdy, but the naughtiness doesn't actually take place on the stage.

LORELEI
(1974)

New book by Kenny Solms and Gail Parent; from *Gentlemen Prefer Blondes* by Anita Loos   *Music* by Jule Styne   *Lyrics* by Leo Robin; *additional lyrics* by Betty Comden and Adolph Green   *Published libretto*: None   *Condensation*: None   *Anthology*: None   *Vocal selections*: Consolidated Music, 1974   *Licensing agent*: Tams-Witmark   *Recordings*: MGM M3G 55, Verve MV 5097 (original cast)   *Cast*: Large mixed cast

Lorelei Lee is the most famous gold digger of this century. This often reworked Anita Loos story has Lorelei sailing for Europe in the roaring twenties. This is a revision of a 1949 musical, *Gentlemen Prefer Blondes* which was filmed in 1953 with Marilyn Monroe. Carol Channing, however, starred in both stage versions and "Diamonds are a Girl's Best Friend" became her signature. Careful attention should be given to costume, set design and choreography (tap, charleston, nightclubs in Paris, etc). The music is bouncy and fun; "Bye, Bye Baby" is one of the hit songs from the score. This is a real "audience show" with a strong Lorelei.

LOST IN THE STARS
(1949/1958/1968/1972)

Book and lyrics by Maxwell Anderson; based on Alan Paton's novel, Cry, the Beloved Country   Music by Kurt Weill   Published libretto: Sloan (Anderson House), 1950 ☆ Theatre Arts (magazine), December 1950   Condensation: The Burns Mantle Best Plays of 1949–1950. John Chapman, ed. Dodd, Mead, 1950   Anthology: Great Musicals of the American Theatre, vol. 2. Stanley Richards, ed. Chilton, 1976   Piano-vocal score: Chappell, 1950   Licensing agent: Rodgers and Hammerstein Theatre Library   Recording: MCA 2071E (original cast)   Cast: Large mixed cast, primarily black

This is a serious look at South Africa and the apartheid system there in the 1940s. Absalom, a young black from a rural area, comes to Johannesburg. He becomes involved in a robbery and is sentenced to be hanged. For the 1972 revival the stage was a circular platform with bleachers on each side and screens overhead for projected images. African flavor is expected in the costumes and choreography. The cast is primarily black, including a young boy who sings "Big Mole." Clive Barnes of the New York Times called the Kurt Weill score (his last) a "considerable piece of musical theater." There was a film version in 1974 with Melba Moore.

LOVE FROM JUDY
(1952)

Book by Eric Maschwitz and Jean Webster; based on Daddy Long Legs by Jean Webster   Music by Hugh Martin   Lyrics by Hugh Martin and Timothy "Jack" Gray   Published libretto: None   Condensation: None   Anthology: None   Vocal selections: Chappell, 1947–1952   Licensing agent: Samuel French   Recording: Box Office LP JJA 19743 (London original cast)   Cast: 7 M; 8 F; chorus

This show was a big success in London in 1952. The American premiere was at the University of Alabama in 1957. The action is set in New Orleans in 1903. The story is about an orphan girl taken from her grim surroundings by an unknown benefactor with whom she subsequently falls in love. The score is by Americans, although this has not been done on Broadway. Some rousing numbers are "Go and Get Your Old Banjo" and "Mardi Gras."

LOVELY LADIES, KIND GENTLEMEN
(1970)

Book by John Patrick; based on *The Teahouse of the August Moon* by Vern J. Sneider and the play by John Patrick   *Music and lyrics* by Stan Freeman and Franklin Underwood   *Published libretto*: Samuel French, 1971   *Condensation*: None   *Anthology*: None   *Vocal selections*: None   *Licensing agent*: Samuel French   *Recording*: None   *Cast*: Large mixed cast

Since this musical is set in 1946 on Okinawa (Japan) an Oriental cast will help, but is not required. A goat is required for "Lady Astor." Most people are probably familiar with the plot of the American forces of occupation knee-deep in black-market operations and home brew. Sakini, the narrator and con-man extraordinary, was once played by Marlon Brando in a non-musical film version of the play. A Captain is sent to Westernize a native village, but instead of building a school they end up building a tea house. The sets and costumes of the Broadway production were praised for their Oriental beauty. The musical style is both exotic and boogie-woogie.

LUTE SONG
(1946/1959)

Book by Sidney Howard and Will Irwin; adapted from *Pi-Pa-Ki* by Kao-Tong-Kia   *Music* by Raymond Scott   *Lyrics* by Bernard Hanighen   *Published libretto*: Dramatic, 1955   *Condensation*: *Burns Mantle Best Plays of 1945–1946*. Burns Mantle, ed. Dodd, Mead, 1946   *Anthology*: None   *Vocal selections*: None   *Licensing agent*: Dramatic (specify musical version)   *Recording*: Decca 8030 (original cast)   *Cast*: 9 M; 6 F; chorus

Based on a 600-year-old Chinese drama, this musical originally starred Mary Martin and Yul Brynner on Broadway. It is the story of a poor but brilliant scholar during the Ming Dynasty who leaves his wife and family to make his fortune. The scholar succeeds but is ordered by the Emperor to remain in the capital and marry a princess. A revival was hailed as an example of how simple sets and costumes can be used to evoke splendor and richness. The show features parades, pageantry, and dance. "Mountain High, Valley Low" is a familiar song from the score.

MACK AND MABEL
(1974)

Book by Michael Stewart; based on an idea by Leonard Spigelgass   *Music and lyrics* by Jerry Herman   *Published libretto*: Samuel French, 1976   *Condensation*: None   *Anthology*: None   *Vocal selections*: Morris, 1974 (Hal Leonard)   *Licensing agent*: Samuel French   *Recording*: ABC ABCH 830 (original cast)   *Cast*: 10 M; 5 F; singers; dancers

Mabel Norman was working in a Brooklyn delicatessen back in 1911 when she was discovered by Mack Sennett ("Look What Happened to Mabel"). The plot follows them to California and the big days of silent films. There are bathing beauties, Keystone Kops, the unsolved murder of William Desmond Taylor, the coming of sound musicals ("Tap Your Troubles Away") and drugs. Robert Preston was Mack and Bernadette Peters was Mabel. A spectacular Broadway production of the tragic lives of some real Hollywood personalities.

THE MAD SHOW
(1966)

Book by Larry Siegel and Stan Hart; based on *Mad* (magazine)   *Music* by Mary Rodgers   *Lyrics* by Marshall Barer, Larry Siegel, Steven Vinaver and Esteban Ria Nido (Stephen Sondheim)   *Published libretto*: Samuel French, 1973   *Condensation*: None   *Anthology*: None   *Vocal selections*: None   *Licensing agent*: Samuel French   *Recording*: Columbia OS 2930 (original cast)   *Cast*: 3 M; 2 F; extras

This musical revue's basis was a popular comic book, and it was staged in a "pop art" comic book style. The various skits are directed at babysitters, children's television programs, the bossa nova, Bob Dylan, and Christmas gifts. Curiously, there is very little political satire. This can be simply staged and will appeal to the college crowd. A talented cast is needed.

MLLE. MODISTE
(1905/1929/1978)

Book and lyrics by Henry Blossom   *Music* by Victor Herbert   *Pubished libretto*: None   *Condensation*: None   *Anthology*: None   *Piano-vocal score*: Witmark, 1905   *Vocal selections*: *The Music of Victor Herbert*. Warner Brothers Music, 1976   *Licensing agent*: Tams-Witmark   *Recording*: Readers Digest RD 40-N1 (studio cast)   *Cast*: Large mixed cast

Fifi is employed at Madame Cecile's hat shop on the Rue de la Paix in turn-of-the-century Paris. She loves Etienne, who is forbidden to marry beneath his social level. Through the help of an American millionaire, Fifi becomes a famous singer and eventually weds Etienne. The role of Fifi was written for opera star Fritzi Scheff, and she introduced "Kiss Me Again," which is considered one of the great American songs. Although this was originally a big Broadway production with a cast of 85 it was later simply staged by the Light Opera of Manhattan. The 1930 film version was called *The Toast of the Legion*.

MAGGIE FLYNN
(1968/1976)

Book, music and lyrics by Hugo Peretti, Luigi Creatore and George David Weiss; book in collaboration with Morton Da Costa; based on an idea by John Flaxman   *Published libretto*: Samuel French, 1968   *Condensation*: None   *Anthology*: None   *Vocal selections*: Valando, 1968   *Licensing agent*: Samuel French   *Recording*: RCA LSOD 2009 (original cast) *Cast*: 12 M; 6 F; chorus; children

The heroine of this musical is a girl in charge of a Negro orphanage in New York City in 1863. The plot involves her husband, an actor, and a Colonel in the U.S. Army. Race riots and draft-dodgers are major plot elements, and there are obvious comparisons to the 1960s and Vietnam, as noted by the critics. But this is basically an old-fashioned musical and a family show. It includes a big circus parade and provides an opportunity for colorful period costumes and sets. Shirley Jones, Jack Cassidy and Stephanie Mills were in the original Broadway cast.

MAME
(1966/1983)

Book by Jerome Lawrence and Robert E. Lee; based on the novel *Auntie Mame* by Patrick Dennis and the play *Auntie Mame* by Lawrence and Lee *Published libretto*: Random House, 1967   *Condensation: American Musicals: Willson and Herman*. Time-Life, 1982   *Anthology*: None *Piano-vocal score*: Big Three (Morris, 1967)   *Licensing agent*: Tams-Witmark   *Recordings*: Columbia KOS 3000, Time-Life STL–AM13 (original cast)   *Cast*: Large mixed cast

Everyone knows "Auntie Mame." She was introduced in a novel, then returned in a play, in this musical version, and finally in a film musical. She is the madcap aunt of Patrick Dennis who loses her fortune in the

1929 stock market crash, meets wealthy Beauregard while clerking in a department store, and goes South to meet his aristocratic family. It is a funny book with some sensational songs including "Mame" and "We Need a Little Christmas." Angela Lansbury was "Mame" (but Rosalind Russell, Bea Lillie, Lucille Ball, and many others can also claim the part) and this show is a big musical with 1920s and 1930s ambiance for the whole family.

MAN OF LA MANCHA
(1965/1972/1977)

Book by Dale Wasserman; suggested by the life and works of Miguel de Cervantes y Saavedra   *Music* by Mitch Leigh   *Lyrics* by Joe Darion   *Published libretto*: Random House, 1966   *Condensation*: *The Best Plays of 1965–1966*. Otis L. Guernsey, Jr., ed. Dodd, Mead, 1966   *Anthology*: *The Great Musicals of the American Theatre*, vol. 2. Stanley Richards, ed. Chilton, 1976   *Piano-vocal score*: Cherry Lane Music (S. Fox, 1968)   *Vocal selections*: Cherry Lane Music (S. Fox, 1965)   *Licensing agent*: Tams-Witmark   *Recordings*: MCA 2018 (original cast) ☆ 2-MCA 10010 (London cast)   *Cast*: Large mixed cast

This musical play about Cervantes and his "Don Quixote" had a long initial run of over 2,000 performances. It has returned to Broadway several times and has been performed all over the world and filmed in 1972 with Peter O'Toole. The setting is Spain at the end of the sixteenth century. It was originally presented on a thrust stage without intermission. "The Impossible Dream" is a well-known song from the score. The show is an old-fashioned, sentimental extravaganza which was called a "ten hankerchief" play. Audiences love it.
Tony Award Winner (Best Musical)

MAN WITH A LOAD OF MISCHIEF
(1966/1974)

Book by Ben Tarver; adapted from the play by Ashley Dukes   *Music* by John Clifton   *Lyrics* by John Clifton and Ben Tarver   *Published libretto*: None   *Condensation*: None   *Anthology*: None   *Vocal selections*: None   *Licensing agent*: Samuel French   *Recording*: Kapp KRS 5508 (original cast)   *Cast*: 3 M; 3 F

This off-Broadway musical was almost an operetta, with much charm and appeal. It is based on an English play and the title is the name of a roadside inn in the early nineteenth century. The plot is simply about a a lord who makes love to a maid and a servant who makes love to a lady. A revival used a four piece ensemble for accompaniment and a set that swung around from the inn to a garden. The score was described as lovely and enchanting.

MARCH OF THE FALSETTOS
(1981)

Music and lyrics by William Finn   *Published libretto*: Samuel French, 1981
Anthology: None   *Condensation*: None   *Vocal selections*: None
Licensing agent: Samuel French   *Recording*: DRG SBL 12581 (original
cast); includes libretto   *Cast*: 3 M; 1 F; 1 young boy

This is a mini-opera-like musical (and only one part of a trilogy) that is entirely sung and performed for about one hour without an intermission. The hero is Marvin, who is Jewish, married, and has a young son. The plot finds Marvin leaving his family for a male lover, while his psychiatrist takes up with his wife. The *New York Daily News* described the music as "soft-rock" with "cascading melodies, intricate harmonies, complex arrangements and show-stopping deliveries." This is a simple show to stage (the scenery consists of chairs and tables) but is demanding, adult entertainment.

MARRY ME A LITTLE
(1980)

Conceived and developed by Craig Lucas and Norman Rene   *Music and*
lyrics by Stephen Sondheim   *Published libretto*: None   *Condensation*:
None   *Anthology*: None   *Vocal selections*: None   *Licensing agent*:
Music Theatre International   *Recording*: RCA ABL1-4159 (original cast);
includes lyrics   *Cast*: 1 M; 1 F

A one-hour musical (without intermission) made up of bits and pieces of Sondheim scores dropped from other shows. The set is a run-down studio apartment and the cast of two are both on stage, although they are both meant to be alone in their own apartments. There is no spoken dialogue. Through the songs we learn of their lives and loneliness. The 16 Sondheim songs are the main reason for this show. It can be simply staged with only a piano accompaniment.

MARY
(1920/1979)

Book and lyrics by Otto Harbach and Frank Mandel   *Music* by Louis Hirsch   *Published libretto*: None   *Condensation*: None   *Anthology*: None   *Vocal selections*: None   *Licensing agent*: Tams-Witmark   *Recording*: None   *Cast*: Large mixed cast

The hero Jack has bought the plans for a portable, detachable house (this is back in 1920) and figures out a way to construct it cheaply. Mary, his mother's social secretary and daughter of the college president, helps him. Mary is forced into an engagement to a wealthy young man when Jack's investment seems lost. But everything works out as expected to the strains of "Love Nest." The revival production had colorful cut-out scenery and period costumes. This family show is all innocent, tuneful, deliciously foolish, and charming.

ME AND JULIET
(1953/1970)

Book and lyrics by Oscar Hammerstein, II   *Music* by Richard Rodgers   *Published libretto*: Random House, 1953   *Condensation*: None   *Anthology*: *Six Plays by Rodgers and Hammerstein*. Random House, 1955 ☆ Modern Library, 1959   *Piano-vocal score*: Williamson Music, 1953   *Licensing agent*: Rodgers and Hammerstein Theatre Library   *Recording*: RCA LOC 1012 (original cast)   *Cast*: 17 M; 13 F; chorus

This is a musical about backstage show business—a show-within-a-show. There are two romances: one is between a dancer and a stage manager, and the other between an understudy and a young staff assistant. The sets for the original production were praised for their ingenious way of showing the stage, the wings, and even the lobby during intermission. "No Other Love" is the big song. A revival was called a spoof on 1950s-style musicals. Rodgers and Hammerstein musicals are always good family entertainment.

THE ME NOBODY KNOWS
(1970)

Music by Gary William Friedman   *Lyrics* by Will Holt   *Based on the book* edited by Stephen M. Joseph   *Published libretto*: None   *Condensation*: None   *Anthology*: None   *Vocal selections*: New York

Times Music, 1970   *Licensing agent*: Samuel French   *Recording*:
Atlantic SD 1566 (original cast)   *Cast*: 6 M; 6 F

"These are children's voices from the ghetto. In their struggle lies their
hope, and ours. They are the voices of change" (program note). There is
no story line in the usual sense in this show; it is based upon writings
from school classes of ghetto children. The off-Broadway cast (which
later moved to Broadway) was composed of twelve children, eight black
and four white. Their lives are surrounded by poverty, drugs and oppres-
sion. They recite poems and prose reflections, sing songs, and perform
simple dance routines. Some of this is poignant, sad, happy, and humorous. The Broadway production used projected photographs and paint-
ings, while the set was basically a dim alleyway in a slum area of a big city.
Off Broadway (OBIE) Award Winner

MEET ME IN ST. LOUIS
(1944 film adapted for the stage)

Book by Sally Benson; based on her *Kensington Stories* and the 1944 MGM
film   *Music and lyrics* by Hugh Martin and Ralph Blane   *Published
libretto*: None   *Condensation*: None   *Anthology*: None   *Vocal
selections*: None   *Licensing agent*: Tams-Witmark   *Recording*: AEI 3101
(original film score)   *Cast*: Large mixed cast

This is the story of the Smith family in St. Louis. There are four daughters
in the family and they are all excited about the World's Fair to be held
there in the summer of 1904. For a time it looks like they will be leaving
St. Louis before the fair opens, but it all works out well. "The Boy Next
Door" and "The Trolley Song" are two very famous songs from the score.
The 1944 film was adapted for the stage. Judy Garland was the star of the
film and Jane Powell starred in the 1959 TV version. This stage version has
been performed by the St. Louis Municipal Opera. The homespun,
turn-of-the-century show is family entertainment.

MERRILY WE ROLL ALONG
(1981)

Book by George Furth; based on the play by George S. Kaufman and Moss
Hart   *Music and lyrics* by Stephen Sondheim   *Published libretto*:
Dodd, Mead, 1982   *Condensation*: None   *Anthology*: None   *Vocal
selections*: Revelation Music (Valando), 1981   *Licensing agent*: Music
Theatre International   *Recording*: RCA CBL 1-4197 (original cast)   *Cast*:
A young cast of 27

Based on a 1934 play, this musical tells the story of some young hopefuls (song writers and novelist) and their careers over a 25-year period. An unusual technique of going backwards in time is used. The story begins when one of the leads comes back to address the graduating class at his old high school; the plot continues in reverse until he is graduating. The Broadway set was "high tech" style bleachers with skyline projections. Members of the young cast wore T-shirts with their names or titles on them. "Not a Day Goes By" is one of the better songs from the Sondheim score.

THE MERRY WIDOW
(1907/1921/1943/1964)

Book and lyrics by Charles George   *Music* by Franz Lehar   *Published libretto*: Samuel French   *Condensation*: Mark Lubbock. *The Complete Book of Light Operas*. Putnam (London), 1962   *Anthology*: None *Vocal selections*: Chappell, 1977 (lyrics by Sheldon Harnick)   *Licensing agent*: Tams-Witmark ☆ Samuel French   *Recording*: London OSA 1172 (1978 London version—in English)   *Cast*: Large mixed cast

Perhaps the most famous of all Viennese operettas, this show has been revived and filmed many times. The reviewer for an opulent 1943 production at the Majestic Theatre in New York felt the show would have been buried years ago except for the lilting Lehar music. The plot involves the very wealthy widow whose millions draw suitors like flies. But she marries the heir to the throne of an impoverished little kingdom just because she loves him. Set in turn-of-the-century Paris, costumes and sets can be lavish. The third act is set at the famous Maxim's Restaurant. Everyone will exit the theater humming the beautiful "Merry Widow Waltz." This was presented by the New York City Opera in 1982.

MILK AND HONEY
(1961)

Book by Don Appell   *Music and lyrics* by Jerry Herman   *Published libretto*: None   *Condensation*: None   *Anthology*: None *Piano-vocal score*: Big Three, 1963   *Vocal selections: Jerry Herman Songbook*. Morris, 1974   *Licensing agent*: Tams-Witmark   *Recording*: RCA LSO 1065 (original cast)   *Cast*: Large mixed Cast

Modern-day Israel is the setting for this musical that involves some Sabras (native-born Israelis) and some American tourists. The dance numbers include the hora and the big number celebrates Israeli Independence Day. The settings include a street in Jerusalem, a cafe in Tel Aviv and a kibbutz. Besides the expected costumes, there is a Yemenite wedding scene with three gorgeously clad couples married in parallel ceremonies. For humor there is the American widow (played on Broadway by the famous Yiddish star, Molly Picon) in search of a new mate. This was Jerry Herman's first Broadway score.

MINNIE'S BOYS
(1970)

Book by Arthur Marx and Robert Fisher; based on the lives of the Marx Brothers   *Music* by Larry Grossman   *Lyrics* by Hal Hackady *Published libretto*: Samuel French   *Condensation*: None   *Anthology*: None   *Vocal selections*: New York Times Music, 1970   *Licensing agent*: Samuel French   *Recording*: Project 3 TS 6002 SD (original cast)   *Cast*: Large mixed cast

The setting is New York City from the early twentieth century to the 1920s. Minnie Marx has five sons. They are lazy, stealing trouble-makers. Minnie comes from a show business background, so she decides to put her kids on the stage. We follow their misadventures in vaudeville until the "Marx Brothers" begin to take shape. The critics particularly liked the actors cast as the brothers and the re-creation of some of their routines with Margaret Dumont. The production needs the usual backstage and vaudeville sets of the period. Minnie Marx also sings and dances, and performs one number with the boys in which she is dressed as a giant white rabbit.

MR. PRESIDENT
(1962)

Book by Howard Lindsay and Russel Crouse   *Music and lyrics* by Irving Berlin   *Published libretto*: None   *Condensation*: None   *Anthology*: None   *Vocal selections*: None   *Licensing agent*: Music Theatre International   *Recording*: Columbia KOS 2270 (original cast)   *Cast*: Large mixed cast

Irving Berlin's last Broadway musical dealt with the First Family (everyone was wondering if it was based on the Kennedys). The first act is about their home life while in office, while the second concerns retirement after two terms in office. President Henderson is unbelievably noble and blessed with courage in his confrontations with the Russians. This is basically a flag-waving comedy with a First Lady who yearns for her hometown supermarket, a son who likes fast cars and belly dancers, and a daughter about to marry a Middle Eastern wheeler-dealer. This big musical features a formal White House Ball among the production numbers.

MR. WONDERFUL
(1956)

Book by Joseph Stein and Will Glickman   *Music and lyrics* by Jerry Bock, Larry Holofcener and George Weiss   *Published libretto*: None *Condensation*: None   *Anthology*: None   *Vocal selections*: Valando, 1956   *Licensing agent*: Music Theatre International   *Recording*: Decca DL 9032 (original cast)   *Cast*: Large mixed cast

Sammy Davis, Jr. was "Mr. Wonderful" and this show was tailored for him. In fact, at one point the show stopped and Sammy and the Will Mastin Trio entertained with his songs and impersonations. This show could be considered for a nightclub entertainer who wants to try a book show. The thread of a plot is about a young performer who lacks self-confidence. The locales include New York City, Union City, New Jersey and Miami, Florida. "Too Close for Comfort" and the title song were both quite popular. Wolcott Gibbs, however, started off his review by asking, "Mr. Who?"

THE MOONY SHAPIRO SONGBOOK
(1981)

Book by Monty Norman and Julian More   *Music* by Monty Norman *Lyrics* by Julian More   *Published libretto*: Samuel French *Condensation*: None   *Anthology*: None   *Vocal selections*: None *Licensing agent*: Samuel French   *Recording*: Pye NSPL 18609 (London original cast)   *Cast*: 3 M; 2 F; back-up singers

Done originally in London and titled simply *Songbook*, this musical chronicles the career of a fictional songwriter and includes pastiche versions of popular songs of the thirties and onward. The five cast members play a total of about 90 different roles. The show is a retrospective of the life and career of Moony, and is a mild spoof of the "side by side" type shows recently devoted to a composer's work. The spoof extends to film, television, Broadway, Hollywood, and numerous composers and performers. The New York production used a blue set with a white piano and projected backgrounds.

THE MOST HAPPY FELLA
(1956/1979)

Book, music and lyrics by Frank Loesser; based on Sidney Howard's play, *They Knew What They Wanted*   *Published libretto*: *Theatre Arts* (magazine), October 1958   *Condensation*: *Theatre '56*. John Chapman, ed. Random House, 1956 ☆ *American Musicals: Loesser*. Time-Life, 1981 *Anthology*: None   *Piano-vocal score*: Frank Music, 1957   *Vocal selections*: Frank Music, 1956   *Licensing agent*: Music Theatre International   *Recordings*: Columbia OS 2330, Time-Life STL-AM08 (original cast excerpts) ☆ Columbia 03L-240 (original cast complete) *Cast*: Large mixed cast

This musical version of the famous play is about a middle-aged Italian wine grower in California who sends off a picture of his young, handsome foreman to get a mail-order bride for himself. This is almost an opera, and it was successfully revived and performed on television in 1980. Some popular songs from the score are "Standing on the Corner" and "Big D." There are 33 musical numbers which require genuine singing ability. There are three acts, with colorful sets and costumes.

MUSIC IN THE AIR
(1932/1951)

Book and lyrics by Oscar Hammerstein, II   *Music* by Jerome Kern *Published libretto*: None   *Condensation*: None   *Anthology*: None *Piano-vocal score*: Harms, 1933   *Licensing agent*: Tams-Witmark *Recording*: RCA LK 1025 (1951 studio cast)   *Cast*: Large mixed cast

An elderly, genial music teacher in rural Switzerland has written a pleasant tune, and the local school teacher has composed some lyrics for it. They set off for Zurich with a walking club to see about getting the song published. The plot thickens when they meet a prima donna of a forthcoming show. This is an old-fashioned, sentimental, and nostalgic show. The sets should be the colorful never-never world of European operetta (the programs for the 1951 Broadway revival stated, "the present time"). The Jerome Kern score contains several well-remembered songs, including "I've Told Every Little Star" and "The Song Is You." There was a 1934 film version with Gloria Swanson.

THE MUSIC MAN
(1957/1965/1980)

Book, music and lyrics by Meredith Willson; story by Meredith Willson and Franklin Lacey   *Published libretto*: Putnam, 1958   *Condensation*: *Broadway's Best, 1958*. John Chapman, ed. Doubleday, 1958 ☆ *American Musicals: Willson and Herman*. Time-Life, 1982.   *Anthology*: None *Piano-vocal score*: Frank Music, 1958   *Licensing agent*: Music Theatre International   *Recordings*: Capitol SW 990, Time-Life STL-AM13 (original cast)   *Cast*: Large mixed cast

This show needs a fast-talking, high-stepping song and dance man. He plays a confidence man out in the pre-World War I Midwest. Along the way he falls in love with a librarian. Robert Preston created the part of Professor Harold Hill and also played the role in the 1962 film version. There are a number of popular tunes from this show, including "Seventy-Six Trombones" and "Till There Was You." This family show is a big slice of Americana, with a barbershop quartet, lots of kids (including one sizable role for a boy with a lisp), flashy costumes, and production numbers.
Tony Award Winner (Best Musical)

MUSICAL CHAIRS
(1980)

Book by Barry Berg, Ken Donnelly and Tom Savage; based on an original story concept by Larry J. Pontillo   *Music and lyrics* by Tom Savage *Published libretto*: Samuel French, 1982   *Condensation*: None *Anthology*: None   *Vocal selections*: None   *Licensing agent*: Samuel French   *Recording*: Original Cast OC 8024 (original cast)   *Cast*: 9 M; 7 F

It is opening night for a new play. The author is a Pulitzer and Tony award winner who hasn't done so well recently and is trying a comeback. The cast of this musical plays the audience which includes ex-wives, lovers, and the critics. The cast of the New York production sat in chairs on a steeply raked stage and looked out at the audience. Each cast member has his own number to explain his problem or predicament.

MY FAIR LADY
(1956/1976/1981)

Book and lyrics by Alan Jay Lerner; adapted from George Bernard Shaw's *Pygmalion*   *Music* by Frederick Lowe   *Published libretto*:

Coward-McCann, 1956 ☆ New American Library, 1956   *Condensation: The Best Plays of 1955–1956.* Louis Kronenberger, ed. Dodd, Mead, 1956 ☆ *American Musicals: Lerner and Loewe.* Time-Life, 1981.   *Anthology:* None *Piano-vocal score:* Chappell, 1969   *Vocal selections: The Best of Lerner and Loewe.* Chappell, 1974   *Licensing agent:* Tams-Witmark *Recordings:* Columbia CSP XOL 5090, Time-Life STL-AM04 (original cast) ☆ Columbia PS 2015 (London cast) ☆ Columbia PS 34197 (1976 revival) *Cast:* Large mixed cast

Henry Higgins, an expert on dialects, makes a wager with his friend, Colonel Pickering, that he can take a cockney girl and pass her off as a lady through speech instruction. The place is London in 1912. The scenes include a Covent Garden flower market, Ascot, an embassy ballroom, and Higgins' study. The most popular song from the score is "On the Street Where You Live." Rex Harrison was the original Higgins and starred in the 1964 film. This show has everything: wonderful songs, excellent roles, a classic book, endless opportunities for elegant and colorful sets and costumes, and several big dance numbers.
Tony Award Winner (Best Musical)

MY OLD FRIENDS
(1979)

Book, music and lyrics by Mel Mandel and Norman Sachs   *Published libretto:* Samuel French, 1980   *Condensation:* None   *Anthology:* None *Vocal selections:* None   *Licensing agent:* Samuel French   *Recording:* None   *Cast:* 7 M; 4 F

A new "inmate" in an old people's home and hotel resists the tendency to succumb to the mood of the place. The title of the show refers to the pills and medicines he must take. Eventually he has enough and leaves, and again takes up life as a carpenter. This is a show for a mature cast and an audience that will appreciate its humor and messages. It is performed without intermission, with sets consisting of a few chairs and painted flats. There are 13 musical numbers. The New York production used only a piano and bass.

NAUGHTY MARIETTA
(1910/1929/1971/1979)

Book and lyrics by Rida Johnson Young   *Music* by Victor Herbert *Published libretto:* None   *Condensation:* None   *Anthology:* None *Piano-vocal score:* M. Witmark, 1910   *Licensing agent:* Tams-Witmark

Recordings: Columbia CSP P 13707, Smithsonian Album N026 (1026) (studio cast)   *Cast*: Large mixed cast

Familiar songs from this score include "Tramp, Tramp, Tramp" and "The Italian Street Song." Jeanette MacDonald and Nelson Eddy are remembered for their roles in the 1935 film, but this operetta is frequently revived and was recently presented by the New York City Opera. The time is "about 1870" and the place is old New Orleans. A shipload of "casket girls" arrive from France seeking husbands. Hidden among them is the runaway Contesse Marietta. This operetta has been staged simply "in the round" and elaborately at Jones Beach (New York). This family show ends happily to the strains of "Ah, Sweet Mystery of Life."

NEW GIRL IN TOWN
(1957)

Book by George Abbott; based on the play *Anna Christie* by Eugene O'Neill
Music and lyrics by Bob Merrill   *Published libretto*: Random House, 1958
Condensation: None   *Anthology*: None   *Vocal selections*: Chappell,
1957   *Licensing agent*: Music Theatre International   *Recording*: RCA
LSO 1027 (original cast)   *Cast*: Large mixed cast

The time is the early 1900s. Anna, a prostitute, arrives on the New York waterfront to join her father, a barge captain she hasn't seen in many years. She meets and falls in love with a sailor and is redeemed by true love. The New York production was a big, colorful dancing show with Bob Fosse doing the choreography and Gwen Verdon as the star. Most reviews mentioned a ballet-dream sequence. They all praised Thelma Ritter in the meaty role of "Marthy." The sets and costumes were called eye-smacking.

NEW MOON
(1928/1944/1976/1983)

Book and lyrics by Oscar Hammerstein, II, Frank Mandel and Lawrence
Schwab   *Music* by Sigmund Romberg   *Published libretto*: None
Condensation: None   *Anthology*: None   *Piano-vocal score*: Harms,
1928   *Vocal selections*: *The Music of Sigmund Romberg*. Warner Brothers
Music, 1977   *Licensing agent*: Tams-Witmark   *Recordings*:
Monmouth-Evergreen MES 7051 (original London cast) ☆ Columbia CSP
P 13878 (studio cast)   *Cast*: Large mixed cast

The plot deals with the adventures of Robert Mission and is set in New Orleans in 1791. He is a French nobleman and political refugee who is indentured to the wealthy Monsieur Beaunoir. Mission is in love with Beaunoir's daughter, Marianne. They sail on the ship *The New Moon*, go through a mutiny, and end up in Florida. "Softly As in the Morning Sunrise" and "Lover Come Back to Me" are some familiar songs from the score. The show was filmed in 1930 with Grace Moore and in 1940 with Jeanette MacDonald and Nelson Eddy. A concert version was performed at Town Hall in New York City. Fully staged productions require elaborate costumes and wigs.

A NIGHT IN VENICE
(1884/1953/1982)

Original German libretto by F. Zell and R. Genee; *English book and lyrics* by Ruth and Thomas Martin (for Jones Beach); William Mount-Burke and Alice Hammerstein Mathias (for Light Opera of Manhattan)   *Music* by Johann Strauss   *Published libretto*: None   *Condensation*: None   *Anthology*: None   *Piano-vocal score*: Edition Cranz 656, 1967 (English and German)   *Licensing agent*: Tams-Witmark   *Recordings*: Everest SDBR 3028 (Jones Beach cast recording) ☆ Columbia M2 35908 (studio recording)   *Cast*: 4 M; 5 F; chorus; dancers

The Duke of Palobino arrives in Venice in 1750 for an annual visit to host a gala ball during the Carnival. Since the Duke's amorous adventures are well-known, the husbands decide that their wives will not attend; but the ladies plan otherwise. After much confusion, all ends happily. There was a spectacular Mike Todd production in 1952 at Jones Beach (New York) with gondolas, fireworks, and a water ballet. A revised, much more modest production was staged in 1982 by the Light Opera of Manhattan.

NIGHTCLUB CANTATA
(1977)

Conceived, composed and directed by Elizabeth Swados   *Published libretto*: None   *Condensation*: None   *Anthology*: None   *Vocal selections*: None   *Licensing agent*: Dramatists Play Service   *Recording*: None   *Cast*: 4 M; 4 F

This musical entertainment was originally performed in a cabaret setting. It lasts a bit over an hour and was described as all-singing, all-dancing, all-acting. There are some mild gymnastic feats performed by the men. The 20 numbers are primarily by Swados, but the works of Sylvia Plath, Frank O'Hara, Carson McCullers, and others are also utilized. The sets, lighting and costumes were minimal and unobtrusive. The accompaniment consisted of Swados on guitar, a piano and percussion. Some critical comments referred to the show as avant-garde and as "bohemian vaudeville."

NINA ROSA
(1930/1937)

Book by Otto Harbach   *Music* by Sigmund Romberg   *Lyrics* by Irving Caesar   *Published libretto*: None   *Condensation*: None   *Anthology*: None   *Piano-vocal score*: Harms, 1934   *Licensing agent*: Tams-Witmark   *Recording*: None   *Cast*: Large mixed cast

The setting for this musical is Peru, and the plot involves the Inca Indians and how they affect a group of tourists and some gold mine owners. The original Broadway production was a lavish one, with much publicity given to some of the exotic dancers in the cast. The unusual locale lends itself to sets and costumes in vivid colors and theatrical glamor. There are a Cafe de los Gauchos, an ornamental hacienda, and a cave of the Incas where the mood is pagan and ceremonial. There have been lavish outdoor productions of this show at Jones Beach (New York) and the St. Louis Municipal Opera.

THE 1940's RADIO HOUR
(1979)

Written by Walton Jones   *Published libretto*: Samuel French, 198–   *Condensation*: None   *Anthology*: None   *Vocal selections*: None   *Licensing agent*: Samuel French   *Recording*: None   *Cast*: 10 M; 5 F

Performed without intermission, this is actually a play about a group preparing a radio show broadcast on December 21, 1942, from the Astor Hotel in New York City. When the show actually goes on the air a number of familiar songs ("I'll Be Seeing You," "Boogie-Woogie Bugle Boy," "That Old Black Magic," etc.) are spiritedly performed by the cast along with some hilarious commercials. When the show is over, they all pack up and go home. There are some threads of plots involving the various performers. This can be simply staged and costumed, and all nostalgia buffs will have a great time.

NO, NO, NANETTE
(1925/1971)

Book by Otto Harbach and Frank Mandel   *Music* by Vincent Youmans
Lyrics by Irving Caesar and Otto Harbach   *Published libretto*: None
Condensation: None   *Anthology*: None   *Piano-vocal score*: Warner
Brothers Music, 1972   *Vocal selections*: Warner Brothers Music, 197–
Licensing agent: Tams-Witmark   *Recording*: Columbia S 30563 (1971
revival cast)   *Cast*: Large mixed cast

Back in New York City in 1925, bible publisher Jimmy Smith and his wife
have taken on a schoolgirl ward, Nanette, to raise as a lady. Nanette wants
to go to Atlantic City with her friends for the weekend, but the Smiths say,
"no." Through a series of misunderstandings, everyone turns up in
Atlantic City for Act II. "Tea for Two" and "I Want to Be Happy" are just
two popular songs from the score. The 1971 New York revival was a
lavish Busby Berkeley production starring Ruby Keeler. The cast recording includes a number of color photographs of the sets and costumes,
excellent notes, and, of course, the score.

NO STRINGS
(1962/1972)

Book by Samuel Taylor   *Music and lyrics* by Richard Rodgers
Published libretto: Random House, 1962   *Condensation*: None
Anthology: None   *Piano-vocal score*: Williamson Music, 1962
Licensing agent: Rodgers and Hammerstein Theatre Library   *Recordings*:
Capitol SO 1695 (original cast) ✰ Stet DS 15013 (London original cast)
Cast: 5 M; 5 F

This is Richard Rodgers' only solo musical. Set in contemporary Paris, it is
about a black fashion model and a writer on the skids. There is no
mention of the racial situation until the very end. In the Broadway
production the orchestra (without any strings!) was located on the stage
and musicians wandered on and off as the situation warranted. The sets
were highly stylized. This is a bittersweet romance that doesn't end
happily, with very stylish people and places. It has an excellent score,
although there are no standards.

NOW IS THE TIME FOR ALL GOOD MEN
(1967/1971)

Book and lyrics by Gretchen Cryer   *Music* by Nancy Ford   *Published
libretto*: Samuel French, 1969   *Condensation*: None   *Anthology*: None

Vocal selections: None   *Licensing agent*: Samuel French   *Recording*: Columbia OS 3130 (original cast)   *Cast*: 6 M; 6 F

A young man has been court-martialed out of the Army for refusing to do battle. He gets a job as a school teacher in a small town, where he teaches his students to question established values, causes one boy to refuse the draft, and becomes involved with the music teacher. This is a look at middle America during the Vietnam crisis and does not have a happy ending. This was the first musical by these composers; they have gone on to write several others, always with something relevant to say. This was simply staged off-Broadway with no dances, and with only a piano, bass, and percussion for accompaniment.

OF THEE I SING
(1931/1952/1968)

Book by George S. Kaufman and Morrie Ryskind   *Music* by George Gershwin   *Lyrics* by Ira Gershwin   *Published libretto*: Knopf, 1932 ☆ Samuel French, 1959   *Condensation: American Musicals: Gershwin.* Time-Life, 1982   *Anthology: The Pulitzer Prize Plays.* Kathryn Coe and William Cordell, eds. Random House, 1940 ☆ *Ten Great Musicals of the American Stage.* Stanley Richards, ed. Chilton, 1973   *Piano-vocal score*: New World Music, 1932   *Licensing agent*: Samuel French   *Recordings*: Capitol T 11651, Time-Life STL-AM09 (1952 revival cast) ☆ Columbia S 31763 (1972 TV cast)   *Cast*: 14 M; 5 F; chorus

John P. Wintergarden is elected President ("Wintergreen for President") on a platform of love ("Love Is Sweeping the Country"). This is a satire on Presidential campaigns which is well remembered for its Gershwin score. "Who Cares" is another fine song. It is a big musical and dressy costumes and snappy dance routines are necessary. A TV version in 1972 featured Carroll O'Connor. Most critics seem to feel that this should be done as a 1930s period show.
Pulitzer Prize

OH! BOY!
(1917/1979)

Book and lyrics by Guy Bolton and P. G. Wodehouse   *Music* by Jerome Kern   *Published libretto*: None   *Condensation*: None   *Anthology*: None   *Vocal selections*: None   *Licensing agent*: Tams-Witmark   *Recording*: None   *Cast*: 9 M; 8 F

The 1979 off-Broadway production of this Jerome Kern musical featured a score (piano and cello) that included "Till the Clouds Roll By." The time is 1917 during World War I. The plot, which was compared to that of a French farce, concerns a secretly married bachelor. During a party given by his best friend, an actress chased by the police comes in through an open window. Misunderstandings abound. The second act is set at the Country Club, and all ends well. This is one of the "Princess" musicals (originally performed at the Princess Theater), and was intended as an intimate production with no big numbers and a small chorus.

OH! BROTHER!
(1981)

Book and lyrics by Donald Driver; based on works by William Shakespeare and Plautus   *Music* by Michael Valenti   *Published libretto*: Samuel French, 1982   *Condensation*: None   *Anthology*: None   *Music publisher*: Mac Music (Schirmer), 1982   *Licensing agent*: Samuel French   *Recording*: Original Cast Records OC8342 (original cast)   *Cast*: 7 M; 3 F; chorus; dancers

The place is the Persian Gulf and the time is "today" (meaning 1981 with Arab-Israeli-Iranian-energy problems). This is another musical version of *A Comedy of Errors* about the identical twins who were separated at birth and not quite meeting (until the end of the show) but causing a great deal of confusion and hilarity. This show has a lot of topical humor (including the Ayatollah), some exotic dancers, and a nice score. It is all played in one basic set of sand dunes without intermission. Critics called it mindless fun.

OH CAPTAIN!
(1958)

Book by Al Morgan and Jose Ferrer; based on the screenplay *The Captain's Paradise* by Alec Coppel   *Music and lyrics* by Jay Livingston and Ray Evans   *Published libretto*: None   *Condensation*: None   *Anthology*: None   *Vocal selections*: None   *Licensing agent*: Tams-Witmark   *Recording*: Columbia CSP AOS 2002 (original cast)   *Cast*: Large mixed cast

This is the musical tale of a British freighter captain with a wife at home and a mistress in Paris. Unexpectedly, the wife visits Paris, meets the mistress, and they connive to teach the captain a lesson. The contemporary settings include a town near London, on shipboard, and then Paris. This big Broadway musical had sets that moved on treadmills, but it can be simply staged. Atmosphere is important.

OH COWARD!
(1972/1981)

Music and lyrics by Noel Coward; *production devised* by Roderick Cook
Published libretto: Doubleday, 1974   *Vocal selections*: *Noel Coward Songbook*. Simon and Schuster, 1953 ☆ *Sir Noel Coward, His Words and Music*. Chappell, 1973   *Condensation*: None   *Anthology*: None
Licensing agent: Music Theatre International   *Recording*: Bell 9001 (original cast)   *Cast*: 2 M; 1 F

This revue is made up of songs and witty observations by Noel Coward performed by a cast of three. It is organized into a biographical outline of the famous writer/actor/composer/wit. The show begins with "the boy actor" and proceeds through sections on "music hall," "travel," "theater," "love," etc. The off-Broadway production used only twin pianos and percussion. The setting can be a very simple Victorian proscenium with a few props and formal attire. This is sophisticated adult entertainment. Your cast should primarily be actors who are able to carry off the outrageous and sentimental moments.

OH! KAY!
(1926/1960)

Book by Guy Bolton and P. G. Wodehouse   *Music* by George Gershwin
Lyrics by Ira Gershwin   *Published libretto*: None   *Condensation*:
American Musicals: Gershwin. Time-Life, 1982   *Anthology*: None
Vocal selections: Harms, 1926   *Licensing agent*: Tams-Witmark
Recordings: Smithsonian R 011 (original cast recording) ☆ Columbia CSP ACL 1050, Time-Life STL-AM09 (studio cast); ☆ Stet DS 15017 (1960 revival cast)
Cast: 8 M; 8 F

The story is about a titled Englishman and his sister who get mixed up with prohibition and bootleggers back in 1926 out on Long Island. The original Broadway production featured Gertrude Lawrence singing "Someone to Watch over Me." The off-Broadway revival was an attempt to recreate the style and atmosphere on a less grand scale. One critic declared that no Gershwin song ever gets old, and this show includes "Clap Yo' Hands," "Maybe," and "Do, Do, Do."

OH! LADY! LADY!
(1918/1974)

Book and lyrics by Guy Bolton and P. G. Wodehouse   *Music* by Jerome Kern   *Published libretto*: None   *Condensation*: None   *Anthology*: None   *Piano-vocal score*: Harms, 1918   *Licensing agent*: Tams-Witmark   *Recording*: None   *Cast*: 10 M 10 F

This is a Jerome Kern "Princess" musical from 1918. The "Princess" refers to the theater where it was originally done and indicates a small, intimate production. The most famous song from the score is "Bill," although it was dropped and later used in *Show Boat*. The plot deals with a mix-up between a young man and his fiancee. There are two sets. One is the heroine's Long Island home and the other is the terrace of a Greenwich Village penthouse. There are some jewel thieves, and it is all giddy, obvious and fun.

OKLAHOMA!
(1943/1951/1963/1979)

Book and lyrics by Oscar Hammerstein, II; based on *Green Grow the Lilacs* by Lynn Riggs   *Music* by Richard Rodgers   *Published libretto*: Random House, 1943   *Condensation*: *Burns Mantle Best Plays 1942–1943*. Burns Mantle, ed. Dodd, Mead, 1944 ✩ *American Musicals: Rodgers and Hammerstein*. Time-Life, 1980   *Anthology*: *Six Plays by Rodgers and Hammerstein*. Random House, 1955 ✩ Modern Library, 1959   *Piano-vocal score*: Williamson Music, 1943   *Licensing agent*: Rodgers and Hammerstein Theatre Library   *Recordings*: MCA 2030, Time-Life STL-AM01 (original cast) ✩ RCA CBL 1-3572 (1979 revival cast)

The action takes place in the Indian Territory (now Oklahoma) just after the turn of the century. This show changed the form and direction of musical theater; plot, music, and dancing were all integrated. The plot deals with the rivalry between the farmers and the cattlemen. The dances were Agnes de Mille ballets. "Oh What a Beautiful Mornin'" and "People Will Say We're in Love" are well-known songs from the score. The popular film version in 1955 starred Gordon MacRae. The title song was made the state's official song. This is a show for the entire family.

OLIVER!
(1963/1984)

Book, music and lyrics by Lionel Bart; freely adapted from *Oliver Twist* by Charles Dickens   *Published libretto*: None   *Condensation*: None

Anthology: None   *Piano-vocal score*: Hollis Music, 1960   *Vocal selections*: Hollis Music, 1968 (motion picture edition)   *Licensing agent*: Tams-Witmark   *Recordings*: Decca (British) SKL 4105 (London original cast) ☆ RCA AYL1 4113 (Broadway cast)   *Cast*: Large mixed cast

This British musical is about a young boy adrift in London around 1850 who falls in with the "Artful Dodger" and Fagin's gang of thieves. The plot includes the adult story of Nancy and Bill Sikes. This show was revived several times in London, had a very successful New York run, and was filmed in 1968. Some of the popular songs are "Consider Yourself" and "It's a Fine Life." This was a lavish production with some elaborate sets, but it can be staged on a simple scale. Costumes, however, need to be Dickensian. A number of young boys are required for the cast.

ON A CLEAR DAY YOU CAN SEE FOREVER
(1965/1979)

Book and lyrics by Alan Jay Lerner   *Music* by Burton Lane   *Published libretto*: Random House, 1966   *Condensation*: None   *Anthology*: None   *Piano-vocal score*: Chappell, 1967   *Vocal selections*: Chappell, 1970   *Licensing agent*: Tams-Witmark   *Recording*: RCA LSOD 2006 (original cast)   *Cast*: 14 M; 7 F; chorus

A young college student tries hypnosis to stop smoking. She turns out to have a subconscious memory of an earlier life. Thus the time and place shift back and forth from New York in the present to eighteenth century London. The critics liked the score, calling it one of the loveliest heard in years, and the beautiful sets and costumes. There is a great deal of humor in the book, although some critics wondered if it was basically a comedy. The film version in 1970 starred Barbra Streisand.

ON THE TOWN
(1944/1959/1971)

Book and lyrics by Betty Comden and Adolph Green; based on a Jerome Robbins ballet, *Fancy Free*   *Music* by Leonard Bernstein   *Published libretto*: None   *Condensation*: None   *Anthology*: *Comden and Green on Broadway*. Drama Book Specialists, 1981   *Music for dance episodes*: Schirmer, 1945   *Licensing agent*: Tams-Witmark   *Recordings*: Decca DL 8030 (original cast) ☆ Columbia CSP AS 31005 (1960 studio recording)   *Cast*: Large mixed cast

The adventures of three sailors on 24-hours' leave in New York City are featured in this popular musical. It was filmed in 1949 with Gene Kelly and Frank Sinatra. There was a recent revival on Broadway with Bernadette Peters. "New York, New York" and "Lucky to Be Me" are some popular songs from the score. Called a classic musical, this show requires a lot of dancing. Sets are numerous, from museums to taxis to streets to subways to apartments. The 1944 setting should include zoot suits and wedgies.

ON THE TWENTIETH CENTURY
(1978)

Book and lyrics by Betty Comden and Adolph Green; based on Twentieth Century by Ben Hecht and Charles MacArthur and The Napoleon of Broadway by Bruce Millholland   Music by Cy Coleman   Published libretto: Drama Book Specialists, 1981 ☆ Samuel French   Condensation: None   Anthology: None   Music publisher: Notable Music, 1978 Licensing agent: Samuel French (specify musical version)   Recording: Columbia 35330 (original cast)   Cast: Large mixed cast

Based on the play Twentieth Century, this is a wild, madcap train ride from Chicago to New York. The main characters are theater impresario Oscar Jaffee and Lily Garland, a Hollywood star. Jaffee needs Garland for a play. This show is set in the early 1930s, and critics praised the art deco designs of the sets and costumes. There are a number of flamboyant parts and some tap-dancing train porters. The music is unusually challenging with several large production numbers. A critic at a local paper called it "a real musical comedy, and a truly grand one at that."

ON YOUR TOES
(1936/1954/1983)

Book by Richard Rodgers, Lorenz Hart and George Abbott   Music by Richard Rodgers   Lyrics by Lorenz Hart   Published libretto: None Condensation: None   Anthology: None   Vocal selections: Chappell, 1936   Licensing agent: Rodgers and Hammerstein Theatre Library Recordings: Stet DS 15024E (1954 revival cast) ☆ Polydor 813 667 1 Y 1 (1983 revival cast)   Cast: Large mixed cast

This was the first musical to make important use of ballet. Two major ballet numbers (including "Slaughter on Tenth Avenue") are required, plus one big tap number to the title tune. In the plot of this famous musical, Junior has once danced in vaudeville with his parents but has now settled down to teaching music. It is the mid-1930s and a famous

Russian ballet is soon to perform at the Cosmopolitan Opera House. Junior is torn between his love for one of his students and the tempestuous ballerina, Vera Baronova. "There's a Small Hotel" and "It's Gotta Be Love" are just two of the popular songs from the famous score. The 1983 revival on Broadway was a big hit with Natalia Makarova and George de la Pena dancing the George Balanchine choreography. There was a 1939 film version with Vera Zorina.

ONCE UPON A MATTRESS
(1959)

Book by Jay Thompson, Marshall Barer, Dean Fuller; based on "The Princess and the Pea"   *Music* by Mary Rodgers   *Lyrics* by Marshall Barer
Published libretto: Theatre Arts (magazine), July 1960.   *Condensation*: None   *Anthology*: None   *Piano-vocal score*: Chappell, 1967   *Vocal selections*: Chappell, 1960   *Licensing agent*: Music Theatre International
Recording: MCA 37097 (original cast)   *Cast*: Large mixed cast

Carol Burnett starred in this musical, first off-Broadway, then on Broadway, and twice (in 1964 and 1972) on television. The plot of this family musical is based on the fairy tale about the princess being put to a test to see if she can feel a pea through 20 mattresses. Costumed in the never-never medieval land of fairy tales, this tongue-in-cheek farce includes a court wizard who longs for the good old days of vaudeville, and a Harpo Marx-type mute King. There is sophistication for the adults, and fun for the kids.

110 IN THE SHADE
(1963/1974/1982)

Book by N. Richard Nash; based on his play *The Rainmaker*   *Music* by Harvey Schmidt   *Lyrics* by Tom Jones   *Published libretto*: None   *Condensation*: None   *Anthology*: None   *Piano-vocal score*: Chappell, 1964   *Vocal selections: The Best of Schmidt and Jones.* Chappell, 1975   *Licensing agent*: Tams-Witmark   *Recording*: RCA LSO 1085 (original cast)   *Cast*: 8 M; 8 F; children; townspeople

A handsome confidence man collects $100 on the premise that he will make it rain within 24 hours. He also convinces the ugly-duckling daughter of a wealthy rancher that she is really beautiful. Settings should create the atmosphere of the great Southwest around 1900 with parched land, small towns, and colorful western costumes. Some numbers suggest a revival meeting. The dancing is "hoedown" style.

ONE TOUCH OF VENUS
(1944/1952/1983)

Book by S. J. Perelman and Ogden Nash   *Music* by Kurt Weill   *Lyrics* by Ogden Nash   *Published libretto*: Little, 1944   *Condensation*: *American Musicals: Weill*. Time-Life, 1982   *Anthology*: *Ten Great Musicals of the American Stage*. Stanley Richards, ed. Chilton, 1973   *Vocal selections*: None   *Licensing agent*: Tams-Witmark   *Recordings*: AEI 1136, Time-Life STL-AM10 (original cast) ☆ *Kurt Weill Revisited*. Painted Smiles Records 1375, 1376 (studio cast recordings of additional songs) *Cast*: Large mixed cast

This story concerns a priceless statue of Venus which suddenly vanishes from a New York museum. It seems that while the museum owner was admiring his new treasure he was also having his morning shave. When he was called from the room for a moment, the barber tried out the engagement ring he bought for his sweetheart on the statue. The statue comes to life! Mary Martin was Venus on Broadway during World War II, and "Speak Low" is just one of the many beautiful songs from the score. There were several ballets by Agnes de Mille. There was a film version with Ava Gardner in 1948 but without most of the songs.

THE ONLY GIRL
(1917/1934)

Book by Henry Blossom; adapted from Frank Mandel's comedy *Our Wives* *Music* by Victor Herbert   *Published libretto*: None   *Condensation*: None   *Anthology*: None   *Vocal selections*: *The Music of Victor Herbert*. Warner Brothers Music, 1976   *Licensing agent*: Tams-Witmark *Recording*: None   *Cast*: 5 M; 13 F

A young female composer lives in the apartment above a librettist. The setting is Times Square and even in a 1945 revival in California the time was still "the present." Even though he has many amours and marriage is described in the song "When You Wear a Ball and Chain" they fall in love and all ends well. "While You're Away" is a well-remembered song from the original score.

OUT OF THIS WORLD
(1950/1955/1962)

Book by Dwight Taylor and Reginald Lawrence; freely adapted from the Amphitryon myth   *Music and lyrics* by Cole Porter   *Published libretto*: None   *Condensation*: None   *Anthology*: None   *Vocal selections*: None   *Licensing agent*: Tams-Witmark   *Recording*: Columbia CSP CML 4390 (original cast)   *Cast*: Large mixed cast

A young couple are on their honeymoon in Greece. The young man is also looking for information for a news story about a gangster. From high above on Mount Olympus, Jupiter, the King of the Gods, sees the young bride and takes a fancy for her. So the newlyweds are involved with Greek Gods and gangsters in this opulent Broadway musical. Cole Porter's songs are even more sophisticated than usual making this bawdy farce adult entertainment. Modestly staged versions of this musical have been done off-Broadway.

OVER HERE!
(1974)

Book by Will Holt   *Music and lyrics* by Richard M. Sherman and Robert B. Sherman   *Published libretto*: Samuel French, 1979   *Condensation*: None   *Anthology*: None   *Vocal selections*: New York Times Music, 1974   *Licensing agent*: Samuel French   *Recording*: Columbia KS 32961 (original cast)   *Cast*: 10 M; 8 F; chorus

With this musical Broadway took a nostalgic look at World War II "B" movies. The plot involves a sister act that entertains the boys at camps. The Andrews Sisters did just that and made movies about it, too. They returned to the limelight to star in this show. There is an attractive German spy who sings with the girls and adds to the plot. While the score is original, it sounds like the popular "big-band" music of the era. On Broadway the Andrews Sisters also sang a medley of their biggest hits. Costumes and sets (including a cross-country railroad trip) should be in keeping with the period.

PACIFIC OVERTURES
(1976/1984)

Book by John Weidman; additional book material by Hugh Wheeler   *Music and lyrics* by Stephen Sondheim   *Published libretto*: Dodd, Mead, 1977   *Condensation*: *The Best Plays of 1975–1976*. Otis L. Guernsey, Jr., ed. Dodd, Mead, 1976   *Anthology*: None   *Piano-vocal score*: Revelation Music, 1977   *Licensing agent*: Music Theatre International   *Recording*: RCA ARL 1-1367 (original cast)   *Cast*: Large male cast

Performed in the style of the Japanese Kabuki theater, this is the story of Commodore Perry's "opening up" of Japan in 1853. The original production (with an all-male cast, some in female roles) was highly praised for its costumes and sets. The Sondheim score commands a great deal of attention. A jump at the finale brings the story to the present. This is a real challenge.

PAINT YOUR WAGON
(1951/1962)

Book and lyrics by Alan Jay Lerner   *Music* by Frederick Loewe
Published libretto: Coward-McCann, 1952 ☆ *Theatre Arts* (magazine),
December 1952   *Condensation*: None   *Anthology*: None
Piano-vocal score: Chappell, 1951   *Licensing agent*: Tams-Witmark
Recording: RCA LSO 1006E (original cast)   *Cast*: 8 M; 6 F; chorus

Ben Rumson and his daughter are out in California panning for gold in
1853. She finds a nugget, and the rush is on. When she falls in love with
one of the miners, Ben sends her back East to school. "I Talk to the Trees"
was a popular song from the score. Agnes de Mille staged the dances for
the original production and they were called explosive and sensational,
particularly the one involving the "fancy ladies" that come into town. To
add to the pioneer atmosphere, the press agent for this production grew
a beard and greeted the customers in the lobby! Clint Eastwood starred in
the 1969 film.

THE PAJAMA GAME
(1954/1957/1973)

Book by George Abbott and Richard Bissell; based on *7½ Cents* by Richard
Bissell   *Music and lyrics* by Richard Adler and Jerry Ross   *Published
libretto*: Random House, 1954 ☆ *Theatre Arts* (magazine), September 1955
Condensation: *Theatre '54*. John Chapman, ed. Random House, 1954
Anthology: None   *Piano-vocal score*: Frank Music, 1955   *Vocal
selections*: Frank Music, 1954   *Licensing agent*: Music Theatre
International   *Recording*: Columbia S 32606 (original cast)   *Cast*:
12 M; 6 F; chorus

"Hey There" and "Steam Heat" are two big hit songs from this show. With
a contemporary setting in Iowa, the plot concerns a new superintendent
at the Sleep-Tite Pajama Factory and his problems with the workers'
union. Along the way he falls in love with the chief of the grievance
committee. There are many wonderful numbers (remember "Hernan-
do's Hideaway"?) and considerable dancing talent is required. There was
a faithful film version with Doris Day and the original cast in 1957.
Tony Award Winner (Best Musical)

PAL JOEY
(1940/1952/1963/1976/1983)

Book by John O'Hara   *Music* by Richard Rodgers   *Lyrics* by Lorenz
Hart   *Published libretto*: Random House, 1952   *Condensation*:
American Musicals: Rodgers and Hart. Time-Life, 1981   *Anthology*: None

Piano-vocal score: Chappell, 1962   *Licensing agent*: Rodgers and Hammerstein Theatre Library   *Recordings*: Columbia CSP 4364, Time-Life STL-AM06 (studio cast) ☆ Capitol 310 (1952 revival cast)   *Cast*: 10 M; 15 F; chorus

Joey is a nightclub performer and a heel. He would like to own his own club and becomes friendly with the older and wealthy Vera when she agrees to finance him. But its just a fling for her and he loses in the end. This realistic, unpleasant story helped change the direction of American musicals. The famous score includes "Bewitched" and "I Could Write a Book." Joey is basically a dancing role and there are several tacky nightclub numbers. This is a sophisticated, adult musical. The 1959 film with Sinatra changed the plot and score considerably.

PANAMA HATTIE
(1940/1976)

Book by Herbert Fields and B. G. De Sylva   *Music and lyrics* by Cole Porter   *Published libretto*: None   *Condensation*: None   *Anthology*: None   *Music publisher*: *Music and Lyrics by Cole Porter*. 2 vols. Chappell, 1972–1975   *Licensing agent*: Tams-Witmark   *Recording*: Sandy Hook SH 2043 (1954 TV cast)   *Cast*: Large mixed cast

Hattie is a dance-hall hostess with a heart of gold. A widower with an eight-year-old daughter is in love with her. He is employed in the operations of the Panama Canal. There are three sailors "on the town" who detect some spies trying to sabotage the Canal. All this is just at the beginning of World War II. Some of the songs include "Let's Be Buddies" and "Make It Another Old Fashioned, Please." The original production was described as rowdy, replete with sex and sumptuous sets. Ethel Merman was Hattie and repeated her role on television in the 1950s. There was also a film version in 1942 with Ann Sothern.

PARK
(1970/1971)

Book and lyrics by Paul Cherry   *Music* by Lance Mulcahy   *Published libretto*: Samuel French, 1970   *Condensation*: None   *Anthology*: None   *Vocal selections*: None   *Licensing agent*: Samuel French   *Recording*: None   *Cast*: 2 M; 2 F

Four strangers meet near a bandstand in a park and proceed to tell each other their secrets and indulge in a form of group therapy. It turns out they are a family—mother, father, son, and daughter trying to work out problems of communication within the family. The Broadway production used a simple set and a small rock band. There was very little dancing. It was called an intimate "minimusical."

PEACE
(1969)

Book and lyrics by Tim Reynolds; based on the play *Peace* by Aristophanes *Music* by Al Carmines   *Lyrics* adapted by Al Carmines   *Published libretto*: None   *Condensation*: None   *Anthology*: None   *Vocal selections*: CAAZ Music (Chappell), 1969   *Licensing agent*: Samuel French *Recording*: Metromedia MP 33001 (original cast)   *Cast*: 8 M; 7 F

During the 1960s and 1970s a Greenwich Village assistant church minister composed a number of rollicking off-Broadway musicals. They were entertainments with messages. This adaptation from Aristophanes is about a "heedless monster" who is about to push a panic button and explode the world. Trygaeus decides to fly up to heaven on the back of a giant green beetle to see what the gods are going to do about the situation. Described as a blend of humor, satire and bawdiness, this avant-garde minstrel musical is perhaps most suitable for adult audiences.

PERFECTLY FRANK
(1980)

Book by Kenny Solms   *Music and lyrics* by Frank Loesser; with additional music and lyrics by various collaborators   *Published libretto*: None *Condensation*: None   *Anthology*: None   *Vocal selections*: *The Frank Loesser Songbook*. Simon and Schuster, 1971 (see also various show titles) *Licensing agent*: Music Theatre International   *Recording*: None (see recordings under show titles)   *Cast*: 5 M; 5 F

Frank Loesser wrote songs for over 60 Hollywood films and five Broadway shows. This revue is made up of 55 of the hundreds of songs he wrote. The numbers are arranged into his Hollywood studio period, World War II, Broadway, and such categories as "marriage" and "blues" and joined together by "mini skits" and narrative material. The costumes were described by critics as functional and casual. The Broadway set was an arrangement of platforms and arches. *Guys and Dolls, Hans Christian Andersen, Most Happy Fella,* and *Where's Charley?* are just some of the shows that are included.

PETER PAN
(1954/1979)

Music by Moose Charlap; additional music by Jule Styne; based on the play by James M. Barrie   *Lyrics* by Carolyn Leigh; additional lyrics by Betty Comden and Adolph Green   *Published libretto*: None   *Condensation*: None   *Anthology*: None   *Vocal selections*: Big Three (Morris, 1974)   *Licensing agent*: Samuel French   *Recording*: RCA LSO 1019E (original cast)   *Cast*: Large mixed cast, including children

The charm of Barrie, of Peter and Tinker Bell and the children and the pirates in "Never Never Land" are all rolled up in a musical version with such songs as "I've Got to Crow" and "I'm Flying." This last one may present a problem as the audience will expect Peter to "fly" (Sandy Duncan in the Broadway revival "flew" out over the audience)! Mary Martin was the original, and she also performed on television in 1955. This is a show of tremendous magic and one that children love.

PHILEMON
(1975)

Book and lyrics by Tom Jones   *Music* by Harvey Schmidt   *Published libretto*: None   *Condensation*: None   *Anthology*: None   *Vocal selections*: None   *Licensing agent*: Music Theatre International   *Recording*: Gallery OC-1 (original cast)   *Cast*: 4 M; 3 F

This story is based upon an incident that took place in the Roman city of Antioch in 287 A.D. A cheap street clown is arrested and forced to impersonate Philemon, a great Christian leader. There is some humor, but the story is essentially a tragic one. This was very simply staged off-Broadway, with piano and percussion for accompaniment. The emphasis is on the music and words, rather than the scenery (some scaffolding) and costumes (leotards and capes). This musical is for adults as well as young people. There was a TV production in 1976.

PIAF
(1981)

Book by Pam Gems   *Music* by various composers   *Published libretto*: Samuel French   *Condensation*: None   *Anthology*: None   *Vocal selections*: None   *Licensing agent*: Samuel French   *Recording*: None   *Cast*: 9 M; 5 F

The life of the famous French chanteuse Edith Piaf was neither happy nor wholesome. She started out as a streetwalker, sang on street corners and in cafes, and eventually became an international star. Along the way she had numerous affairs, automobile accidents, drug problems, and cancer. When she died at age 47, she was penniless. All this is graphically portrayed with occasional songs from the Piaf repertory. The London and Broadway productions used a raked platform stage for the acting area with the cast, costumes and props all around the sides and back. The cast double up on small parts, and only assume their characterization while in the acting area. This is a sensational part for the star, but it is strictly adult entertainment. This was shown on cable television in 1982.

PIANO BAR
(1978)

Music by Rob Fremont; story by Doris Willens and Rob Fremont   *Lyrics* by Doris Willens   *Published libretto*: Samuel French, 1978
Condensation: None   *Anthology*: None   *Vocal selections*: None
Licensing agent: Samuel French   *Recording*: Original Cast OC 7812 (original cast)   *Cast*: 4 M; 2 F

The contemporary setting is Sweet Sue's Piano Bar in Manhattan. It is a rainy night and four customers meet and unburden their problems. The other two characters are the piano player and a silent bartender. The show is just one song after another with very few spoken lines. Eventually the four customers pair off and leave. The off-Broadway production was a simple one. The critics found the score pleasant and enjoyed the tango and the inebriated waltz.

PIPE DREAM
(1955)

Book and lyrics by Oscar Hammerstein, II; based on *Sweet Thursday* by John Steinbeck   *Music* by Richard Rodgers   *Published libretto*: Viking, 1956
Condensation: None   *Anthology*: None   *Piano-vocal score*: Williamson Music, 1956   *Licensing agent*: Rodgers and Hammerstein Theatre Library
Recording: RCA LOC 1023 (original cast)   *Cast*: 17 M; 10 F

Set on the California coast in Monterey County, Steinbeck's tale concerns a waterfront bohemian who gathers and sells marine specimens, a young homeless girl, and a bordello madam. There is a large assortment of vagrants, waterfront denizens, and prostitutes to liven up the evening. There's a costume party and opportunities for colorful locales. While the score is far better than most musicals can offer, the critics found it "minor key" and there are no standard songs.

PIPPIN
(1972)

Book by Roger O. Hirson   *Music and lyrics* by Stephen Schwartz
Published librettos: Drama Book Specialists, 1975 ☆ Bard (paperback), 1977
Condensation: None   *Anthology*: None   *Vocal selections*: Belwin-Mills,
1972   *Licensing agent*: Music Theatre International   *Recording*:
Motown M760L (original cast)   *Cast*: 11 M; 3 F; chorus

The year is 780 A.D. Pippin is the oldest son of Charlemagne and heir to
the Holy Roman Empire. "Magic to Do" is the famous opening number,
performed by Ben Vereen in the original Broadway production. "No
Time at All" is a show-stopping number performed by Pippin's grand-
mother. The critics liked the style of the production—a commedia
dell'arte atmosphere with sensational choreography by Bob Fosse. This
stylized rock musical has been extremely popular with young audiences,
and has been done on cable television.

THE PIRATES OF PENZANCE
(1980)

Lyrics by W. S. Gilbert   *Music* by Arthur Sullivan   *A contemporary
adaptation* by William Elliott   *Published libretto*: None   *Condensation*:
None   *Anthology*: None for the Elliott adaptation but a different version is
found in the *Complete Plays of Gilbert and Sullivan*. Norton, 1976
Piano-vocal score: Chappell, 192– (a non-Elliott version)   *Licensing
agent*: Music Theatre International ☆ Samuel French (non-Elliott version)
Recording: Electra VE-601 (original 1980 cast)   *Cast*: Large mixed cast

This popular version of the Gilbert and Sullivan operetta was first presented in Central Park as part of the New York Shakespeare Festival, and
then moved to Broadway for a long and prosperous run. One review
mentions a "Mack Sennett wackiness" that has been interjected into the
tale of Frederic, the unwilling pirate apprentice. Still, certain traditional
expertise is required to pull off the difficult "Modern Major General" and
other numbers. The Broadway scenery was described as "twopence-
coloured" cut-outs. The modern musical arrangements were called ami-
ably sacrilegious by some, but overwhelmingly successful by all. Costumes are Victorian in the traditional Gilbert and Sullivan fashion. The
film version featured Angela Lansbury and the original cast.

PLAIN AND FANCY
(1955/1980)

Book by Joseph Stein and Will Glickman   Music by Albert Hague
Lyrics by Arnold B. Horwitt   Published libretto: Random House, 1955 ☆
Samuel French, 1956 ☆ Theatre Arts (magazine), July 1956   Condensation:
None   Anthology: None   Piano-vocal score: Chappell, 1956
Licensing agent: Samuel French   Recordings: Capitol S603 (original cast)
☆ Dot DLP 3048 (London cast)   Cast: Large mixed cast

This contemporary musical is set in an Amish community in Pennsylvania. The plot deals with a young New York couple who arrive in the area for a real estate deal and become involved in the romantic problems of two young brothers. All ends happily, with lots of song and dance in rustic Americana style. "Young and Foolish" was a very popular song from the score. There is a barn-raising sequence with on-stage construction. Amish costumes need to be reasonably authentic.

PORGY AND BESS
(1935/1953/1964/1976/1983)

Book by DuBose Heyward; based on the play Porgy by Dorothy and DuBose
Heyward   Music by George Gershwin   Lyrics by Ira Gershwin
Published libretto: None   Condensation: None   Anthology: Ten Great
Musicals of the American Stage. Stanley Richards, ed. Chilton, 1973
Piano-vocal score: Chappell, 1935   Vocal selections: Chappell, 1935
Licensing agent: Tams-Witmark   Recording: RCA ARL 3-2109 (1976 revival
cast); includes libretto   Cast: Large mixed cast

Walter Kerr says that this is an opera. But it's a Gershwin opera that has graced the stages of several Broadway houses. The score is legendary, with "Summertime" and "It Ain't Necessarily So" just two of the many famous songs. Set in a Negro slum in Charleston, South Carolina, it takes place around 1935. Porgy is a crippled beggar in love with Bess. She stays with him briefly, but then leaves for New York City. He sets out after her as the final curtain falls. The leading roles are called grueling and a strong cast is needed. The score is vocally demanding. There was a 1959 film version with Sidney Poitier, but his singing was dubbed by Robert McPherrin.

PRETZELS
(1974)

Music and lyrics by John Forster   Book by Jane Curtin, Fred Grandy and
Judy Kahan   Published libretto: Samuel French, 1975   Condensation:

None   *Anthology*: None   *Vocal selections*: None   *Licensing agent*:
Samuel French   *Recording*: None   *Cast*: 2 M; 2 F

Called sparkling and urbane, this little show carries on that endangered species—the revue, with satirical sketches and catchy songs. The critics found it more personal than political and recommended it for the college crowd. Some highlights were: a foreign actress applying for unemployment, "the cockroach song," a class reunion, and a section called "classical music" performed by the pianist. A performance was taped and shown on cable television.

THE PRINCESS PAT
(1915/1981)

Music by Victor Herbert   *Book* by Henry Blossom   *Published libretto*:
None   *Condensation*: None   *Anthology*: None   *Vocal selections*:
The Music of Victor Herbert. Warner Brothers Music, 1976   *Piano-vocal score*: Witmark, 1915   *Licensing agent*: Tams-Witmark   *Recording*:
None   *Cast*: 11 M; 7 F

Set on Long Island around 1915, the plot concerns the daughter of a politician spending the weekend in Southhampton where she tries to win back her husband, a down-and-out Italian prince. This is an intimate type musical with a small cast. It was revived by Manhattan's Bel Canto Opera and received a good deal of publicity about its attempts to present an authentic reproduction of the 1915 production. The program noted the original book was "unperformable today" and was considerably revised. The costumes and music indicate a period that was just moving into the jazz age.

PRIVATES ON PARADE
(1977)

Book and lyrics by Peter Nichols   *Music* by Dennis King   *Published libretto*: Samuel French, 1977   *Condensation*: None   *Anthology*: None
Vocal selections: None   *Licensing agent*: Samuel French   *Recording*:
EMI (British) EMC 3233 (original London cast)   *Cast*: 10 M; 1 F

This spoof on British colonial army life in and around Singapore in 1948 was a big hit when performed by the Royal Shakespeare Company in London. It was done at the Long Wharf Theatre in Connecticut in 1979, but not on Broadway. The plot involves a group of soldiers, some of whom are homosexual, putting on a camp show for the boys. Some female impersonation is required. This is actually a comedy with music. It was called boisterous and outrageous and perhaps a "bit too English."

The costumes are British (tropical) military and female 1940s attire. The sets are simple. An on-stage quartet provides the music. There was a 1982 film version with members of the original cast.

PROMENADE
(1969)

Book and lyrics by Maria Irene Fornes   *Music* by Al Carmines
Published libretto: None   *Condensation*: None   *Anthologies*: *Great Rock Musicals*. Stanley Richards, ed. Stein and Day, 1979 ✮ *Promenade and Other Plays*. Maria Irene Fornes. Winter House, 1971   *Vocal selections*: CAAZ Music (Chappell), 1970   *Licensing agent*: Samuel French *Recording*: RCA LSO 1161 (original cast)   *Cast*: 10 M; 5 F

Two prisoners escape from jail and promenade through life, illuminating the comic lunacy of attitudes toward sex, war, fashion, nudity and wealth. There are satiric jabs at modern society, which is depicted as an Alice in Wonderland world of cynicism and cruelty. The score is the thing, ranging in style from the tango to a plaintive tune, reminding the critics of Weill and Brecht. The costumes were described as everything from Elinor Glyn to Carnaby Street. The set included a collage of bicycle wheels. The show includes 32 songs and very little dancing.

PROMISES, PROMISES
(1968/1983)

Book by Neil Simon; based on the screenplay *The Apartment* by Billy Wilder and I. A. L. Diamond   *Music* by Burt Bacharach   *Lyrics* by Hal David *Published libretto*: Random House, 1969   *Condensation*: None *Anthology*: *The Comedy of Neil Simon*. Random House, 1971   *Piano-vocal score*: Morris, 1969   *Licensing agent*: Tams-Witmark   *Recording*: United Artists UAS 9902 (original cast)   *Cast*: 11 M; 9 F; chorus

A young insurance employee lends his apartment to company executives so they can use it for illicit sex. The cast includes a number of business stereotypes, from the contemptible boss to the understanding secretary. The office setting has been used successfully in many plays and musicals. This show has the added advantage of Neil Simon dialogue and a catchy Burt Bacharach score. "I'll Never Fall in Love Again" is a big number. The modern, Manhattan-style sets include offices, the apartment, and a crowded saloon called "The Grapes of Roth."

PUMP BOYS AND DINETTES
(1981)

Music and lyrics by Jim Wann   *Published libretto*: Samuel French
Condensation: None   *Anthology*: None   *Vocal selections*: None
Licensing agent: Samuel French   *Recording*: CBS FM 37790 (original cast)
Cast: 4 M; 2 F

Called "an idyll of rural innocence" by a critic with the *Village Voice*, this is a revue of 20 country and western songs tied together by a bit of dialogue. The men are filling-station attendants along a North Carolina highway and the women wait tables in a nearby diner. This show was described as a theatrical concert and the setting merely an accessory. The subjects covered in song include love, fishing, drinking beer, and the nearby shopping mall. The mood ranges from the sentimental to the comic. This is folksy, family fun.

PURLIE
(1970/1972)

Book by Ossie Davis, Philip Rose and Peter Udell; based on the play *Purlie Victorious* by Ossie Davis   *Music* by Gary Geld   *Lyrics* by Peter Udell
Published libretto: Samuel French, 1971   *Condensation*: None
Anthology: None   *Vocal selections*: Mourbar Music, 1970   *Licensing agent*: Samuel French   *Recording*: Ampex A 40101 (original cast)
Cast: Large mixed cast

Purlie is a self-taught black preacher who returns home to reopen an abandoned church. Set in the deep South, the show features characters which are caricatures. The story line involves $500 which belonged to a deceased servant and which "evil ol' Cap'n Cotchipee" won't give up. Melba Moore became a star as "Lutiebelle" singing the title song. The sets and costumes depict a run-down Southern plantation. The music frequently has the intensity of a church revival meeting. The dancing should be sensational. There was a TV version.

RAISIN
(1973/1981)

Book by Robert Nemiroff and Charlotte Zaltzberg; based on *A Raisin in the Sun* by Lorraine Hansberry   *Music* by Judd Woldin   *Lyrics* by Robert Brittan   *Published libretto*: Samuel French, 1978   *Condensation*: None
Anthology: None   *Vocal selections*: Blackwood Music, 1974   *Licensing agent*: Samuel French   *Recording*: Columbia KS 32754 (original cast)
Cast: 9 M; 6 F; chorus

With a theme of "black identity" this musical takes place in a black Chicago slum. The plot concerns a proud black matriarch and her family's ambitions to escape their run-down tenement life. She wants to move to a nice (white) suburb. When they receive a $10,000 insurance check, conflicts arise. The set consists of the apartment and fire escapes; the furniture and costumes are simple and worn. Called a picture of a family fighting for life, this show offers a wide range of good parts, from the mother to her grown son, his wife and little boy, and a Nigerian student.

Tony Award Winner (Best Musical)

REALLY ROSIE
(1980)

Book and lyrics by Maurice Sendak   *Music* by Carole King   *Published libretto*: Samuel French   *Condensation*: None   *Anthology*: None
Vocal selections: Columbia Pictures, 1975   *Licensing agent*: Samuel French   *Recording*: Caedmon TRS 368 (original cast)   *Cast*: 4 M; 3 F; extras (all children)

This is a musical about children to be performed by children. Rosie lives in Brooklyn. She entertains herself and her friends by acting out her "show biz" dreams, which include directing and starring in a film and winning an Oscar. Other than a few off-stage voices, there are no adult roles. The basis for this hour-long musical is six Sendak books. The show was originally an animated cartoon TV special. For in-depth information, see Bill Powers' *Behind the Scenes of a Broadway Musical* (Crown, 1982).

THE RED MILL
(1906/1945/1978/1981)

Original book and lyrics by Henry Blossom; *new book* by Milton Lazarus; *additional lyrics* by Forman Brown   *Music* by Victor Herbert
Published libretto: None   *Condensation*: None   *Anthology*: None
Piano-vocal score: Witmark, 1906   *Vocal selections*: *The Music of Victor Herbert*. Warner Brothers Music, 1976   *Licensing agent*: Tams-Witmark
Recording: Turnabout 34766 (studio recording)   *Cast*: Large mixed cast

Two Americans are stranded in Europe in the Dutch port of Katwyk-aan-Zee. They manage to rescue the Burgomaster's daughter from a loveless marriage. This is a very old-fashioned operetta with plenty of opportunity for low comedy and pretty girls. "Moonbeams" and "The Streets of New York" are two popular songs from the score. The time is about 1900 and the scenes include the Inn at the Red Mill and a neighborhood street.

There was a silent film version with Marion Davies back in 1927 and a TV version in 1958.

REDHEAD
(1959)

Book by Herbert and Dorothy Fields, Sidney Sheldon and David Shaw
Music by Albert Hague   *Lyrics* by Dorothy Fields   *Published libretto*:
None   *Condensation*: None   *Anthology*: None   *Piano-vocal score*:
Chappell, 1960   *Licensing agent*: Music Theatre International
Recording: RCA LSO 1104 (original cast)   *Cast*: Large mixed cast

Essie Whimple makes wax figures for a museum operated by her aunts, the Simpson Sisters. It is turn-of-the-century London and this musical "whodunit" is about a fiend who has strangled a chorus girl. This show was tailored for the talents of Gwen Verdon, with choreography by Bob Fosse. It was described as a mixture of old-time melodrama and British music hall. The hero is an American, but English accents predominate. The sets include a theater, a pub and the wax museum. This was a big, handsome musical with lavish costumes. Critics called it funny, fast, opulent and refreshing.
Tony Award Winner (Best Musical)

REGINA
(1949/1953/1958/1978)

Book, music and lyrics by Marc Blitzstein; based on *The Little Foxes* by Lillian
Hellman   *Published libretto*: Chappell, 1953   *Condensation*: None
Anthology: None   *Piano-vocal score*: Chappell, 1954   *Licensing agent*:
Tams-Witmark   *Recording*: Columbia/Odyssey Y3 35236 (1958
production); includes libretto   *Cast*: 6 M; 4 F; townspeople; field workers

This modern opera (or musical drama) is set in Alabama in 1900. Regina needs her sick husband's signature to complete an important deal. He refuses and plans to change his will. She taunts him into a heart attack and lets him die. The three acts take place in the living room, the ballroom and on the veranda of the Giddens home. The book follows the famous play, except for the addition of a party and a bit of time juggling. An off-Broadway production was chided for not having more opulent sets and costumes. The set consisted of an angled white platform with three pillars to suggest a Southern estate.

RIO RITA
(1927)

Music by Harry Tierney   *Words* by Joe McCarthy   *Book* by Guy Bolton
and Fred Thompson   *Published libretto*: Samuel French, 1926

Piano-vocal score: L. Feist   *Condensation*: None   *Anthology*: None
Licensing agent: Tams-Witmark   *Recording*: Monmouth-Evergreen MES
7058 (1930 London cast)   *Cast*: Large mixed cast

Set in the early part of the twentieth century, this romantic story is about
the love of a Texas Ranger for a Mexican girl. The show includes all kinds
of intrigue, a Mexican bandit, and a few weddings. This was a lavish
Ziegfeld musical and some critics were disappointed that revival productions were not up to his standards. Brooks Atkinson of the *New York
Times* wrote that you should have "pretty cabaret girls, beautiful dancing
girls, South American troubadours and a Marimba band!" This was filmed
in 1929 and 1942. There was a TV version in 1950.

RIVERWIND
(1962/1973)

Music and lyrics by John Jennings   *Published libretto*: None
Condensation: None   *Anthology*: None   *Vocal selections*: None
Licensing agent: Music Theatre International   *Recording*: London AMS
78001 (original cast)   *Cast*: 3 M; 4 F

Reviews of an off-Broadway revival called this show simple, non-neurotic
and old-fashioned. The dialogue is clever and contains homespun phi-
losophy. The setting is a run-down motel in Indiana. The cast includes the
widow who owns and runs the motel, her daughter, a young local boy in
love with the daughter, and two visiting couples (one married, one not).
The various stages and ages of love are all settled by the final curtain. The
set is divided into a guest house bedroom, the yard, and a corner of the
main house.

THE ROAR OF THE GREASEPAINT—THE SMELL
OF THE CROWD
(1965/1969)

Book, music and lyrics by Leslie Bricusse and Anthony Newley   *Published
libretto*: None   *Condensation*: None   *Anthology*: None   *Vocal
selections*: Musical Comedy Productions, 1965   *Licensing agent*:
Tams-Witmark   *Recording*: RCA LSO 1109 (original cast)   *Cast*: 4 M;
2 F; chorus

The theme of this musical is playing the game of life. The Little Man is
"Cocky" and "Sir" is the maker of the rules. Sir always gets, and Cocky is
always bested. These two characters carry the bulk of the show, with

topics covering religion, hunger, work, success, etc. The cast includes an assortment of urchins, a girl, a bully, and a black. For the Broadway production the set was a series of platforms with a central playing area. In that production a great deal of mime was used by the star, Anthony Newley, and he reminded many of Chaplin. Most critics did not feel this show had anything new to say, but found it most entertaining with some wonderful songs, including "Who Can I Turn To" and "The Joker."

THE ROBBER BRIDEGROOM
(1975/1983)

Book and lyrics by Alfred Uhry; based upon the novella by Eudora Welty *Music* by Robert Waldman   *Published libretto*: None   *Condensation*: None   *Anthology*: None   *Vocal selections*: Schirmer, 1976 *Licensing agent*: Music Theatre International   *Recording*: Columbia CSP P 14589 (original cast)   *Cast*: Large mixed cast

This is a country western musical that combines backwoods legends and fairy tales. Set in Mississippi, the story deals with a girl in love with a bandit. They do not know that the marriages being arranged for them are with each other. A square dance is going on when the folks begin to tell the tale of "The Robber Bridegroom." The production includes an on-stage fiddler, a small country band, "hoedown" costumes and dancing, and very simple sets. The Broadway production included some nudity and earthy dialogue.

ROBERT AND ELIZABETH
(1964)

Book and lyrics by Ronald Millar; based on *The Barretts of Wimpole Street* by Rudolph Besier   *Music* by Ron Grainer   *Published libretto*: Samuel French, 1967   *Condensation*: None   *Anthology*: None   *Piano-vocal score*: Erle Music (London), 1967   *Licensing agent*: Samuel French *Recording*: Stet DS 15021, AEI 1111 (London cast)   *Cast*: 30 M; 10 F; chorus

Set in London in 1845, this is the love story of Elizabeth Moulton-Barrett and Robert Browning. The conflict is with her tyrannical father who tries to stop the romance. This was a big hit in London and has been staged in a number of other countries (including the USA) but not on Broadway. The Victorian settings include interiors and gardens, the stage of the Theatre Royal, and Vauxhall Station. This show was performed in Portland, Maine, in 1978 with a cast of 26, twin pianos, and percussion.

ROBERTA
(1933/1937/1984)

Book and lyrics by Otto Harbach; adapted from *Gowns by Roberta* by Alice Duer Miller   *Music* by Jerome Kern   *Published libretto*: None *Condensation: American Musicals: Kern*. Time-Life, 1981.   *Anthology*: None   *Piano-vocal score*: Harms, 1933, 1950   *Licensing agent*: Tams-Witmark   *Recordings*: Columbia CSP COS 2530E, Time-Life STL-AM03 (studio cast)   *Cast*: Large mixed cast

A young American football player inherits a famous Parisian fashion salon. He falls in love with one of the employees who is a Russian princess in exile. This was filmed twice (in 1935 with Fred Astaire and Ginger Rogers and in 1952 with Gower Champion and Ann Miller) and was done as a TV special in 1969. Some of the famous songs include "Smoke Gets in Your Eyes" and "Yesterday." A big fashion show is a necessity for this production, even if the 1930s script is updated. This musical has been particularly successful in lavish summer productions in such locations as Jones Beach (New York), St. Louis, and Dallas.

THE ROCKY HORROR SHOW
(1975)

Book, music and lyrics by Richard O'Brien   *Published libretto*: Samuel French   *Condensation*: None   *Anthology*: None   *Vocal selections*: Columbia Pictures Publications, 1974   *Licensing agent*: Samuel French *Recording*: Ode SP 77026 (Tim Curry and the original Roxy cast); includes lyrics.   *Cast*: 7 M; 3 F

The title of this British musical refers to horror films, which it ridicules, and rock music. This was not particularly successful on Broadway, but the 1975 film version has become a cult favorite. The grotesque cast includes Dr. Frank N. Furter (a bisexual drag queen), a hump-backed dwarf, and some groupies. A straight young American couple turn up to take refuge at the castle. This show runs about 90 minutes without an intermission. While this is not a family show, adolescents love it.

RODGERS AND HART
(1975)

Music by Richard Rodgers   *Lyrics* by Lorenz Hart   *Concept* by Richard Lewine and John Fearnley   *Published libretto*: None   *Condensation*: None   *Anthology*: None   *Music publishers*: *The Best of Rodgers and*

Hart. Chappell, 1974 ☆ *The Rodgers and Hart Songbook.* Simon and
Schuster, 1951   *Licensing agent:* Rodgers and Hammerstein Theatre
Library   *Recording:* None   *Cast:* 3 M; 3 F

This salute to the great musical stage collaborators features 59 of their
songs. "Manhattan," "My Heart Stood Still" and "Lover" are just a few of
them. There is no master of ceremonies and almost no dialogue. There
are a few brief dance numbers. The Broadway stage setting was a simple
arrangement of platforms and steps. The costumes were modern and
informal. This is one of many salutes to composers that take songs from a
career and put them into what is really a non-stop concert. The material is
top class. A talented and energetic cast is needed for this show.

ROSALIE
(1928/1957/1983)

Book by William Anthony McGuire and Guy Bolton   *Lyrics* by P. G.
Wodehouse and Ira Gershwin   *Music* by Sigmund Romberg and George
Gershwin   *Published libretto:* None   *Condensation:* None
Anthology: None   *Vocal selections:* None   *Licensing agent:*
Tams-Witmark   *Recording:* None   *Cast:* Large mixed cast

The original plot deals with a princess from the mythical kingdom of
Romanza who falls in love with an American flyer. It was a lavish Ziegfeld
production with Marilyn Miller. A later production was not lavish, but
entertaining and was staged outdoors in Central Park. One of the Gershwin songs featured is "Oh Gee, Oh Joy." (The 1937 film version
featured a different score by Cole Porter, and some songs from it are
sometimes interpolated into revival productions.)

ROSE-MARIE
(1924/1982)

Book and lyrics by Otto Harbach and Oscar Hammerstein, II   *Music* by
Rudolf Friml and Herbert Stothart   *Published libretto:* None
Condensation: None   *Anthology:* None   *Music publisher:* Harms, 1924
Licensing agent: Tams-Witmark   *Recordings:* Columbia CSP P 13878, RCA
LSO 1001 (studio cast)   *Cast:* 7 M; 4 F; chorus

The time is 1924 and the setting is Canada. Rose-Marie is a favorite of both
the Mounties and the trappers up in Saskatchewan, but she really loves
Jim, who is accused of murder. But virtue is triumphant and evil is
destroyed! There have been several film versions (featuring Jeanette

MacDonald in 1936 and Howard Keel in 1954). This is a costume show; in addition to the famous red uniforms of the Mounties, the trappers and flappers, there are lots of Indians for the elaborate "Totem Tom-Tom" number. The show includes an elaborate fashion show, a formal ball at the Chateau Frontenac, and a big wedding scene. The score is full of familiar tunes, and most of the audience will exit happily singing the "Indian Love Call."

THE ROTHSCHILDS
(1970)

Book by Sherman Yellen; based on *The Rothschilds* by Frederic Morton *Music* by Jerry Bock   *Lyrics* by Sheldon Harnick   *Published libretto*: None   *Condensation*: *American Musicals: Bock and Harnick*. Time-Life, 1982   *Anthology*: None   *Vocal selections*: Valando, 1970   *Licensing agent*: Samuel French   *Recordings*: Columbia S 30337, Time-Life STL-AM14 (original cast)   *Cast*: 29 M; 4 F; chorus

This is the musical story of the founding and growth of the House of Rothschild, with a strong Jewish theme of the indomitable character of an oppressed people. The Broadway production was called an opulent production with sets ranging from the ghetto to stately palaces. The staging and choreography were described as discreet. The story begins in Germany in 1772 and proceeds up to 1818. This is a musical about wealth, and should have an elegant, stylish production.

RUNAWAYS
(1978)

Book, music and lyrics by Elizabeth Swados   *Published libretto*: Samuel French, 1980   *Condensation*: None   *Anthology*: None   *Vocal selections*: None   *Licensing agent*: Samuel French   *Recording*: Columbia JS 35410 (original cast)   *Cast*: 11 M; 9 F

Called a musical collage in two acts, this show is about runaway children. The cast in New York was primarily made up of non-professionals between the ages of 11 and 24 with diverse ethnic and financial backgrounds. The show has no actual plot and consists of songs and monologues dealing with runaway experiences. The music is a combination of rock, blues, salsa, country, and western. The themes of abandonment, anger, and bewilderment are intertwined with those of bravery, humor, and opportunism.

SALAD DAYS
(1958)

Book and lyrics by Dorothy Reynolds and Julian Slade   *Music* by Julian
Slade   *Published libretto*: Samuel French, 1961   *Condensation*: None
Anthology: None   *Vocal selections*: None   *Licensing agent*:
Tams-Witmark   *Recording*: London 5765 (London original cast)   *Cast*:
6 M; 6 F

This 1954 British musical was a favorite of Princess Margaret and had a
long run in London. A Canadian cast presented it off-Broadway in 1958.
The plot involves a tramp with a piano in a park. The piano has magical
powers and brings happiness to everyone. Members of the small cast
portray approximately 40 characters, in the manner of British revue or
repertory. Most critics found the puns and the odd walks just a bit too
slapstick, but also found it imaginative, fanciful, and youthful. This is a
family show that can be simply staged.

SALLY
(1920/1948/1982)

Book by Guy Bolton   *Music* by Jerome Kern; with ballet music by Victor
Herbert   *Lyrics* by Clifford Grey and B. G. De Sylva   *Published libretto*:
None   *Condensation*: None   *Anthology*: None   *Piano-vocal score*:
Harms, 1921   *Licensing agent*: Tams-Witmark   *Recording*:
Monmouth-Evergreen 7053 (London original cast)   *Cast*: 7 M; 7 F; chorus

Sally is an orphan who goes to work as a dishwasher in a cafe. Here she
sings the famous "Look for the Silver Lining." At the cafe she meets and
falls in love with Blair. Through a series of misunderstandings she
masquerades as a famous singer at a party, is unmasked, and ends up a
Ziegfeld star! In a 1982 New York revival, this was done without any sets
and only a suggestion of costume. Yet the audience was charmed and
thoroughly enjoyed the seldom-heard Kern score. There was a film
version in 1929 and a London revival in 1942 under the title *Wild Rose*.

SALVATION
(1969)

Book, music and lyrics by Peter Link and C. C. Courtney   *Published
libretto*: None   *Condensation*: None   *Anthology*: None   *Vocal
selections*: Chappell, 1969   *Licensing agent*: Music Theatre International
Recording: Capitol SO 337 (original cast)   *Cast*: 4 M; 4 F; rock band

The New York critics liked the music and the cast better than the theme of this 1960s rock musical. The idea is that organized religion no longer meets the needs of the individual. There was some nudity and sex with appropriate Biblical quotations. The plot line involves a southern evangelist who attempts to turn a group of young people away from their evil ways. There are 19 songs, including "There Ain't No Flies on Jesus." Psychedelic slides were used in the New York production. The critic of the *Chelsea Clinton News* suggested, "Keep your Bible-quoting maiden aunt away."

SAY, DARLING
(1958)

Book by Richard Bissell, Abe Burrows and Marian Bissell; based on the novel by Richard Bissell   *Music* by Jule Styne   *Lyrics* by Betty Comden and Adolph Green   *Published libretto*: None   *Condensation*: None *Anthology*: None   *Vocal selections*: None   *Licensing agent*: Tams-Witmark   *Recording*: RCA LOC 1045 (original cast)   *Cast*: Large mixed cast

A writer from the Midwest becomes involved with "show biz" when his novel is turned into a musical comedy. Some of the other leading parts include a beautiful but slipping Hollywood star trying to go "legit" and a young (and not so sincere) boy producer. This is actually a satire on the author's experiences when his first novel became *The Pajama Game*. It is a comedy about a musical with many of the numbers and the main dance routines presented as part of the show being rehearsed. The Broadway production used only two pianos although the cast recording features a full orchestra.

SCRAMBLED FEET
(1979)

By John Driver and Jeffrey Haddow   *Published libretto*: Samuel French *Condensation*: None   *Anthology*: None   *Vocal selections*: None *Licensing agent*: Samuel French   *Recording*: DRG 6105 (original cast) *Cast*: 3 M; 1 F; 1 duck

This revue was done at New York's Village Gate nightclub on a small proscenium stage fringed by tiny light bulbs. The cast of four (and Hermione, the duck) go through 22 numbers about various aspects of the theater—mostly spoofs but with a couple of serious moments. Some skits include auditioning for a Latin American road company of *Annie*, a "Public Theater Playwriting Kit," and Elizabeth Swados' greatest hits. The show is structured around getting to the theater, what we see, and ending with a perhaps insincere curtain call. The only on-stage prop is a grand piano.

THE SECRET LIFE OF WALTER MITTY
(1964/1973)

Book by Joe Manchester; based on the story by James Thurber   *Music* by Leon Carr   *Lyrics* by Earl Shuman   *Published libretto*: Samuel French, 1968   *Condensation*: None   *Anthology*: None   *Vocal selections*: None   *Licensing agent*: Samuel French   *Recording*: Columbia OS 2720 (original cast)   *Cast*: 5 M; 6 F

Walter Mitty is America's everyman. As he approaches his 40th birthday, nagged by his wife and bullied by his boss, he finds escape in his daydreams. So we have Mitty as a surgeon, an astronaut, and even producing the "Folies de Mitty" in Paris. This off-Broadway musical can be economically staged and offers several good parts, including Mitty's ten-year-old daughter. The critics liked the score, made up of marches, hymns, jazzy little waltzes, and ballads.

SEESAW
(1973/1981)

Book by Michael Bennett; based on the play *Two for the Seesaw* by William Gibson   *Music* by Cy Coleman   *Lyrics* by Dorothy Fields   *Published libretto*: Samuel French, 1975   *Condensation*: None   *Anthology*: None   *Vocal selections*: Notable Music (Big Three, 1973)   *Licensing agent*: Samuel French   *Recordings*: Columbia CSP X 15563, Buddah 95006-1-OC (original cast)   *Cast*: 4 M; 4 F; chorus; dancers

A fancy-free lawyer from Nebraska is in New York making a new start. He meets and has an affair with a dancer from the Bronx. The bittersweet ending has him going back home to Nebraska and his wife. A secondary part had Tommy Tune as a choreographer; he always stopped the show with his balloon dance. There is also a good part for a young Spanish boy with a big voice. "The essence of *Seesaw* is its very New Yorkishness," wrote John Beaufort of the *Christian Science Monitor*. It's a big, brassy show with big numbers and a good score.

SEVEN BRIDES FOR SEVEN BROTHERS
(1982)

Book by Lawrence Kasha and David Landay; based on the 1954 MGM film and *The Sobbin' Women* by Stephen Vincent Benet   *Music* by Gene de Paul; new songs by Al Kasha and Joel Hirschhorn   *Lyrics* by Johnny Mercer   *Published libretto*: None   *Condensation*: None   *Anthology*: None   *Vocal selections*: None   *Licensing agent*: Music Theatre International   *Recording*: None   *Cast*: Large mixed cast

The setting is the Pacific Northwest in the 1850s. Adam desperately needs a wife to take care of himself and his six brothers. Milly marries him without knowing about the brothers, so she sets out to find brides for all of them. This was a popular film in 1954 with Jane Powell and Howard Keel, although this stage version retains only four songs from the film. The Broadway production featured elaborate sets and athletic dances.

SEVENTEEN
(1951/1962)

Book by Sally Benson; based on the novel by Booth Tarkington   *Music* by Walter Kent   *Lyrics* by Kim Gannon   *Published libretto*: Samuel French, 1954   *Condensation*: None   *Anthology*: None   *Vocal selections*: None   *Licensing agent*: Samuel French   *Recording*: RCA CBM 1-2034 (original cast)   *Cast*: 13 M; 12 F; extras

The famous summertime "puppy love" story set in Indiana in 1907 was musicalized for Broadway. The plot concerns Lola Pratt, visiting for the summer and causing all sorts of problems with the local teenagers and their parents. Called by Brooks Atkinson (*New York Times*) a "touching and uproarious portrait of the torture of adolescence," it is a show for the entire family. The sets and costumes need to suggest the pre-World War I period, and the whole show should have charm, style, and innocence.

70, GIRLS, 70
(1971)

Book by Fred Ebb and Norman L. Martin; based on the play *Breath of Spring* by Peter Coke   *Music* by John Kander   *Lyrics* by Fred Ebb   *Published libretto*: None   *Condensation*: None   *Anthology*: None   *Vocal selections*: Valando, 1971   *Licensing agent*: Samuel French   *Recording*: Columbia S 30589 (original cast)   *Cast*: 11 M; 13 F

The girls in the title are all in the vicinity of being seventy years old and live in a seedy retirement hotel on New York's Upper West Side. They decide to fix things up a bit by shoplifting and specialize in stores that stock expensive furs. Occasionally, the actors step out of their roles and speak to the audience. In the New York production the orchestra wore colorful jerseys and the piano player ("Hit it, Lorraine") was onstage. There are banjo and other vaudeville-type numbers. The only young person in the cast is the bellhop.

1776
(1969)

Book by Peter Stone   *Music and lyrics* by Sherman Edwards
Published libretto: Viking, 1970   *Condensation: The Best Plays of 1968–1969*. Otis L. Guernsey, Jr., ed. Dodd, Mead, 1969   *Anthologies: Ten Great Musicals of the American Stage*. Stanley Richards, ed. Chilton, 1973 ☆ *Best American Plays*, 7th series. Clive Barnes, ed. Crown, 1975   *Vocal selections*: Schirmer, 1969   *Licensing agent*: Music Theatre International   *Recording*: Columbia BOS 3310 (original cast)   *Cast*: 25 M; 2 F

All the delegates are there—John Adams, John Hancock, Ben Franklin— the object is to get the Second Continental Congress to draft and adopt the Declaration of Independence. At the final curtain the group freezes in the pose of the familiar Trumbull painting of the event. The two women in the cast are Abigail Adams and Martha Jefferson. The script was described as "touching, funny, endearing, frank and truthful." There is no chorus and only an impromptu waltz for choreography. There was a film version in 1972. Even the most jaded sophisticate cannot help but be touched and inspired by this show.
Tony Award Winner (Best Musical)

SHE LOVES ME
(1963/1976/1977/1980)

Book by Joe Masteroff; based on the play *Parfumerie* by Miklos Laszlo *Music* by Jerry Bock   *Lyrics* by Sheldon Harnick   *Published libretto*: Dodd, Mead, 1964   *Condensation: The Best Plays of 1962–1963*. Henry Hewes, ed. Dodd, Mead, 1963   *Anthology*: None   *Vocal selections*: Valando, 1963   *Licensing agent*: Tams-Witmark   *Recordings*: Stet DS 15008, MGM SE 41180C-2 (original cast)   *Cast*: 13 M; 8 F

This charming musical is set in Budapest in the 1930s. A young clerk who works in a shop carries on a romance by mail with a girl he doesn't know. By chance, she comes to work in the same shop and complications develop. This show (and recording) have reached a cult status. It has been revived several times, including a "concert" version at Town Hall

(New York City). There was also a slightly abridged version on Public Television. The delightful, if somewhat challenging score includes "Ice Cream" which Barbara Cook introduced.

SHELTER
(1973)

Book and lyrics by Gretchen Cryer   *Music* by Nancy Ford   *Published libretto*: Samuel French, 1973   *Condensation*: None   *Anthology*: None *Music publisher*: Belwin-Mills, 1973   *Licensing agent*: Samuel French *Recording*: None   *Cast*: 3 M; 3 F; off-stage voices

A television writer and a model meet in a TV studio and spend the night there. He prefers the TV sets to his own home, and through the use of the equipment can provide a sky of stars, crickets chirping, or whatever mood he wants. There is also a talking computer. So this shelter from the real world is a psychological metaphor and the themes involved include time and reality. The sets should include a convincing studio with excellent projections for the required effects. Critics described the show as an intimate musical, with a soft rock score.

SHENANDOAH
(1975)

Book by James Lee Barrett, Peter Udell and Philip Rose; based on the 1965 film; original screenplay by James Lee Barrett   *Music* by Gary Geld *Lyrics* by Peter Udell   *Published libretto*: Samuel French, 1975 *Condensation*: None   *Anthology*: None   *Piano-vocal score*: Morris, 1977   *Vocal selections*: Morris, 1975 (Hal Leonard)   *Licensing agent*: Samuel French   *Recording*: RCA AGL 1-3763 (original cast)   *Cast*: 11 M; 3 F; children; chorus

Charlie Anderson, a widower with six sons and a daughter, lives with his family on a Virginia farm in the Shenandoah Valley. When the Civil War begins, Charlie does not let his sons enlist; he believes that war violates the will of God. Then his youngest son is kidnapped by Yankee soldiers. This musical (which is based on a 1965 film with Jimmy Stewart) was described as traditional and old-fashioned. Most critics compared it to the works of Rodgers and Hammerstein. A prologue includes a ballet in which the opposing soldiers face each other in a military drill. The New York sets were described as semi-abstract. The score includes country tunes, love songs, hymns, and lullabies.

SHOW BOAT
(1927/1946/1966/1976/1983)

Book and lyrics by Oscar Hammerstein, II; based on *Show Boat* by Edna Ferber   *Music* by Jerome Kern   *Published libretto*: None *Condensation: American Musicals: Kern*. Time-Life, 1981   *Anthology*: None   *Piano-vocal score*: Harms, 1927 (Cherry Lane)   *Licensing agent*: Rodgers and Hammerstein Theatre Library   *Recordings*: Columbia OS 2220, Time-Life STL-AM03 (studio cast) ☆ RCA LSO 1126 (1966 Lincoln Center cast) ☆ Stanyan 2SR 10048 (1971 London cast)   *Cast*: 14 M; 19 F; singers; dancers

This world-famous musical begins in Natchez, Mississippi on the Mississippi River, around 1880. The following scenes include The Chicago World's Fair in 1883, New Year's Eve at the Trocadero in 1905, and back to the Show Boat in 1927. The plot concerns Magnolia, who sings on the Show Boat, and her unfortunate marriage to Gaylord Ravenal. This musical is frequently presented in outdoor summer theaters, usually on a lavish scale. The Lincoln Center production had a Show Boat that moved out onto the stage! The score is legendary, containing such classics as "Ol' Man River," "Can't Help Lovin' Dat Man," and "Only Make Believe." The most recent film version was in 1951 with Howard Keel and Kathryn Grayson. Irene Dunne starred in a 1936 film version.

SHOW ME WHERE THE GOOD TIMES ARE
(1970)

Book by Lee Thuna; suggested by Moliere's *The Imaginary Invalid*   *Music* by Kenneth Jacobson   *Lyrics* by Rhoda Roberts   *Published libretto*: Samuel French, 1970   *Condensation*: None   *Anthology*: None *Vocal selections*: None   *Licensing agent*: Samuel French   *Recording*: None   *Cast*: 6 M; 4 F; extras

Moliere's play has been transformed into a Jewish musical comedy. It is Spring, 1913, on New York's Lower East Side. Aaron is the imaginary invalid (reminding many critics of Groucho Marx) and Bella is his scheming wife, anxious for him to die and leave her his fortune. Annette is their daughter who doesn't want to marry the doctor's son. There is a touch of ragtime in the score which evokes the early 1900s and was performed by a seven-piece orchestra in the off-Broadway production. For one number, the audience was encouraged to sing along. The lively choreography and colorful period costumes were noted in the reviews.

SIDE BY SIDE BY SONDHEIM
(1977)

Music and lyrics by Stephen Sondheim (with additional music by various collaborators); continuity by Ned Sherrin   *Published libretto*: None   *Condensation*: None   *Anthology*: None   *Music publisher*: The Hansen Treasury of Stephen Sondheim Songs. Hansen, 1974   *Licensing agent*: Music Theatre International   *Recording*: RCA CBL 2-1851 (original cast)   *Cast*: 2 M; 2 F

This revue was conceived and first presented in Great Britain. It was a great success on Broadway, however, and has been presented in many locations since that time. There is a cast of four—three singers and a "wry narration" and perhaps a song by the fourth. According to director and star Ned Sherrin, "We wanted to explore three propositions. Sondheim as the best lyric writer . . . the most adventurous composer of musicals, and the most considerable musical dramatist." *Company, Follies,* and *Anyone Can Whistle* are the main sources of material, although such obscure titles as *The Seven Percent Solution* and *Evening Primrose* are included. A simple set with stools and two pianos is all that is required.

SILK STOCKINGS
(1955/1977)

Book by George S. Kaufman, Leueen MacGrath and Abe Burrows; suggested by *Ninotchka* by Melchior Lengyel   *Music and lyrics* by Cole Porter   *Published libretto*: None   *Condensation*: None   *Anthology*: None   *Vocal selections*: Chappell, 1954   *Licensing agent*: Tams-Witmark   *Recording*: RCA LOC 1102 (original cast)   *Cast*: Large mixed cast

This 1930s film comedy was updated to the 1950s for a Broadway musical. Three Russian agents are sent to Paris to bring back a leading— and defecting—Soviet composer. When the three agents do not return, Ninotchka is sent to bring them all home. But once in Paris she meets Hollywood agent Canfield and falls in love. There is also a subplot about a Hollywood swimming star making a film version of *War and Peace.* Some of the Cole Porter songs include "Paris Loves Lovers," "All of You," and the title song. An off-Broadway production used a simple rotating staircase as the set. There was a film version with Fred Astaire in 1957.

SIMPLY HEAVENLY
(1957/1978)

Book and lyrics by Langston Hughes; based on the "Simple" stories by Langston Hughes   *Music* by David Martin   *Published libretto*:

Dramatists Play Service, 1959   *Condensation*: None   *Anthology*: *Five Plays by Langston Hughes*. Webster Smalley, ed. Indiana University Press, 1963   *Vocal selections*: None   *Licensing agent*: Dramatists Play Service *Recording*: Columbia OL 5240 (original cast)   *Cast*: 11 M; 8 F

In Harlem, Jess Simple is trying to raise enough money to divorce a wife he doesn't love in order to remarry. The set is two rooms divided by Paddy's Bar. Simple is described as a comical and lovable barroom philosopher with many things to say about the Negro in American life. Langston Hughes presents Harlem and the New York Negro as they really were and as no outsider would see them. This is family entertainment. The score includes blues, calypso, and early rock and roll. The cast album also includes some of Simple's monologues.

SING OUT, SWEET LAND!
(1944)

Book by Walter Kerr   *Music composed and arranged* by Elie Siegmeister *Published libretto*: Baker, 1949   *Condensation*: None   *Anthology*: None *Vocal selections*: None   *Licensing agent*: Baker's Plays   *Recording*: AEI 1137 (original cast)   *Cast*: Large mixed cast

Called a saga of American folk and popular music, this show starred Alfred Drake and Burl Ives when the Theatre Guild presented it on Broadway. Some of the songs used were composed for the show. Others are by such well-known composers as W. C. Handy; but the majority of the songs are those whose origins and authors are unknown. Some of these are "Frankie and Johnny," "Blue Tail Fly," and "Big Rock Candy Mountain." There is a slight plot line about Barnaby Goodlove, condemned to go through the ages singing and dancing. The original production had choreography by Charles Weidman and Doris Humphrey. The cast can double up on the parts, and a simple piano could work as well as a full orchestra.

SKYSCRAPER
(1965)

Book by Peter Stone; based on *Dream Girl* by Elmer Rice   *Music* by James van Heusen   *Lyrics* by Sammy Cahn   *Published libretto*: Samuel French, 1967   *Condensation*: None   *Anthology*: None   *Vocal selections*: Harms, 1965   *Licensing agent*: Samuel French   *Recording*: Capitol SVAS 2422 (original cast)   *Cast*: 11 M; 5 F; chorus

This musical about New York was praised for capturing the personality of the city. The title refers to the building Tim Bushman would construct if only Georgina Allerton would sell her brownstone. Georgina is dedicated to preserving old New York. Georgina also daydreams, so the show includes her numerous fantasies—cavaliers fighting over her, she is Scarlett O'Hara, etc. This is a big musical and the fantasies require special costuming. Some of the Michael Kidd dances involve construction workers with jackhammers and a foreman beating out the rhythm on a big oil drum. Another number depicts the typical New York delicatessen during the lunch hour rush. The New York production also included a filmed sequence satirizing Italian movies.

SMITH
(1973)

Book by Dean Fuller, Tony Hendra and Matt Dubey   *Music and lyrics* by Matt Dubey and Dean Fuller   *Published libretto*: Samuel French, 1972 *Condensation*: None   *Anthology*: None   *Vocal selections*: None *Licensing agent*: Samuel French   *Recording*: None   *Cast*: 6 M; 4 F; chorus

This is the story of a man whose life assumes the form of a musical comedy! Smith is a staid young botanist who, after firing a lab assistant, finds a musical comedy script about his life. This comedy takes him to the South Seas. The New York production included an erupting volcano. The costumes include not only chic New York but grass skirts for the islanders. The action is interrupted by stage hands moving the sets and prompting forgetful actors. Some critics felt that this was all a satire on the big musicals of the 1950s.

SNOOPY
(1982)

Book by Charles M. Schulz; based on his comic strip *Peanuts*   *Music* by Larry Grossman   *Lyrics* by Hal Hackady   *Published libretto*: None *Condensation*: None   *Anthology*: None   *Vocal selections*: Chappell, 1984   *Licensing agent*: Tams-Witmark   *Recordings*: DRG 6103 (San Francisco cast) ☆ That's Entertainment Records TER 1073 (London cast) *Cast*: 5 M; 2 F

After the great success of *You're a Good Man, Charlie Brown* it was decided to develop another musical revue from the *Peanuts* material and to concentrate on the dog Snoopy. This new show started out in San Francisco in 1976. After much traveling and changing it finally opened off Broadway in 1982. Once again, the format is merely quick bits and tunes, briskly and simply staged. The dialogue is carefully based on the comic strip. Some of the characters are a bit more cynical than in the earlier show. This will appeal to adults as well as to children.

SOMETHING'S AFOOT
(1976)

Book, music and lyrics by James McDonald, David Vos and Robert Gerlach; additional music by Ed Linderman   *Published libretto*: Samuel French, 1975   *Condensation*: None   *Anthology*: None   *Vocal selections*: Hansen, 1976   *Licensing agent*: Samuel French   *Recording*: None   *Cast*: 6 M; 4 F

The plot of this musical farce is a tribute to the British "whodunit," particularly the works of Agatha Christie. In an isolated mansion with a missing host, a strange assortment of guests are successively bumped off. A chandelier even falls on one victim! The setting is a country estate in the English Lake District in 1935, and the musical numbers spoof musicals of the thirties. *New York Magazine* described the production as full of "manic movement, scenery-climbing and eyeball rolling" and considered it an audience show. Someone like Tessie O'Shea would be a good choice for the Miss Marple-type character.

SONG OF NORWAY
(1944/1958/1981)

Book by Milton Lazarus; from a play by Homer Curran   *Music* by Edvard Grieg   *Lyrics and musical adaptation* by Robert Wright and George Forrest   *Published libretto*: None   *Condensation*: None   *Anthology*: None   *Piano-vocal score*: Chappell, 1951   *Licensing agent*: Tams-Witmark   *Recordings*: MCA 2023E (original cast) ☆ Columbia CL 1328 (Jones Beach cast)   *Cast*: Large mixed cast

Based on incidents in the life of Edvard Grieg, the story begins in Troldhaugen on Midsummer's Eve in 1860. Grieg and his friend Nordraak share the dream of making Norway more important in the world of music and literature. But Grieg is attracted to the Countess Louise, a tempestuous opera star, and follows her to Rome. This lavish musical was presented outdoors at Jones Beach with Viking ships and icebergs, as well as by the New York City Opera with choreography by Eliot Feld. The musical score, not an easy one to sing, includes the popular "Strange Music." There are dancing villagers in folk costumes and a Peer Gynt ballet. This family show was filmed in 1970.

THE SOUND OF MUSIC
(1959/1967/1979/1980)

Book by Howard Lindsay and Russel Crouse; suggested by *The Trapp Family Singers* by Maria Augusta Trapp   *Music* by Richard Rodgers   *Lyrics* by Oscar Hammerstein, II   *Published libretto*: Random House, 1960   *Condensation*: None   *Anthology*: None   *Piano-vocal score*: Williamson Music, 1960   *Vocal selections*: Williamson Music, 1960   *Licensing agent*: Rodgers and Hammerstein Theatre Library   *Recording*: Columbia S 32601 (original cast)   *Cast*: 9 M (2 boys); 15 F (4 girls); chorus

Set in Austria during the months which immediately preceded the outbreak of the second world war, this is the story of Maria Rainer, a postulant who is not ready to take her final vows. She is sent to the home of widower Captain von Trapp as a governess to his seven children. Maria falls in love with the captain and they marry as the Nazi menace threatens. Some critics were irritated by the sentimentality of this tale, but that same quality has endeared it to the masses. It has become one of the select giants of the musical stage. Although revivals tend to be lavish, an off-Broadway production proved that the music and the children will carry the most simple production. Many people know all the songs and remember the Julie Andrews 1965 film version.
Tony Award Winner (Best Musical)

SOUTH PACIFIC
(1949/1955/1961/1967)

Book by Oscar Hammerstein, II, and Joshua Logan; adapted from *Tales of the South Pacific* by James A. Michener   *Music* by Richard Rodgers   *Lyrics* by Oscar Hammerstein, II   *Published libretto*: Random House, 1949   *Anthologies*: *Six Plays by Rodgers and Hammerstein*. Random House, 1955 ☆ Modern Library, 1959 ☆ *Representative American Plays*, 7th ed. Arthur H. Quinn, ed. Appleton, 1953   *Condensation*: *American Musicals: Rodgers and Hammerstein*. Time-Life, 1980   *Piano-vocal score*: Williamson Music, 1949   *Licensing agent*: Rodgers and Hammerstein Theatre Library   *Recordings*: Columbia S 32604, Time-Life STL-AM01 (original cast)   *Cast*: 22 M; 15 F; 2 children; islanders; sailors

Set on a tropical island during World War II, the plot revolves around two love affairs that offer a lesson in human tolerance and understanding. Nellie Forbush, the nurse from Arkansas, falls in love with Emile de Becque, a mature expatriot French planter. Meanwhile, young Seabee Lieutenant Joe Cable falls in love with Liat, a lovely native girl. Nellie sings "I'm Gonna Wash That Man Right outa My Hair" and traditionally does so on stage. Emile sings "Some Enchanted Evening" in operatic fashion and

the young lieutenant sings "Younger Than Springtime." Another big number, "Bali Ha'i," is sung by the wily Bloody Mary. *Variety* called this "one of the great shows of legit history." A two-piano arrangement is available. The show was filmed by Todd-A-O in 1958.
Tony Award Winner (Best Musical)
Pulitzer Prize

SPOKESONG (or The Common Wheel) (1979)

Book and lyrics by Stewart Parker   *Music* by Jimmy Kennedy
Published libretto: Samuel French, 1980   *Condensation*: None
Anthology: None   *Vocal selections*: None   *Licensing agent*: Samuel
French   *Recording*: None   *Cast*: 4 M; 2 F

This musical is set in and around a bicycle shop in Belfast, Northern Ireland. The shop is used as a metaphor to point out the problems of Northern Ireland, and in fact, modern civilization. This folk comedy is really a play with songs, rather than a musical. The off-Broadway production featured a one-man band, and fine cycling from the entire cast. In addition to the new songs, "A Bicycle Built for Two" is also used. The other numbers were described as music-hall types. The "loose-jointed" form of this show includes flashbacks to the hero's grandparents and a mustached man on a unicycle who rides in and out, singing and commenting on the action.

STARTING HERE, STARTING NOW (1977)

Lyrics by Richard Maltby, Jr.   *Music* by David Shire   *Published libretto*:
None   *Condensation*: None   *Anthology*: None   *Vocal selections*:
Fiddleback Music, 1978   *Licensing agent*: Music Theatre International
Recording: RCA ABL 1-2360 (original cast)   *Cast*: 1 M; 2 F; (some
productions have used 5 M; 4 F)

Presented off-Broadway in a theater-restaurant, this is a cabaret revue of songs composed by Maltby and Shire. One cast member described it as a show about how people cope with life. A critic thought it was about love, lost and found. In any case, it has no plot or dialogue but consists of 25 numbers done as solos, duets and big production numbers. Some numbers were written for this show, but others were written earlier. Barbra Streisand sang the title song on her TV special, "Color Me Barbra." Musical support can be a piano and a bass (sometimes switching to a guitar).

THE STINGIEST MAN IN TOWN
(1956 TV musical adapted for the stage)

Book and lyrics by Janice Torre; based on *A Christmas Carol* by Charles Dickens   *Music* by Fred Spielman   *Published libretto*: None   *Condensation*: None   *Anthology*: None   *Piano-vocal score*: Warner Brothers Music, 1957   *Licensing agent*: Music Theatre International   *Recording*: Columbia CL 950 (original TV cast)   *Cast*: Large mixed cast, including children

This musical version of *A Christmas Carol* is done in the traditional Dickensian style and period. The songs and dances were described as modernistic interpolations, but never mind that. This is a family show that is just right for the holiday season. In addition to the original telecast with Basil Rathbone as Scrooge, this same score was used for an animated version telecast in 1978.

STOP THE WORLD—I WANT TO GET OFF
(1962/1969/1978)

Book, music and lyrics by Leslie Bricusse and Anthony Newley   *Published libretto*: None   *Condensation*: *The Best Plays of 1962–1963*. Henry Hewes, ed. Dodd, Mead, 1963   *Anthology*: None   *Vocal selections*: Ludlow Music, 1961 ✫ *The Songs of Leslie Bricusse*. Chappell, 1976   *Licensing agent*: Tams-Witmark   *Recordings*: London 88001 (original cast) ✫ Warner Brothers Records HS 3214 (1978 cast)   *Cast*: 1 M; 10 F; 2 boys

This musical combines British music-hall style with commedia dell'arte as it tells the story of Littlechap using clown-show acts. He is the only male in the cast (except for children) and the women in his life are all played by the same female. The chorus is composed of assorted beautiful girls. There are three popular songs from the score: "Gonna Build a Mountain," "Once in a Lifetime," and "What Kind of Fool Am I?" In the original production the costumes were leotards and clown outfits, although the Sammy Davis revival featured more conventional street wear. An off-Broadway production was noted for its elegant and effective set, a raised ring in the center of the stage which provided focus for the implied circus atmosphere. The original production employed a great deal of panto-mime in the style of Marcel Marceau. A 1966 film version preserved the original costumes and style of this popular show.

STREET SCENE
(1947/1959/1978/1982)

Book by Elmer Rice; based on his Pulitzer Prize-winning play   *Music* by Kurt Weill   *Lyrics* by Langston Hughes   *Published libretto*: None *Condensation*: None   *Anthology*: None   *Piano-vocal score*: Chappell, 1948   *Licensing agent*: Rodgers and Hammerstein Theatre Library *Recording*: Columbia COL 4139 (original cast)   *Cast*: 18 M; 15 F; extras

The romantic tragedy of urban alienation was turned into an American opera by Kurt Weill in 1947. The single setting is a tenement street in New York. The plot follows the murder of an adulterous woman and her lover, and the romance of her daughter with a young Jewish intellectual. Originally done on Broadway, this was later performed by the New York City Opera and was telecast on October 27, 1979. The challenging score contains some American jazz phrases.

THE STREETS OF NEW YORK
(1963)

Book and lyrics by Barry Alan Grael; based on the play by Dion Boucicault *Music* by Richard B. Chodosh   *Published libretto*: Samuel French, 1965 *Condensation*: None   *Anthology*: None   *Vocal selections*: None *Licensing agent*: Samuel French   *Recording*: None   *Cast*: 8 M; 7 F; chorus

Based on a "hearts-and-flowers" nineteenth-century play, this musical is set in New York City around 1880 and is about a hard-hearted banker and his scheming daughter. She wants to marry a young aristocrat whose fortune has been stolen by the banker. The off-Broadway production was noted for its handsome production, colorful costumes, and the excellent voices of the entire cast. The scenery was described as simple and smart. The score contains a hint of Gilbert and Sullivan, as well as a Mexican ballad, Christmas carols, and madrigals. This is a family musical melodrama of incorruptible virtue and "hissable" villainy. A two-piano accompaniment is used.

STRIDER
(1979)

Book by Mark Rozovsky; adapted from a story by Leo Tolstoy; English stage version by Robert Kalfin and Steve Brown   *Music composed* by M. Rosovsky and S. Vetkin   *Published libretto*: Samuel French, 1981

Condensation: None   *Anthology*: None   *Vocal selections*: Schirmer, 1980   *Licensing agent*: Samuel French   *Recording*: None   *Cast*: 12 M; 7 F; 4 musicians (some doubling)

Tolstoy's allegory of a century ago has been musicalized. It is the story of a beaten and abused horse, who, like the Russian peasant he represents, is indefatigable. There are two challenges in the staging of this show. First, the actors must portray horses—nuzzle, twitch tails, and whinny through skillful use of mime. The title role is a real challenge. The second challenge is locating a small on-stage gypsy ensemble to provide atmosphere and accompaniment for the songs and lively folk dances. There are people in the story, including the prince who owns Strider and the ballerina he loves. A number of critics mentioned that, while this is an unusual attraction, children will adore it.

THE STUDENT GYPSY, OR THE PRINCE OF LIEDERKRANZ (1963)

Book, music and lyrics by Rick Besoyan   *Published libretto*: None
Condensation: None   *Anthology*: None   *Vocal selections*: None
Licensing agent: Samuel French   *Recording*: None   *Cast*: Large mixed cast

Described by the critic of *Variety* as "a large, ornate imitation antique," this is a spoof on the light operas of the 1920s. The wildly convoluted plot is meant to be ridiculous; it concerns the adopted daughter of the monarch of a mythical kingdom and a prince disguised as a soldier. In this "Never Never Land" the "painted trees should look like painted trees" and bright-eyed maidens dance "in their beruffled and beflowered peasant dresses." There are the soldiers, the gypsies and the royal court to be costumed, as well. The musical score is richly melodic, with amusing love songs, drinking songs, bell songs (the cast should include a bell ringer) and a "seventh heaven waltz." A full orchestra or two pianos can be used.

THE STUDENT PRINCE (1924/1943/1961/1980)

Book and lyrics by Dorothy Donnelly; based on the play *Old Heidelberg* by Wilhelm Meyer-Forster   *Music* by Sigmund Romberg   *Published libretto*: None   *Condensation*: None   *Anthology*: None
Piano-vocal score: Chappell, 1932 ☆ Harms, 1932   *Vocal selections*: *The Music of Sigmund Romberg*. Warner Brothers Music, 1977   *Licensing*

agent: Tams-Witmark   *Recordings*: Odyssey Y 32367, Angel S 37318
(studio cast) ☆ RCA LSC 2339 (Mario Lanza and studio cast)   *Cast*: Large
mixed cast

This musical romance is set in 1860 and relates the sentimental story of
the love of a prince for a waitress at a students' inn. Unfortunately, duty
calls, and he gives her up in favor of a wedding with a princess from a
neighboring country. It's not possible to modernize a story like this one,
so the production must have the colorful peasant costumes, the student
drinking songs, and the "schmaltz." The required settings are the garden
of the Inn of the Three Golden Apples, the prince's sitting room at the
inn, and a state room at the royal palace. The famous score includes
"Deep in My Heart," "Golden Days," and "Just We Two." There have been
several film versions, including one in 1954 with the voice of Mario
Lanza. A perennial favorite, this show was performed in 1980 by the New
York City Opera.

SUGAR
(1972)

Book by Peter Stone; based on the screenplay *Some Like It Hot* by Billy
Wilder and I. A. L. Diamond; from a story by Robert Thoeren   *Music* by
Jule Styne   *Lyrics* by Bob Merrill   *Published libretto*: None
Condensation: None   *Anthology*: None   *Vocal selections*: None
Licensing agent: Tams-Witmark   *Recording*: United Artists UAS 9905
(original cast)   *Cast*: Large mixed cast

This story begins in Chicago in 1931 as a couple of musicians witness the
St. Valentine's Day massacre. In their efforts to escape being rubbed out
themselves, they masquerade as women and join a women's orchestra
traveling to Florida. There's a lot of humor in this "theatrical drag" show.
Other major roles are Sugar (the band's singer), Sweet Sue (the band-
leader), a naughty old millionaire and a tap-dancing gangster. This was an
old-style Broadway musical, staged and choreographed by Gower Champion. The scenery was described as modest and mobile, and includes
Pullman berths. If done with good taste, this is plain popular theater with
lots of laughs.

SUGAR BABIES
(1979)

Book by Ralph G. Allen; based on traditional burlesque material   *Music*
by Jimmy McHugh   *Lyrics* by Dorothy Fields and Al Dubin   *Published*

libretto: Samuel French   *Condensation*: None, but see *The Best Plays of 1979–1980* for one skit from the play. Dodd, Mead 1980   *Anthology*: None   *Vocal selections*: Jimmy McHugh Music   *Licensing agent*: Samuel French   *Recording*: B'Way Entertainment BE 8302-R (original cast)   *Cast*: 8 M; 2 F; chorus girls; extras

Described by Julius Novick (*Village Voice*) as "somewhere between recollection and parody," this is a tribute to the burlesque show of yesteryear. There is a great deal of humor in the gags, the pitch man selling postcards down in front of the house, the chorus girls, and the specialty acts. The original New York production featured a hilarious dog act, later replaced by a comic juggler, so it's possible to interpolate. The songs are mostly standards like "On the Sunny Side of the Street" and "I Can't Give You Anything but Love." There are affectionate salutes to Sally Rand and her fan dance and other "greats." There's plenty of corn, risqué one-liners, slap-stick, cute chorines, and a patriotic red-white-and-blue finale.

SUNNY
(1925)

Book and lyrics by Otto Harbach and Oscar Hammerstein, II   *Music* by Jerome Kern   *Published libretto*: None   *Condensation*: None   *Anthology*: None   *Piano-vocal score*: Chappell, 1925, 1934 ☆ Harms, 1925, 1934   *Licensing agent*: Tams-Witmark   *Recording*: Stanyan SR 10035 (1926 London cast)   *Cast*: Large mixed cast

The settings for this 1920s musical include a circus in England, aboard the "S. S. Triumphant," and finally in Florida. The big song from the score is "Who?" (which was done by Judy Garland in a circus setting in the film *Till the Clouds Roll By*). A group of American ex-soldiers have been revisiting the French battlefields of World War I. While in England and on their way home, they notice that a circus bareback rider is "Sunny," the little entertainer for their outfit in France. She decides to see them off, and ends up as a stowaway. This was originally a lavish production, and in England it was described as a spectacular revue. A 1972 Goodspeed Opera revival in Connecticut reproduced *Sunny* without condescension or kidding, with a succession of songs, and dancing of all varieties from acrobatic to "soft-shoe" to tap. Marilyn Miller was the original "Sunny" and starred in a 1930 film version. There was another film in 1941 with Anna Neagle.

SUSAN B!
(1981)

Book by Jules Tasca   *Lyrics* by Ted Drachman   *Music* by Thomas Tierney   *Published libretto*: None   *Condensation*: None   *Anthology*: None   *Vocal Selections*: None   *Licensing agent*: Dramatic *Recording*: None   *Cast*: 3 M; 3 F

The off-Broadway production of this one-act musical featured a cast of six in multiple roles (a larger cast can be used) and recorded music for accompaniment. The plot concerns Susan B. Anthony and her fight for women's rights. It is presented through a series of biographical vignettes with Horace Greeley as a narrator.

SWEENEY TODD THE DEMON BARBER OF FLEET STREET
(1979)

Book by Hugh Wheeler; based on a version of *Sweeney Todd* by Christopher Bond   *Music and lyrics* by Stephen Sondheim   *Published libretto*: Dodd, Mead, 1979   *Condensation*: *The Best Plays of 1978–1979*. Otis L. Guernsey, Jr., ed. Dodd, Mead, 1979   *Anthology*: None   *Piano-vocal score*: Revelation Music, 1981   *Vocal selections*: Revelation Music, 1979 *Licensing agent*: Music Theatre International   *Recording*: RCA CBL 2-3379 (original cast); includes libretto   *Cast*: Large mixed cast

A cut-throat barber practices above a pie shop supplying it with cheap and easy meat! Todd is an escaped convict who was unjustly sentenced so that the Judge could have Mrs. Todd. He returns to find his wife a suicide and his daughter the ward of the Judge. Victorian London is presented as a plague-spot—a dark grotesque underworld. This needs to be awesome, staggering, epic, monumental—a huge factory signifying the Industrial Revolution covers the stage and center stage becomes the pie shop, a lunatic asylum, the wharf, the basement furnace, the barber shop, and the street. There is no choreography. It is almost completely sung. This is one of the more challenging shows to produce; it is also a challenge vocally. There was a cable telecast in 1982 with Angela Lansbury.
Tony Award Winner (Best Musical)

SWEET CHARITY
(1966)

Book by Neil Simon; based on the film, *The Nights of Cabiria* by Frederico Fellini, Tullio Pinelli and Ennio Flaiano   *Music* by Cy Coleman   *Lyrics* by Dorothy Fields   *Published libretto*: Random House, 1966 *Condensation*: None   *Anthology*: None   *Vocal selections*: Notable Music, 1969   *Licensing agent*: Tams-Witmark   *Recording*: Columbia KOS 2900 (original cast)   *Cast*: 22 M; 12 F; extras

This sensational dancing show starred Gwen Verdon as a Times Square dance-hall hostess. The honky-tonk atmosphere should be shown in both the sets and costumes. Charity, our luckless heroine, has several unfortunate encounters with men. All she wants is to be loved for herself. She sings "If My Friends Could See Me Now" when she goes home with her movie star idol. "Big Spender" is performed by all the dance-hall girls. "The Rhythm of Life" is a big number by members of a religious cult. Bob Fosse did the very stylish choreography and the Broadway production had the "gut thrill of big time Broadway" (Martin Gottfried, *Women's Wear Daily*). Shirley MacLaine starred in the 1969 film.

SWEETHEARTS
(1913/1929/1947/1977/1983)

Book by Harry B. Smith and Fred De Gresac   *Music* by Victor Herbert *Lyrics* by Robert B. Smith   *Published libretto*: None   *Condensation*: None   *Anthology*: None   *Piano-vocal score*: Chappell, 1913   *Music publisher*: *The Music of Victor Herbert*. Warner Brothers Music, 1976 *Licensing agent*: Tams-Witmark   *Recording*: RCA LK 1015 (studio cast) *Cast*: 9 M; 9 F; chorus; dancers

Considered to be one of Herbert's most ambitious scores, this is very close to being an opera. (Tams-Witmark has a simplified version suitable for high schools.) The locale is the city of Bruges, Belgium, around the turn of the century. A woman finds an abandoned infant in a tulip garden. The baby grows into a beautiful young lady. Prince Franz, about to ascend the throne of Zilania, meets and falls in love with her, not knowing that she is the long-lost crown princess. Bobby Clark, Gil Lamb, and other comedians have starred in revivals of this operetta. A rollicking wooden shoe episode is one of the show's highlights. The 1938 film with Jeanette MacDonald and Nelson Eddy has a modern setting. In 1983 there was a concert version given at Town Hall in New York City.

TAKE ME ALONG
(1959)

Book by Joseph Stein and Robert Russell; based on the play *Ah, Wilderness* by Eugene O'Neill   *Music and lyrics* by Robert Merrill   *Published libretto*: None   *Condensation*: None   *Anthology*: None   *Vocal selections*: None   *Licensing agent*: Tams-Witmark   *Recording*: RCA LSO 1050 (original cast)   *Cast*: Large mixed cast

The setting is Centerville, Connecticut, around the Fourth of July back in 1906. A brother-in-law who drinks a bit too much visits his relatives for the holiday. Another important character is the 16-year-old son of the family who has his first taste of liquor and women. Based on O'Neill's only comedy, this was described as bright, warm-hearted and likable. There are some rousing numbers, but overall this is a quiet, nostalgic musical. Jackie Gleason and Walter Pidgeon did a "soft-shoe" to the title tune.

TARANTARA! TARANTARA!
(1975)

Book by Ian Taylor   *Music* by Arthur Sullivan   *Lyrics* by W. S. Gilbert   *Published libretto*: Broadway Play Publishing, Inc., 1983   *Condensation*: None   *Anthology*: None   *Vocal selections*: None   *Licensing agent*: Broadway Play Publishing, Inc.   *Recording*: None   *Cast*: 5 M; 3 F; extras

This musical was first presented by the Bristol Old Vic and then moved on to London in 1975. It has not been done in New York. One critic felt that he had learned all he would ever need to know about the Gilbert and Sullivan partnership, but did enjoy the musical numbers from 13 of their famous comic operas, in chronological order. The plot begins with a rehearsal at the Savoy Theatre in 1888 and then goes back in time. This is not a history or anthology of the Savoy operas, nor a comedy or critical examination of their careers, but a bit of all of these elements. There are three main characters (the third being D'Oyly Carte) with the others changing costumes taken from wicker hampers to assume a variety of parts. The music is provided by an on-stage pianist.

TENDERLOIN
(1960/1975)

Book by George Abbott and Jerome Weidman; based on the novel by Samuel Hopkins Adams   *Music* by Jerry Bock   *Lyrics* by Sheldon

Harnick   *Published libretto*: Random House, 1961   *Condensation*:
None   *Anthology*: None   *Vocal selections*: Valando, 1957   *Licensing
agent*: Tams-Witmark   *Recording*: Capitol SWAO 1492 (original cast)
Cast: 15 M; 12 F; chorus

The minister of a New York church in the 1890s decides to close down
the nearby red-light district. He is joined by a young reporter for a
scandal sheet who also warns the crooked politicians who run the
"Tenderloin." Maurice Evans was the minister who sang about "Good
Clean Fun." The naughty ladies sang about "Little Old New York." And
the reporter wins them over with his heart-rending ballad, "Artificial
Flowers." The off-Broadway revival featured a cast of 25, two pianos and a
drum, and simple but appropriate sets.

THEY'RE PLAYING OUR SONG
(1979)

Book by Neil Simon   *Music* by Marvin Hamlisch   *Lyrics* by Carole
Bayer Sager   *Published libretto*: Random House, 1980 ☆ Samuel French,
1980   *Condensation*: None   *Anthology*: None   *Vocal selections*:
Chappell, 1979   *Licensing agent*: Samuel French   *Recording*:
Casablanca NBLP 7141 (original cast)   *Cast*: 1 M; 1 F; back-up group of 6,
1 offstage voice

He is an established pop composer. She is younger and an aspiring
lyricist. As they work together, they fall in love. Can an older man open
himself to a younger woman? These two are backed up by their "voices"
or alter egos that appear in costumes appropriate to the plot situation.
The critics all liked Lucie Arnaz—a "kook" from 18th Street wearing
costumes left over from various shows, and Robert Klein—a neurotic,
demanding egomanic. The show, like the music, is lively and modern.
The two leads should have both talent and charm.

THIRTEEN DAUGHTERS
(1961)

Book, music and lyrics by Eaton Magoon, Jr.; additional book material by
Leon Tokatyan   *Published libretto*: None   *Condensation*: None
Anthology: None   *Vocal selections*: None   *Licensing agent*: Music
Theatre International   *Recording*: Mahalo M 3003 (Hawaiian original cast)
Cast: Large mixed cast

The action takes place in Hawaii in the late nineteenth century. The
composer of this musical was born and raised in Hawaii where this show
was first presented. Don Ameche and Sylvia Syms starred in the Broad-

way production. In the plot, a young Chinese merchant marries a Hawaiian Princess. The natives resent him as a foreigner, and predict that he will have 13 daughters, but no sons. Described as a lush and ornate musical with energetic, rousing dances, this provides the opportunity for Polynesian atmosphere and the hula. The critic for the *New York Daily News* described the music as having "more of Hawaii than Tin Pan Alley—which is high praise!" In New York on opening night, the orchestra conductor sported a lei around his neck.

THREE MUSKETEERS
(1928/1975)

Book by William Anthony McGuire; adapted from the novel by Alexandre Dumas   *Music* by Rudolf Friml   *Lyrics* by P. G. Wodehouse and Clifford Grey   *Published libretto*: None   *Condensation*: None *Anthology*: None   *Piano-vocal score*: Chappell, 1932 ✩ Harms, 1932 *Licensing agent*: Tams-Witmark   *Recording*: Monmouth Evergreen MES 7050 (1930 London cast)   *Cast*: Large mixed cast

A review of the original Ziegfeld production indicates that this musical retains most of the original Dumas plot. Naturally it was a lavish production with a good, rambunctious score. Dennis King and Vivienne Segal were the stars. There are 12 scenes with locales including the garden of the Tuilleries, Cardinal Richelieu's chambers, and the Duke of Buckingham's palace in England. The score does not contain any Friml standards, although some people may recognize "Ma Belle." In addition to the ornate fifteenth-century court costumes, the production should include a certain amount of on-stage sword play.

THREE WISHES FOR JAMIE
(1952)

Book by Charles O'Neal and Abe Burrows; based on the novel by Charles O'Neal   *Music and lyrics* by Ralph Blane   *Published libretto*: None *Condensation*: None   *Anthology*: None   *Vocal selections*: None *Licensing agent*: Samuel French   *Recording*: Capitol S 317 (original cast) *Cast*: 12 M (1 boy); 5 F; extras

This musical version of a Christopher Award novel concerns Jamie McRuin who is granted three wishes. The first is to travel, the second is to marry the girl of his dreams, and the third is to have a son who can speak the old Gaelic tongue. So he leaves Ireland and turns up at a horse traders' camp in Georgia in 1896. The Broadway production was applauded for its colorful settings and handsome costumes. The "Trottin' to the Fair" number was one of the highlights of the production, being both vigorous and imaginative. There is also a comic ballet depicting the agony of expectant fatherhood. The production has plenty of Irish wit and humor.

THE THREEPENNY OPERA
(1933/1955/1972/1976)

Book by Bertolt Brecht; English adaptation of book and lyrics by Marc Blitzstein; based on *The Beggar's Opera* by John Gay   *Music* by Kurt Weill   *Published libretto*: Vintage Books, 1976   *Condensation: The Best Plays of 1975–1976*. Otis L. Guernsey, Jr., ed. Dodd, Mead, 1976 ☆ *American Musicals: Weill*. Time-Life, 1982   *Anthology*: Brecht, Bertolt. *Collected Plays*, vol. 2. Vintage, 1977   *Piano-vocal score*: Universal Edition (Wein), 1928 (German)   *Vocal selections*: Universal Edition (Wein), 1928 (German)   *Licensing agent*: Tams-Witmark (Marc Blitzstein translation)   *Recordings*: MGM S 3121 OC, Time-Life STL AM10 (Marc Blitzstein translation)   *Cast*: Large mixed cast

Revived many times and in different translations, this particular version was first presented off-Broadway in 1955 with Lotte Lenya, and it was a sensation. The original premiere was in Berlin in 1928 and the first Broadway production was in 1933. The setting is London's Soho before and during the coronation of Queen Victoria. The master criminal Macheath marries Polly Peachum, and his old flame, Jenny, turns him in to the police. The cast is largely made up of criminals, beggars and tarts. Brecht is interested in exposing corrupt officials of a sad and vicious society. But the Kurt Weill score is actually what has made this show a classic. Everyone knows the Threepenny Opera theme, "Mack the Knife."

A THURBER CARNIVAL
(1960/1965/1984)

Book by James Thurber   *Music* by Don Elliott   *Published libretto*: Samuel French, 1962   *Condensation: The Best Plays of 1959–1960*. Louis Kronenberger, ed. Dodd, Mead, 1960   *Anthology*: None   *Music selections*: None   *Licensing agent*: Samuel French   *Recording*: Columbia CSP CKOS 2024 (original cast)   *Cast*: 5 M; 4 F (more if desired)

This is a comedy-revue which Samuel French describes as "for those with no musical talent." There is incidental "sweet jazz" music played by a quartet. It supplies accompaniment, commentary and transition between sketches. The show includes some light dancing but no songs. It is made up of skits, monologues and brief episodes taken from Thurber's writings. They include "The Unicorn in the Garden," "The Secret Life of Walter Mitty," and "The Last Flower." The billboard-type sets were called cartoons.

Tony Award Winner (Special Award)

TIMBUKTU!
(1978)

Book by Luther Davis; based on the musical *Kismet* by Charles Lederer and Luther Davis; from the play by Edward Knoblock   *Music and lyrics* by Robert Wright and George Forrest; from themes of Alexander Borodin and African folk music   *Published libretto*: None   *Condensation*: None   *Anthology*: None   *Vocal selections*: Blackwood Music, 1978   *Licensing agent*: Music Theatre International   *Recording*: None   *Cast*: Large mixed cast

Once upon a time in the 1950s the team of Wright and Forrest took some themes from Borodin and turned an old play into a smash musical called *Kismet*. It was an Arabian adventure. Now it has been re-set in Africa in the fourteenth century for an all-black cast. The plot is basically the same. A beggar-poet's beautiful daughter meets the Prince and they fall in love. This is an opportunity for exotic costuming, ethnic-based choreography, big voices (Melba Moore and Eartha Kitt starred on Broadway), and "Baubles, Bangles and Beads." The big song hit is "Stranger in Paradise."

TINTYPES
(1980)

Conceived by Mary Kyte, with Mel Marvin and Gary Pearle   *Published libretto*: None   *Condensation*: None   *Anthology*: None   *Vocal selections*: None   *Licensing agent*: Music Theatre International   *Recording*: DRG S2L 5196 (original cast)   *Cast*: 2 M; 3 F

This revue is comprised of various character types who span the period from 1890 to 1920, showing an image of American history through approximately 50 songs of the period. The songs are compartmentalized into such sections as "Arrivals," "Rich and Poor," and "Vaudeville," and include such songs as "Yankee Doodle Boy" and "Bill Bailey, Won't You Please Come Home?" On Broadway this was performed on a stage that was almost bare, with just a few props and some glorious costumes. Accompaniment was provided by an on-stage upright piano. The show has some dialogue, but no book or plot. The various characters include a Jewish immigrant, a black maid, a Broadway star, a U.S. President and a poor but honest working girl. There was a television version in 1983.

TIP-TOES
(1925/1979)

Book by Guy Bolton and Fred Thompson   *Music* by George Gershwin
Lyrics by Ira Gershwin   *Published libretto*: None   *Condensation*: None
Anthology: None   *Vocal selections*: None   *Licensing agent*:
Tams-Witmark   *Recording*: Monmouth-Evergreen 7052E (London original
cast)   *Cast*: 13 M; 8 F

"When Do We Dance?" they sing at the Surf Club in Palm Beach, Florida,
in those golden musical comedy days of the 1920s. Other settings include
the deck of Steve's yacht and the lobby of the Everglades Inn. The Three
Kayes are in Florida for a dancing engagement. Tip-Toes falls in love with
a millionaire and pretends to be of high position herself. The Goodspeed
Opera revival in Brooklyn was noted for its choreography, with tap,
"soft-shoe," Charleston and Peabody routines. There are also some very
corny routines done by the other two Kayes. But the wonderful Gershwin
score makes up for everything—"These Charming People," "Looking for
a Boy" and "Sweet and Low Down" are just a few other gems. There was a
silent film version in 1928!

TOM SAWYER
(1956 TV musical adapted for the stage)

Book adapted by Edward Reveaux, Richard H. Berger and Peter Gurney;
based on the novel by Mark Twain.   *Music and lyrics* by Frank Luther
Published libretto: None   *Condensation*: None   *Anthology*: None
Vocal selections: None   *Licensing agent*: Music Theatre International
Recording: Decca DL 8432 (original TV cast)   *Cast*: Large mixed cast (the
leads should be teenagers)

This version of the classic tale of Missouri teenagers in the nineteenth
century follows the famous novel closely in spirit and outline. Some
reviews felt that the TV production was almost a folk opera. An off-stage
chorus carried the story along with a narrative ballad. In the stage
version, which has been presented by the St. Louis Municipal Opera and
other stock theaters but not in New York, there are 18 songs and 22
musical sequences, including a ballet.

TOP BANANA
(1951)

Book by Hy Kraft   *Music and lyrics* by Johnny Mercer   *Published
libretto*: None   *Condensation*: None   *Anthology*: None   *Vocal*

selections: None   *Licensing agent*: Tams-Witmark   *Recording*: Capitol S
308 (original cast)   *Cast*: Large mixed cast

The plot of this musical features a burlesque comic who has a popular TV show, suggesting perhaps Milton Berle back in the early 1950s. He runs into problems with his soap-opera sponsor when he inadvertently marries off the leading lady to his male singer. There was a recent production of this show in Las Vegas. The show should have some pretty girls for the "Burlesk Kuties," and comics who can handle the campy routines. Your "top banana" will need a brash, hearty and forceful style, and good timing. There are also some secondary roles for good singers. There was a 1954 film featuring Phil Silvers and most of the original cast.

TREEMONISHA
(1975)

Lyrics and music by Scott Joplin   *Published libretto*: see *Recording*
Condensation: None   *Anthology*: None   *Vocal selections*: Chappell,
1975   *Licensing agent*: Dramatic   *Recording*: Deutsche Grammophon
2707 083 (Houston Grand Opera Production); includes libretto   *Cast*:
8 M; 3 F; chorus

Treemonisha is found abandoned under a tree just after the Civil War, and she is adopted by a former slave couple. She grows up and tries to educate her people. There is a "conjur" man who thrives on their superstitions, and opposes her. Described as authentic musical Americana, this all-black story set on an Arkansas plantation is sung, rather than spoken. It is called an opera, and is much more than just ragtime music. Written in 1907, it is a mixture of nineteenth-century music hall and operetta. There is some exciting dancing, including a rousing cakewalk.

TRICKS
(1973)

Book by Jon Jory; based on a one-act play by Moliere   *Music* by Jerry
Blatt   *Lyrics* by Lonnie Burstein   *Published libretto*: Samuel French,
1971   *Condensation*: None   *Anthology*: None   *Vocal selections*:
Chappell, 1972   *Licensing agent*: Samuel French   *Recording*: None
Cast: 6 M; 3 F; 4 musicians; 3 dancers

The action of this story is set in and around Venice during the Renaissance, and the style is a cross between commedia dell'arte and vaudeville. There is juggling, puppetry, acrobatic tumbling, and slapstick. The plot concerns the servant Scapino, a twin set of lovers, and two masters being outwitted. The Broadway costumes were described as bright and vivid. The rock score includes some pop-soul. This production, which came to Broadway by way of regional theater, was designed for a small cast, limited facilities, and a small budget.

TRIXIE TRUE   TEEN DETECTIVE
(1980)

Book, music and lyrics by Kelly Hamilton   *Published libretto*: Samuel French, 1981   *Condensation*: None   *Anthology*: None   *Vocal selections*: None   *Licensing agent*: Samuel French   *Recording*: None   *Cast*: 4 M; 4 F

Two different kinds of entertainment are spoofed in this off-Broadway musical. First of all, there is the "Nancy Drew" type juvenile mystery, and secondly, a far more sophisticated take-off on the style of Hollywood films in the 1940s. The action switches from the publishing offices to a mythical town, as the author of the stories dreams up Trixie's adventures. The plot of "The Secret of the Tapping Shoes" is played out for us, with some doubling up of the cast. The author wants to "kill off" Trixie, so she has him, as well as the Nazis to worry about! The sets may be simply suggested, and music can be provided by a quartet alongside the stage.

THE TRUTH ABOUT CINDERELLA
(1974)

Book by June Walker Rogers; based on *The Cinderella Complex* by Sir Osbert Sitwell   *Music* by Charles Strouse   *Lyrics* by David Rogers   *Published libretto*: Dramatic, 1974   *Condensation*: None   *Anthology*: None   *Vocal selections*: None   *Licensing agent*: Dramatic   *Recording*: None   *Cast*: 9 M; 14 F

Broadway's Charles Strouse occasionally strays into the area of children's theater. He has also composed *Nightingale* for a large cast of children and teenagers. *The Truth about Cinderella* is a family show designed for any age group. The time is the present and the setting is Wilfer Hall in England. The sets are simple and costumes are optional. There are easy-to-play orchestrations. The score is described as a "today sound in rocking, rollicking rhythms." The plot is a reverse of the usual—the stepmother and sisters are desperately trying to drag Cinderella away from her beloved brooms and brushes to the ball!

2 × 5
(1976)

Music by John Kander   *Lyrics* by Fred Ebb   *Published libretto*: None
Condensation: None   *Anthology*: None   *Vocal selections*: None
Licensing agent: Samuel French   *Recording*: None (see individual albums
of titles below)   *Cast*: 2 M; 3 F (1 pianist)

Approximately 30 songs from the shows of Kander and Ebb have been
put together in a cabaret-style revue that was originally presented off-
Broadway in Greenwich Village. Some of the things the critics liked
include the use of flashlights in the dark, lighting up each face from
below for the "Money" song from *Cabaret*; the funny "Class" duet from
Chicago; all the numbers from *Flora the Red Menace*; and the movie
song, "New York, New York." The set was simply a pair of stairs, a few
chairs and tables, and some portable props. These tuneful and intelligent
songs are about the best Broadway has to offer. Five very talented
performers are needed.

TWO BY TWO
(1970)

Book by Peter Stone; based on *The Flowering Peach* by Clifford Odets
Music by Richard Rodgers   *Lyrics* by Martin Charnin   *Published
libretto*: None   *Condensation*: None   *Anthology*: None
Piano-vocal score: Williamson Music, 1971   *Vocal selections*: Williamson
Music, 1970   *Licensing agent*: Rodgers and Hammerstein Music Library
Recording: Columbia S 30338 (original cast)   *Cast*: 4 M; 4 F

The time is before, during and after the biblical Flood. The locales are in
and around Noah's home, the Ark, and atop Mt. Ararat. The Broadway sets
were simple, with projections on a white backdrop. This is a humorous
telling of the biblical story, with "clean dirty jokes and cautiously blas-
phemous God gags" (John Simon, *New York Magazine*). Noah is an old
sot with a dismal wife and three dismal sons. Danny Kaye played Noah,
besieged with dreary domestic problems until the Flood (which occurs
during the intermission). The attractive Richard Rodgers score has not
yet produced any standards. There is no dancing or chorus.

TWO GENTLEMEN OF VERONA
(1971)

Book adapted by John Guare and Mel Shapiro; based on the play by William Shakespeare   *Music* by Galt MacDermot   *Lyrics* by John Guare   *Published libretto*: Holt, 1973   *Condensation*: None   *Anthology*: *Great Rock Musicals*. Stanley Richards, ed. Stein and Day, 1979   *Piano-vocal score*: Chappell, 1973   *Vocal selections*: Chappell, 1972   *Licensing agent*: Tams-Witmark   *Recording*: ABC BCSY 1001 (original cast)   *Cast*: 10 M; 3 F; extras

This popular rock show started off in New York's Central Park as part of the Shakespeare Festival, and then moved to Broadway for a successful run of over 600 performances. It is a love story—Valentine loves Silvia (Who is Silvia? The daughter of the Duke of Milan!). His friend Proteus who loved Julia, a local girl, decides to also love Silvia. This story was considerably modernized, with ethnic actors in the leads. The dialogue is a mixture of Shakespeare and modern passages. The score was described by Julius Novick of the *Village Voice* as "soft-rock-pop-quasi-Latin-semi-soul" and is by the composer of *Hair*. The scenery was "scaffoldy" and costuming "hippie-Renaissance" (see record album photos). The finale features soap bubbles, frisbies, and yoyos.
Tony Award Winner (Best Musical)

THE UNSINKABLE MOLLY BROWN
(1960)

Book by Richard Morris   *Music and lyrics* by Meredith Willson   *Published libretto*: Putnam, 1961 ☆ *Theatre Arts* (magazine) February 1963   *Condensation*: None   *Anthology*: None   *Piano-vocal score*: Frank Music, 1962   *Vocal selections*: Frank Music, 1964   *Licensing agent*: Music Theatre International   *Recording*: Capitol SW 2152 (original cast)   *Cast*: Large mixed cast

Turn-of-the-century Denver and the Rocky Mountain area is the setting for this musical, although Europe, and even the sinking of the Titanic get into the act. Molly the "hillbilly heroine" marries into unexpected wealth and is determined to crash society. There is a bouncy score and opportunities for several energetic dance numbers. Costuming style is both "back hills" and "high society." This big Broadway musical was a triumph for Tammy Grimes, and it was filmed in 1964 with Debbie Reynolds.

UNSUNG COLE
(1977)

Conceived and arranged by Norman L. Berman   *Music and lyrics* by
Cole Porter   *Published libretto*: Samuel French, 1981   *Condensation*:
None   *Anthology*: None   *Music publisher*: *Music and Lyrics by Cole
Porter*. 2 vols. Chappell, 1972–1975   *Licensing agent*: Samuel French
Recording: None   *Cast*: 2 M; 3 F

The seldom-heard songs of Cole Porter are featured in this cabaret-style
revue. This was performed off-Broadway in a simple but elegant setting
with twin pianos for accompaniment. Called a musical entertainment,
there is no plot and only a bit of spoken dialogue. Some of the songs are
from shows like *Mexican Hayride* while others were dropped from such
shows as *Kiss Me, Kate*. Scattered throughout the evening are the risqué
verses from "Nobody's Chasing Me Now" from the show *Out of This
World*. There are familiar songs, as well, and "Friendship" makes a happy
finale.

THE UTTER GLORY OF MORRISSEY HALL
(1979)

Book by Clark Gesner and Nagle Jackson   *Music and lyrics* by Clark
Gesner   *Published libretto*: Samuel French, 1982   *Condensation*: None
Anthology: None   *Vocal selections*: None   *Licensing agent*: Samuel
French   *Recording*: Original Cast OC 7918 (original cast)   *Cast*: 4 M;
18 F (includes 12 schoolgirls)

The setting is a girl's school somewhere in the English countryside. The
atmosphere is reminiscent of the St. Trinian movies. There are all sorts of
problems that the headmistress must resolve; the climax is an all-out war
between the students, using arrows, bombs, and even a cannon! The set is
a large Victorian-Gothic mansion converted into a school; it includes
offices, closets, corridors, and two upstairs rooms. The score has a hint of
Gilbert and Sullivan. Most of the adults are a bit off balance, and the girls
are malevolent!

THE VAGABOND KING
(1925/1943/1961/1979)

Book and lyrics by Brian Hooker and W. H. Post; based on *If I Were a King*
by Justin Huntley McCarthy   *Music* by Rudolf Friml   *Published libretto*:
Samuel French, 1929, 1956   *Condensation*: None   *Anthology*: None

Piano-vocal score: Famous Music, 1926   *Licensing agent*: Tams-Witmark
(for professional productions) ☆ Samuel French (for amateur productions)
Recordings: Monmouth-Evergreen MES 7050 (London original cast) ☆
Reader's Digest RD 40-N8 (studio cast—*Treasury of Great Operettas*, Record
8) *Cast*: 18 M; 11 F; chorus

Set in fifteenth-century France, this is the tale of a poet-thief and his
adventures with royalty, prostitutes with hearts of gold, and comedians.
The hero assumes the kingship of France for a day, and repels a Burgun-
dian invasion. This popular show has had several lavish Broadway productions, and has also been produced around the country and in the
British Isles. There have also been numerous simple versions, with
unpretentious costumes and limited props. It is described as a colorful,
exciting family entertainment with ample opportunity for swordplay.
The famous score includes "Only a Rose," "Love Me Tonight," and "Some
Day." It was filmed in 1930 and again in 1956.

VARIETY OBIT
(1973)

Book by Ron Whyte   *Music* by Mel Marvin   *Lyrics* by Ron Whyte and
Bob Satuloff   *Published libretto*: Samuel French, 1973   *Condensation*:
None   *Anthology*: None   *Vocal selections*: None   *Licensing agent*:
Samuel French   *Recording*: None   *Cast*: 2 M; 1 F

The title of this one-act musical refers to the obituaries of show biz
personalities that appear in *Variety*. It begins with a blow up of the
Variety obit of Danny Jefferson, the last member of an obscure show
business family. We then have the family history done in song and dance.
There are just two performers and a narrator. It is simply staged with a
piano and drum. The off-Broadway production used a number of slide
projections.

VERY GOOD EDDIE
(1915/1975)

Book by Guy Bolton; based on the farce by Phillip Bartholomae   *Music*
by Jerome Kern   *Lyrics* by Schuyler Greene   *Published libretto*: None
Condensation: American Musicals: Kern. Time-Life, 1981   *Anthology*:
None   *Piano-vocal score*: Harms, 1915   *Licensing agent*: Tams-
Witmark   *Recordings*: DRG 6100, Time-Life STL-AM03 (1975 cast)
Cast: 11 M; 7 F

The plot of this musical concerns two honeymooning couples who take a boat to Poughkeepsie, and are separated. The right bride ends up with the wrong groom at Honeymoon Inn. The time is circa 1915. This is another Kern "Princess" musical that was revived and brought to Broadway by the Goodspeed Opera House. The first act is aboard the Hudson River boat and the second act is in the lobby of the hotel. The critics found it dated and innocent. The score of 18 songs is tuneful, but will probably not be familiar to the audience. Lively choreography and simple period costumes and sets will make this a popular, nostalgic attraction.

VIA GALACTICA
(1972)

Book by Christopher Gore and Judith Ross   *Music* by Galt MacDermot
Lyrics by Christopher Gore   *Published libretto*: None   *Condensation*:
None   *Anthology*: None   *Vocal selections*: None   *Licensing agent*:
Samuel French   *Recording*: None   *Cast*: 16 M; 11 F; 2 children

Described as a space age musical, this story is set 1000 years in the future. Most Earthlings are without feeling—they do not love or hate, and commit suicide at the age of 55. But there is one tiny outpost, a small asteroid called Ithaca, made up of some nonconformists. The production in New York was extremely elaborate, with trampolines used to simulate weightlessness, a flying garbage truck, a lot of moving scenery, and blinking lights. The almost non-stop score (all the lines are sung) was described by critics as agreeable and pleasant. A note to the make-up department: all Earthlings have blue skin!

WALKING HAPPY
(1966/1976)

Book by Roger O. Hirson and Kitti Frings; based on the play *Hobson's Choice* by Harold Brighouse   *Music* by James van Heusen   *Lyrics* by Sammy Cahn   *Published libretto*: Samuel French, 1967   *Condensation*: None   *Anthology*: None   *Vocal selections*: Shapiro, Bernstein, 1966 *Licensing agent*: Samuel French   *Recording*: Capitol SVAS 2631 (original cast)   *Cast*: 14 M; 7 F

Hobson is a widowed merchant with three daughters. The original title stems from his choice and their choices for their husbands. Maggie, the oldest, is set on Will Mossop, a bootmaker. He was played on Broadway by the British comedian, Norman Wisdom. This is set in the North

Country of England in the 1870s, so there is a music-hall flavor to the numbers. There was an excellent clog dance, which much later was recreated on Broadway by the American Dance Machine. The Broadway production was praised for its ingenious motor-driven scenery of skyline, chimney pots, and neighborhood pubs. A family show.

WEST SIDE STORY
(1957/1964/1968/1982)

Book by Arthur Laurents; based on a conception by Jerome Robbins *Music* by Leonard Bernstein   *Lyrics* by Stephen Sondheim   *Published libretto*: Random House, 1958 ☆ *Theatre Arts* (magazine) October 1959 *Condensation: Broadway's Best, 1958*. John Chapman, ed. Doubleday, 1958 ☆ *American Musicals: Bernstein*. Time-Life, 1983   *Anthology: Ten Great Musicals of the American Stage*. Stanley Richards, ed. Chilton, 1973 *Piano-vocal score*: Schirmer and Chappell, 1959   *Vocal selections*: Schirmer and Chappell, 1957   *Licensing agent*: Music Theatre International   *Recordings*: Columbia JS 32603, Time-Life STL-AM15 (original cast)   *Cast*: Large mixed cast

This famous musical concerns rival teenage gangs in New York City in the late 1950s. It is a retelling of the *Romeo and Juliet* story with a tragic love affair between Tony and Maria. By now it has become a classic landmark of the American musical theater. The Bernstein score includes the familiar "Tonight," "Maria," and "Something's Coming." Both the stage and the 1961 film versions are noted for their vigorous and athletic choreography. The settings are back streets, alleys, and fire escapes of lower-class Manhattan white and Puerto Rican neighborhoods. This is a great singing show, and a great dancing show.

WHAT MAKES SAMMY RUN?
(1964)

Book by Budd and Stuart Schulberg; based on the novel by Budd Schulberg *Music and lyrics* by Ervin Drake   *Published libretto*: Random House, 1965 *Condensation*: None   *Anthology*: None   *Vocal selections*: Harms, 1964 *Licensing agent*: Tams-Witmark   *Recording*: Columbia COS 2440 (original cast)   *Cast*: Large mixed cast

This is a big musical set in Hollywood and New York in the 1930s. In addition to Grauman's Chinese Theater, studios and offices, there are biblical and South Sea production numbers (for films being made), elegant clothes, and energetic choreography. Sammy is a fast-talking

Lower East Side kid who becomes a big Hollywood producer after taking advantage of almost everybody along the way. Since Schulberg grew up in Hollywood, there may be more fact than fiction to this. Steve Lawrence was very successful in his Broadway debut as Sammy. "A Room without Windows" is a popular hit from the score.

WHAT'S A NICE COUNTRY LIKE YOU DOING IN A STATE LIKE THIS?
(1973)

Music by Cary Hoffman; based on an original concept by Ira Gasman, Cary Hoffman and Bernie Travis   *Lyrics* by Ira Gasman   *Published libretto*: Samuel French, 1975   *Condensation*: None   *Anthology*: None   *Vocal selections*: None   *Licensing agent*: Samuel French   *Recordings*: RMSC 747003 (Canadian cast) ☆ Galaxy GAL 6004 (London original cast)   *Cast*: 3 M; 2 F

"It's a Political-Satirical Revue" is the opening number in this show. There are no sketches—just songs or song scenes. This was called "soft-core" political satire rather than real political cabaret. Some of the subjects covered include liberals, women's liberation, political scandal, life in New York, and changing sex styles. This is simple to stage, but requires talented performers.

WHERE'S CHARLEY?
(1948/1951/1966/1974)

Book by George Abbott; based on *Charley's Aunt* by Brandon Thomas   *Music and lyrics* by Frank Loesser   *Published libretto*: None   *Condensation*: None   *Anthology*: None   *Music publisher*: *The Frank Loesser Songbook*. Simon and Schuster, 1971   *Licensing agent*: Music Theatre International   *Recording*: Monmouth-Evergreen ME 5-7029 (London original cast)   *Cast*: Large mixed cast

"Once in Love with Amy" is the famous "soft-shoe" number performed on Broadway (and the 1952 film version) by Ray Bolger. The plot of this musical is much the same as the famous play. A young Oxford student is forced to masquerade as his Aunt from Brazil and various complications develop. This farce is set in Victorian England. This was performed in-the-round at New York's Circle in the Square. Other song hits from the score include "My Darling, My Darling" and "Lovelier Than Ever." *Charley's Aunt* is a family show which has been a success in any revival or reincarnation.

WHISPERS ON THE WIND
(1970/1975)

Book and lyrics by John B. Kuntz   *Music* by Lor Crane   *Published libretto*: Samuel French, 1971   *Condensation*: None   *Anthology*: None   *Vocal selections*: None   *Licensing agent*: Samuel French   *Recording*: None   *Cast*: 3 M; 2 F

This off-Broadway musical is about growing up, leaving home, and falling in love in the big city. The time is the present and the city is New York. The costumes were described as modish and the setting as handsome ramps and screens. The music was called "plastic rock" and there is very little dancing. The cast of five assume a variety of different roles.

WHITE HORSE INN
(1936)

Book by Hans Mueller   *Music* by Ralph Benatzky   *Lyrics* by Robert Gilbert   *Published libretto*: Samuel French (London), 1957   *Condensation*: None   *Anthology*: None   *Piano-vocal score*: Chappell, 1931   *Licensing agent*: Samuel French   *Recordings*: Angel S 35815 (English studio cast) ☆ Angel SZBX 3897 (German studio cast)   *Cast*: 16 M; 6 F; chorus

There really is a "White Horse Inn" in Austria, and this lavish spectacle set there began in Europe and has since been a popular favorite around the world. New York first saw it at Rockefeller Center in 1936 with Kitty Carlisle. There is very little to the plot. A headwaiter is in love with the lady who operates the inn. There are Tyrolean dancers, mountain crags, lakes, village streets, and wine gardens. The version in New York utilized three revolving stages, numerous settings, and hundreds of performers. In 1954 there was a production on ice at Empress Hall in London. There was also a German language film version in 1956.

WHOOPEE
(1928/1979)

Book by William Anthony McGuire; based on *The Nervous Wreck* by Owen Davis   *Music* by Walter Donaldson   *Lyrics* by Gus Kahn   *Published libretto*: None   *Condensation*: None   *Anthology*: None   *Vocal selections*: Macmillan, 1979   *Licensing agent*: Tams-Witmark   *Recording*: Smithsonian R 012 (original cast recordings)   *Cast*: Large mixed cast

Eddie Cantor starred for Ziegfeld and then made the film version for Goldwyn in 1930. "Makin' Whoopee!" became his theme song. A hypochondriac vacationer at a dude ranch becomes involved with cowboys and Indians and a lovelorn ingenue named Sally. The Goodspeed Opera revived this show and brought it back to Broadway in 1979. "Love Me or Leave Me" was in the original and "Yes Sir, That's My Baby" was added to the revival. There are cardboard auto chases, tap-dancing Indians, and a canoe ride. This is an old-fashioned musical that should be done in period and style.

WILDCAT
(1960)

Book by N. Richard Nash   *Music* by Cy Coleman   *Lyrics* by Carolyn Leigh   *Published libretto*: None   *Condensation*: None   *Anthology*: None   *Piano-vocal score*: Morris, 1964   *Licensing agent*: Tams-Witmark   *Recording*: RCA LSO 1060 (original cast)   *Cast*: 14 M; 5 F; chorus

In 1912, an oil prospector arrives at a southwestern border town called Centavo City, where she hopes to strike it rich to provide for her lame sister. Romance blossoms with a drilling gang foreman. There is also a romantic subplot between the lame sister and a young Mexican. Lucille Ball was "Wildcat Jackson" and the choreography was by Michael Kidd. Most critics liked the sombrero dance and the clowning of Ball. "Hey, Look Me Over!" is Wildcat's opening number. A working rig is assembled onstage during the "Corduroy Road" number.

WISH YOU WERE HERE
(1952)

Book by Arthur Kober and Joshua Logan; based on the play *Having Wonderful Time* by Arthur Kober   *Music and lyrics* by Harold Rome   *Published libretto*: None   *Condensation*: *Theatre '53*. John Chapman, ed. Random House, 1953   *Anthology*: None   *Piano-vocal score*: Chappell, 1955   *Licensing agent*: Music Theatre International   *Recordings*: STET DS (London original cast) ✭ RCA LSO 1108(e) (original cast)   *Cast*: Large mixed cast

Fun, frolic, and romance are the main attractions at Camp Kare-Free in the Catskills. Although the original play was set in the 1930s, this musical version has been updated. The plot concerns a young secretary spending her two weeks' vacation in the pursuit of romance. Among other activities there is a beauty contest alongside the swimming pool. The twenty-foot pool used in the New York production generated a lot of publicity, as did the athletic cast, practicing basketball and swimming. The title song was very popular back in the 1950s.

THE WIZ
(1975)

Book by William F. Brown; based on The Wonderful Wizard of Oz by L. Frank Baum   Music and lyrics by Charlie Smalls   Published libretto: Samuel French, 1979   Condensation: None   Anthology: Great Rock Musicals. Stanley Richards, ed. Stein and Day, 1979   Vocal selections: Fox Fan-Fare, 1975 ☆ Columbia Pictures Publications, 1975   Licensing agent: Samuel French   Recording: Atlantic SD 18137 (original cast)   Cast: 11 principals; singers; dancers

The music is rock, soul, gospel, and rhythm and blues in this black spoof of The Wizard of Oz. Called flamboyant and imaginative the Broadway production was noted for its stylish design and kaleidoscopic dances. The elaborate costumes include blue mushroom-cap munchkins and funky monkeys. A dog is needed for "Toto." "Ease on down the Road" was a popular song from the all-new score. There was a film version in 1978 with Diana Ross.
Tony Award Winner (Best Musical)

THE WIZARD OF OZ
(1939 film adapted for the stage)

Adaptation by Frank Gabrielson; from the MGM film and the stories by L. Frank Baum   Music by Harold Arlen   Lyrics by E. Y. Harburg   Published libretto: None   Condensation: None   Anthology: None   Vocal selections: L. Feist, 1968 (film)   Licensing agent: Tams-Witmark   Recording: MGM E 3996 ST (film sound track)   Cast: Large mixed cast

There have been numerous stage versions of this popular fantasy, but none probably as popular as the Judy Garland film version which is shown regularly on television. This is a stage adaptation of that film with all the famous songs, including "We're Off to See the Wizard," "Ding Dong the Witch Is Dead," and (naturally) "Over the Rainbow." This is billed as suitable for youngsters from 6 to 60! Young people can be cast as munchkins. Costuming of the lion, the scarecrow and the tin woodman will be a challenge. A dog is needed to play "Toto."

WONDERFUL TOWN
(1953/1963/1967/1977)

Book by Joseph Fields and Jerome Chodorov; based on the play *My Sister Eileen* by Joseph Fields and Jerome Chodorov, and the stories of Ruth McKenney   *Music* by Leonard Bernstein   *Lyrics* by Betty Comden and Adolph Green   *Published libretto*: Random House, 1953   *Condensation: The Best Plays of 1952–1953*. Louis Kronenberger, ed. Dodd, Mead, 1953 ☆ *Theatre '53*. John Chapman, ed. Random House, 1953 ☆ *American Musicals: Bernstein*. Time-Life, 1983   *Anthology: Great Musicals of the American Theatre*, vol. 2. Stanley Richards, ed. Chilton, 1976 ☆ *Comden and Green on Broadway*. Drama Book Specialists, 1981   *Vocal selections*: Chappell, 1953   *Licensing agent*: Tams-Witmark   *Recordings*: MCA 2050E, Time-Life STL-AM15 (original cast)   *Cast*: Large mixed cast

Two sisters from Ohio arrive in New York's Greenwich Village in the late 1930s hoping to make their fortunes. Ruth wants to write, and her sister Eileen wants to be an actress. Their adventures have been told several times, including this musical version that starred Rosalind Russell. Some hit numbers from the score include "It's Love" and "One Hundred Easy Ways." A dancing highlight is the famous conga number with some Brazilian sailors.
Tony Award Winner (Best Musical)

WORKING
(1978)

Adapted by Stephen Schwartz and Nina Faso; from the book by Studs Terkel   *Songs* by Craig Carnelia, Micki Grant, Mary Rodgers, Susan Birkenhead, Stephen Schwartz and James Taylor   *Published libretto*: None   *Condensation*: None   *Anthology*: None   *Vocal selections*: None   *Licensing agent*: Music Theatre International   *Recording*: Columbia JS 35411 (original cast)   *Cast*: 10 M; 7 F

This musical was described as being concerned with the longings and frustrations of the working class. The set can be a simple scaffold with the cast moving in and out as they portray many different workers—from cleaning women to firemen to parking lot attendants. There is no plot or story line, but just the thematic link. Taken from actual interviews, this show tells you a lot about America. There are songs and sketches and some dancing. The Broadway production was elaborate, with sliding floor panels, projections, and elevators. There was a television adaptation in 1982.

THE YEARLING
(1965)

Book by Herbert Martin and Lore Noto; based on the novel by Marjorie Kinnan Rawlings   *Music* by Michael Leonard   *Lyrics* by Herbert Martin   *Published libretto*: Dramatic, 1973   *Condensation*: None   *Anthology*: None   *Vocal selections*: Morris, 1966   *Licensing agent*: Dramatic   *Recording*: None   *Cast*: 14 M; 8 F; extras

Anyone who has read the novel will be concerned about the live deer. While the licensing agent assures would-be producers that the deer need not appear, one was used in the Broadway production (along with a dog and a raccoon). The plot concerns a Florida backwoods boy who brings home a fawn. In the 1946 non-musical film, Gregory Peck and Jane Wyman played his parents. The music reminded some of Aaron Copeland's folk themes. There are Christmas festivities and a bit of country dancing. This is a family show that children will particularly enjoy.

YOU NEVER KNOW
(1938/1973)

Book by Rowland Leigh; based on the play *By Candlelight* by Siegfried Geyer and Karl Farkas   *Music* by Cole Porter and Robert Katscher   *Lyrics* by Cole Porter, Rowland Leigh and Edwin Gilbert   *Published libretto*: Samuel French   *Condensation*: None   *Anthology*: None   *Music publisher*: *Music and Lyrics by Cole Porter*. 2 vols. Chappell, 1972–1975   *Licensing agent*: Samuel French   *Recording*: None   *Cast*: 3 M; 3 F; 1 extra

The time is 1938 and the place is Paris. The plot involves a valet and his master who change positions to fool two young ladies. Of course, the young ladies are maid and mistress who have also changed positions. There are a number of Cole Porter songs which may be familiar, including "At Long Last Love," "What Shall I Do?" and "From Alpha to Omega". Revival productions usually interpolate other Porter songs. The silver and white 1930 set was praised in an off-Broadway revival which included an on-stage pianist.

YOUR OWN THING
(1968)

Book by Donald Driver; based on *Twelfth Night* by William Shakespeare   *Music and lyrics* by Hal Hester and Danny Apolinar   *Published libretto*:

Dell, 1970   *Condensation: The Best Plays of 1967–1968*. Otis L. Guernsey, Jr., ed. Dodd, Mead, 1968   *Anthology: All the World's a Stage*. Lowell Swortzell, ed. Delacorte, 1972 ☆ *Great Rock Musicals*. Stanley Richards, ed. Stein and Day, 1979   *Vocal selections*: National General/Shayne, 1968   *Licensing agent*: Tams-Witmark   *Recording*: RCA LSO 1148 (original cast)   *Cast*: 6 M; 3 F

The Shakespearean love tangle involving Orsino, Viola, Olivia, and Sebastian is re-told here in the rock style of the late 1960s. Illyria is now "fun city" and a discotheque is part of the action. The show is about one and one-half hours long, and is performed without intermission. Called "a show about crazy music and clothes and lightshows" the original off-Broadway production used 14 projectors, films, slides, and tapes to create a multimedia experience. The actual voices of well-known personalities were used, with references to Vietnam, the draft, and the generation gap. This was very popular with productions all over the world.

YOU'RE A GOOD MAN CHARLIE BROWN (1967/1971)

Book by John Gordon; based on the comic strip *Peanuts* by Charles M. Schulz   *Music and lyrics* by Clark Gesner   *Published libretto*: Random House, 1967   *Condensation: The Best Plays of 1966–1967*. Otis L. Guernsey, Jr., ed. Dodd, Mead, 1967   *Anthology*: None   *Piano-vocal score*: Jeremy Music, 1972   *Vocal selections*: Jeremy Music, 1967￼ *Licensing agent*: Tams-Witmark   *Recording*: MGM SIE-9 OC (original cast) *Cast*: 4 M; 2 F

This musical revue was a surprise hit off-Broadway where it ran for almost 1,600 performances. The simple staging consists of a bare stage littered with several oversize building blocks, which serve as the dog house or whatever is needed. Charlie Brown, Lucy, and the others go through a disastrous baseball game, book reports on Peter Rabbit, a glee club rehearsal, and other hilarious episodes. Snoopy is concerned with shooting down the Red Baron! A small combo provides the musical accompaniment. This family show was performed on television in 1973.

ZORBÁ (1968/1974/1983)

Book by Joseph Stein; adapted from *Zorba The Greek* by Nikos Kazantzakis *Music* by John Kander   *Lyrics* by Fred Ebb   *Published libretto*: Random House, 1969   *Condensation*: None   *Anthology*: None   *Vocal*

selections: New York Times Music, 1968   *Licensing agent*: Samuel French
Recordings: Capitol SO 118 (original cast) ✰ RCA ABL 1-4732 (1983 revival)
Cast: Large mixed cast

The setting for the story is Piraeus, Greece and the island of Crete in 1924. The curtain rises on a bouzouki circle. Nikos arrives in Greece to reopen an abandoned mine he has inherited. Zorbá (an aging Lothario, philosopher and confidence man) goes with him to Crete. They both experience brief and tragic love affairs, and leave when the mine proves to be worthless. Despite some moments of humor, this is a serious musical drama. The Broadway production included an onstage bouzouki musical group, and dances were described as a series of Greek celebrations. A Greek chorus, all dressed in black, was particularly praised, as was the earthy performance of Herschel Bernardi in the title role.

THE ZULU AND THE ZAYDA
(1965)

Book by Howard Da Silva and Felix Leon; based on a story by Dan Jacobson
Music and lyrics by Harold Rome   *Published libretto*: Dramatists Play
Service, 1966   *Condensation*: None   *Anthology*: None   *Vocal
selections*: Chappell, 1966   *Licensing agent*: Dramatists Play Service
Recording: Columbia KOS 2880 (original cast)   *Cast*: 17 M; 4 F

A Zayda (a Jewish grandfather) is living in present-day (1965) Johannesburg with his son and grandchildren. He likes to go walking about the city, so his son hires a Zulu to keep track of him. This play with music is really about their friendship overcoming their racial and language problems. For the Broadway production, the program included a glossary of the Zulu and the Yiddish phrases used in the play. The musical numbers were a blend of African Yiddish. "You don't have to be Jewish . . . ," a popular New York advertising slogan, applies to the enjoyment of this racially mixed entertainment.

Appendixes

Licensing Agents

All of the titles listed in this directory are available from one of the following companies. Permission must be obtained, and fees and royalties paid before production can begin. These agents will provide scripts and scores.

Baker's Plays
    100 Chauncey Street, Boston, Mass. 02111 (617) 482-1280
Broadway Play Publishing, Inc.
    249 West 29th Street, New York, N.Y. 10001 (212) 563-3820
Dramatic Publishing Company
    4150 N. Milwaukee Ave, Chicago, Ill. 60641 (312) 545-2062
Dramatists Play Service, Inc.
    440 Park Avenue South, New York, N.Y. 10016 (212) 683-8960
Mavin Productions
    Suite 903E, 845 North Michigan Avenue, Chicago, Ill. 60611 (312) 944-5077
Music Theatre International
    1350 Avenue of the Americas, New York, N.Y. 10019 (212) 975-6841
Rodgers and Hammerstein Theatre Library
    598 Madison Avenue, New York, N.Y. 10022 (212) 486-0643
Samuel French, Inc.
    45 West 25th Street, New York, N.Y. 10010 (212) 206-8990

Shubert Organization
234 West 44th Street, New York, N.Y. 10036 (212) 944-3700
Tams-Witmark Music Library
560 Lexington Avenue, New York, N.Y. 10022 (212) 688-2525
Theatre Maximus
1650 Broadway, New York, N.Y. 10019 (212) 765-5913
Titles not listed in this directory may have become available since it was completed. For information regarding a title that is not included, contact any of the listed agents.

Music Publishers

Many of the vocal selections and piano-vocal scores in this directory are out of print. This listing of publishers has been included to assist you in choosing a musical for production. Once the selection has been made, the licensing agent should be able to provide both script and score.

If you and your music dealer are unable to locate a particular publication, you may get some help from:
National Music Publishers Association, Inc.
110 East 59th Street, New York, N.Y. 10022
(212) 751-1930

Belwin-Mills Publishing Corporation
25 Deshon Drive, Melville, N.Y. 11747
Big Three Music Corporation
729 7th Avenue, New York, N.Y. 10036
Blackwood Music, Inc.
1350 Avenue of the Americas, New York, N.Y. 10019
CAAZ Music Company
11 East 44th Street, New York, N.Y. 10017
Carwin *see* United Artists Music Corporation
Cherry Lane Music Company
110 Midland Avenue, Greenwich, N.Y. 10573
Chappell Music Company
810 7th Avenue, New York, N.Y. 10019
Cohan (G. M.) Publishing Company
1790 Broadway, New York, N.Y. 10019
Columbia Pictures Publications
16333 N.W. 54th Avenue, Hialeah, Fla. 33014
Commander Publications *see* Twentieth Century Music
Consolidated Music *see* Music Sales Corporation
Crawford Music *see* Chappell Music Company
Cromwell Music, Inc.
10 Columbus Circle, New York, N.Y. 10019

Damila Music
   40 West 55th Street, New York, N.Y. 10019
Dennison *see* Warner Brothers Music
De Sylva, Brown, and Henderson *see* Chappell Music Company
Erle Music *see* Chappell Music Company
Famous Music
   One Gulf and Western Plaza, New York, N.Y. 10023
Feist (L.) *see* Big Three Music Corporation
Fiddleback Music Publishing Company, Inc.
   1270 Avenue of the Americas, New York, N.Y. 10019
Fox Fan-Fare Music
   1345 Avenue of the Americas, New York, N.Y. 10019
Fox (Sam) Publishing Company, Inc.
   73-941 Highway 111
   Palm Desert, Calif. 92260
Frank Music Corporation
   39 West 54th Street, New York, N.Y. 10019
Hansen *see* Times Square Music Publications Company
Harms, Harms-Witmark *see* Cherry Lane Music Company
Hollis Music, Inc.
   10 Columbus Circle, New York, N.Y. 10019
Irving Berlin Music Corporation
   1290 Avenue of the Americas, New York, N.Y. 10019
Jeremy Music, Inc.
   1889 Palmer Avenue, Larchmont, N.Y. 10538
Jimmy McHugh Music
   170 N.E. 33rd Street, Fort Lauderdale, Fla. 33334
Leonard (Hal) Publishing Company
   8112 West Bluemound Road, Box 13819, Milwaukee, Wis. 53213
Leeds Music Corporation
   445 Park Avenue, New York, N.Y. 10022
Ludlow Music, Inc.
   10 Columbus Circle, New York, N.Y. 10019
MCA Music
   445 Park Avenue, New York, N.Y. 10022
Macmillan Performing Arts Music *see* Schirmer, Inc.
Marks (E. B.) *see* Belwin-Mills Publishing Corporation
Morris (E. H.) *see* MPL Communications
Montage Music Publishers
   Box 806, 1 East 4th Street, Cincinnati, Ohio 45201
Mourbar Music
   17 West 60th Street, New York, N.Y. 10023
MPL Communications
   39 West 54th Street, New York, N.Y. 10019
Music Sales Corporation
   33 West 60th Street, New York, N.Y. 10023

Musical Comedy Productions
  10 Columbus Circle, New York, N.Y. 10019
National General/Shayne *see* Montage Music Publishers
New World Music Corporation
  75 Rockefeller Plaza, New York, N.Y. 10019
New York Times Music Corporation
  655 Madison Avenue, New York, N.Y. 10022
Notable Music Company, Inc.
  161 West 54th Street, New York, N.Y. 10019
Novello *see* Theodore Presser Company
Portfolio Music *see* Chappell Music Company
Revelation Music Publishing Corporation
  1270 Avenue of the Americas, New York, N.Y. 10019
Robbins Music Corporation
  729 7th Avenue, New York, N.Y. 10036
Schirmer, Inc.
  40 West 62nd Street, New York, N.Y. 10023
Sevenoaks, Kent, Novello *see* Theodore Presser Company
Shapiro, Bernstein and Company, Inc.
  10 East 53rd Street, New York, N.Y. 10022
Stratford Music *see* Chappell Music Company
Sunbeam Music *see* Valando
Thackaray Falls Music
  c/o Alexander Broude, 225 West 57th Street, New York, N.Y. 10019
Theodore Presser Company
  Presser Place, Bryn Mawr, Penn. 19010
Times Square Music Publications Company
  1619 Broadway, New York, N.Y. 10019
Twentieth Century Music
  8544 Sunset Boulevard, Los Angeles, Calif. 90096
United Artists Music Corporation
  729 7th Avenue, New York, N.Y. 10036
Universal Edition (Wien) *see* Belwin-Mills Publishing Corporation
Valando Music Publishing Group, Inc.
  1270 Avenue of the Americas, New York, N.Y. 10019
Warner Brothers Music
  75 Rockefeller Plaza, New York, N.Y. 10019
Williamson Music, Inc.
  598 Madison Avenue, New York, N.Y. 10022

Index

Entries are by composer, lyricist, and librettist.

JOHN TAGGART HINCKLEY LIBRARY
NORTHWEST COMMUNITY COLLEGE
POWELL, WYOMING   82435

Richard Chigley Lynch is assistant curator of the Billy Rose Theatre Collection at the New York Public Library. He has written for *Record Collector's Journal, RTS Music Gazette, Kastlemusick*, and *Overtures*.

WITHDRAWN